I0793630

IMAGES
of America

PORTSMOUTH NAVAL PRISON

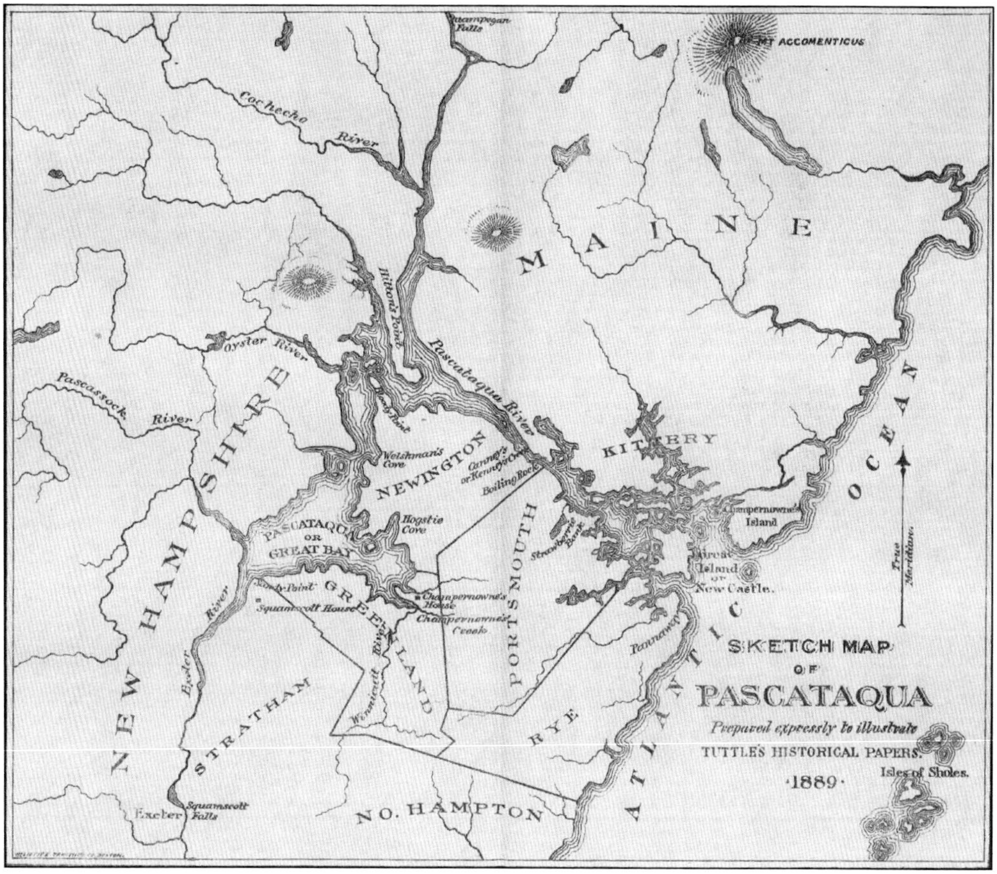

The Piscataqua Region, 1889. This engraving is an 1889 version of an earlier sketch map, originally made by Francis Champernowne in 1699, created to "illustrate Tuyttles Historical Papers." It shows the Piscataqua (Pis-cat'-a-qua) region. The large river of the same name is flowing west to east into the Atlantic Ocean between southern Maine and northeastern New Hampshire. At the mouth of the river is a cluster of smaller islands on which the Portsmouth Naval Shipyard—and the prison—are built. The larger one, originally called Great Island, is New Castle. No fewer than seven rivers feed into Great Bay, Little Bay, and then the Piscataqua River, which empties into Portsmouth Harbor creating a swift current. Ecologically, the Piscataqua region is an estuary. (CMHS.)

On the Cover: The Prison, July 1973. This July 26, 1973, view from the seaward side of the prison shows "the castle" a year before its closing in June 1974. The 10-foot-high fence was originally constructed after World War II. The furious tides of the Piscataqua River, which surrounded the prison on three sides, deterred men from escaping, or drowned them if they tried. In the right foreground is a storage shed. Behind it, to the left, is Building 121, first constructed in 1917 as a mess hall. From 1962 on, it housed the print, tailor, and carpenter shops as well as public works. Both were demolished between 1988 and 1997. (NHHS.)

IMAGES
of America

PORTSMOUTH NAVAL PRISON

Katy Kramer

ARCADIA
PUBLISHING

ISBN 978-1-4671-1667-1

Published by Arcadia Publishing
Charleston, South Carolina

Printed in the United States of America

Library of Congress Control Number: 2015956694

For all general information, please contact Arcadia Publishing:
Telephone 843-853-2070
Fax 843-853-0044
E-mail sales@arcadiapublishing.com
For customer service and orders:
Toll-Free 1-888-313-2665

Visit us on the Internet at www.arcadiapublishing.com

To the memory of my late parents, who one summer took us three kids across the US in a secondhand Plymouth with a map of monuments and museums and a case of tuna fish

"History is the ship carrying living memories into the future."
—Stephen Spender

Contents

ACKNOWLEDGMENTS

I have many people to thank for their generous spirits and depths of expertise and have been most fortunate to have landed in such capable hands. Sincere thanks go to archivist Joan Gearin and the records room staff, National Archives at Boston, for "pulling" annual reports and logbooks for the better part of one summer; the staff at the National Archives and Records Administration, College Park, Maryland, (NARACP) for interpreting the voluminous photograph collection; Lisa Crunk, at the Naval History and Heritage Command, Washington, DC (NHHC), and David Colamaria, photo archivist, who was the quintessential guide and escort for the better part of two days. Gratefully, Jennifer Castro at Quantico fielded my inquiries and Kara Newcomer, photo historian, USMC History Division, and Alisa Whitley, archivist, Archives and Special Collections, Library of the Marine Corps, Quantico, Virginia, (LMCQ) were all instrumental.

Closer to home, Nancy Mason, at the Milne Special Collections and Archives Department, University of New Hampshire Library, Durham (UNHL) graciously, efficiently, and expertly scanned photographs; Tom Hardiman from the Portsmouth Athenaeum Collection (PAC) expedited photograph delivery; and Sophia Yalouris from the Collections of the Maine Historical Society (CMHS) gave generously and expeditiously of her time. Many thanks go to Jim Cerny (JC), New Castle Historical Society (NCHS) and town historian, for explaining and delineating Camp Langdon and providing photographs; and to Rod Watterson, author of *Whips to Walls*, for critical help in explaining military law. Special thanks are extended to Neil Novello for videos, expertise, and time.

Gary Hildreth, public affairs officer; Joe Glukert, historian; Walter Ross; and the volunteers at the Portsmouth Naval Shipyard Museum (PNSYM) have been eternal sources of information.

I owe a monumental debt to Steve Jennison, former control center noncommissioned officer, sergeant of the guard, and "deck daddy," who helped in more ways than I can enumerate.

Caitrin Cunningham at Arcadia Publishing fielded a barrage of my questions with grace and good humor; she is the embodiment of patience and careful explanation.

Finally, thanks go to Bobby Gottfried and Jennifer Kramer for technical assistance and to Tom and Teresa Kramer for lodging, hospitality, transportation, editing, and technical expertise. Without them, this book would remain simply a nice idea.

INTRODUCTION

In Darryl Ponicsan's 1970 novel *The Last Detail,* later made into a movie, First Class Petty Officers Larry "Bad-ass" Buddusky and Richard "Mule" Mulhall (Jack Nicholson and Otis Young) escort Seaman Billy Meadows (Randy Quaid) to the Portsmouth Naval Prison. Meadows has been sentenced to eight years for attempting to steal $40 from the polio box at the post exchange (PX). When they arrive at the prison, after a freewheeling journey from Norfolk, Virginia, the receiving officer of the day (OOD) informs them that the sentence has been reduced to six years for "good behavior." The three brighten at the news, but Buddusky and Mulhall muse that "it's a rare fish that can live for six years in these waters with the sharks and not be chewed up." Thus, if it had not been already established, Ponicsan seals the prison's reputation. Although this scene never made it into the movie (but Nicholson and Quaid were still nominated for Oscars), both the book and screen version underscore the notion that a sentence at Portsmouth Naval Prison was not a walk in the park. Although the characterization has the ring of truth, over its 66-year history, the prison has also been both dynamic and innovative. Individual commandants have influenced what happened there, military necessity has shaped its mission, and emerging naval law has changed day-to-day operations. By any assessment, however, time has largely mitigated the seaman's sentence.

The trek of Buddusky, Mulhall, and Meadows to the prison was, at the time, the last chapter in a thousand years of naval discipline—punishment for dereliction of duty on ships at sea. Separate from civil law, or the rules for ordinary citizens, it has a long and brutal history. Currently, Articles I and II and the Fifth Amendment of the Constitution define the status of military and naval law. And the 1951 enactment of the Uniform Code of Military Justice standardized it throughout the various military branches.

Military law has roots in the Roman Empire but was meticulously codified in 1682, when the first Articles of War were issued in England and a specific court-martial procedure set up to try offenders. The British Navy became adept at dispensing military justice and interpreting and unifying the cases that came before naval officers. The Articles of War were revised in 1749 to simplify the procedures and these were revised once again in 1772 as the Regulations and Instructions Relating to His Majesty's Service at Sea. The intent was to maintain discipline in the ranks, not to ensure the rights of the individual: to fear the officer more than the enemy. England's extensive naval legal tradition became the basis for American articles of war at the 1775 Continental Congress. After several revisions, "An Act for Better Government of the United States Navy" was passed in April 1800, also known as the Articles of War of 1800 or more familiarly "Rocks and Shoals."

Despite Rocks and Shoals' attempt to apply the law equally, sea captains had fewer options than did officers on the ground. Ships had limited space and all hands were needed. There was little tolerance for insubordination and little room to imprison wayward crew. Flogging and the lash were the punishment of choice, but there were an infinite number of barbaric practices that varied from ship to ship and captain to captain—death among them. As a result, desertion rates were high. Sailors routinely jumped ship at port. Without a tracking system, men could leave a tyrant and find better conditions. Captains, on the other hand, felt hamstrung by the poor quality of the crew whom they saw as the dregs of society, with questionable morals and a weak work ethic. Only physical punishment, they felt, kept them in line. In 1850, however, long after the Army had outlawed it 40 years earlier, the Navy banned flogging.

Although this quieted the public uproar over the practice among landlubbers, it created problems at sea. No longer able to administer swift punishment, captains had to devise other methods of discipline, which often proved to be ineffective. Thus began the cry for a permanent naval prison where punishment would finally be meted out. It would be another 50 years before plans for the Portsmouth Naval Prison were drawn up, but it was clear from the beginning that Portsmouth would be synonymous with hard time. Over the years, its brutal reputation was as carefully maintained as its cell block security. But, as many would reluctantly admit, Portsmouth's reputation outside the prison was sometimes far more fearsome than what was actually taking place inside it.

The first prisoners on Seavey's Island, held in a stockade close to the site of the actual prison that opened a decade later, were, ironically, treated well. Approximately 1,800 men captured in Cuba during the Spanish-American War were transported to New Hampshire, with officers taken to the Naval Academy in Annapolis, Maryland. Since the capture of so many was unanticipated, nearer shipyards in Philadelphia and New York were ill-prepared. John D. Long, then secretary of the Navy, grew up in Buckfield, Maine, and attended Hebron Academy before graduating from Harvard. The Portsmouth Naval Shipyard—actually located in Maine—was in his home state. As well, it was summer, and the ocean and offshore breezes seemed a better choice not only for the prisoners but for the Marines who would guard them. Thus, Camp Long was created for the prisoners, and Camp Haywood nearby for the Marines. For the majority of the next century, Marines would remain on Seavey's Island.

As the transition was made from holding seamen in local jails, state prisons, brigs, and Marine Corps barracks to the yet-to-be-built prison in Portsmouth, overcrowding became an issue. As a stopgap measure, two ships, the USS *Topeka* and the USS *Southery*, were brought to the back channel in the shipyard to house those who had committed less serious crimes and whose sentences were short. After the prison was completed, the vessels would serve as intake, quarantine, and discharge centers and then be re-designated.

The cell block and the administration building at Portsmouth were finally commissioned in April 1908 with Allan C. Kelton as its commandant. Hailed as a hero from the recently fought war, Kelton oversaw the building and the opening of the prison before retiring from active duty. Many of the procedures and practices put in place during his tenure remained long after his departure. Subsequent commandants, up until Thomas Mott Osborne's arrival in 1917, would fine-tune and enhance his routine. Basic tenets included sorting prisoners upon arrival as dictated by the Elmira system, popular at the time, and cells built according to the Auburn system, also in vogue. From the beginning, the prison was attuned to advances in the field.

In the early years of the prison, talking among prisoners was prohibited, and some men were marked with red-legged uniforms for repeated rule infractions. Most were kept in the cell block, which was completed after the prison was opened. Neither the commandant nor the Marines would have adequate accommodations until several years later when appropriations, which came in fits and starts, were fully allocated. Thus, security was an issue in the first few years of operation, and eventually, the whole locking system had to be replaced. Marine guards were in short supply, being called away for active duty. Many commandants were also called away right after or during their stint at the prison. Miraculously, there were few escapes.

The early years were hard. Punishment was the watchword. The cell block was kept at 54 degrees, and the breezes that cooled in the summer howled in the winter. Prisoners complained that matches would not stay lit—smoking being one of the few pleasures. Meals were monotonous. The massive gardens that would later dot the grounds and supplement the menu were in the distant future. The workday was long, privileges few, and diversions almost nonexistent. Conversation, education, vocational training, honor barracks, and meaningful work were still a long way off and returning men to active duty rare. It was, in fact, exactly what the sea captains had hoped for: a place where nobody wanted to go.

One

AN IDEAL LOCATION FOR A PRISON

The Piscataqua (Pis-cat'-a-qua), a water boundary between coastal Maine and New Hampshire, is a river to be reckoned with. It has one of the fastest tidal currents among America's navigable waters, making it almost impossible for even a strong swimmer to gain headway. In the spring, the current and the cold water conspire to lay claim to any life that dares to enter it. Even in the summer, a desperate man is no match for its ebb and flood currents. Seven rivers feed the Piscataqua, which empties into Portsmouth Harbor creating the swift current.

Ecologically, the Piscataqua region is an estuary, the place where freshwater rivers mix with saltwater ocean. It is influenced by the tides—another contributor to the dangerous current. Estuaries are usually coastal and partially enclosed areas known for their rich soil and abundant aquatic life—a fact not missed by the early settlers, fishermen from Newfoundland. In 1790, the area was a busy port, known for shipbuilding and fishing industries.

A dozen islands sit in Portsmouth Harbor near the mouth of the river. Over the years, five were joined by landfill—Pumpkin, Clark, Seavey, Jamaica, and Dennetts—to create the 278-acre Portsmouth Naval Shipyard. The yard was established prior to Maine's statehood in 1820, and although its name places it in New Hampshire, the shipyard is actually in Maine, a fact affirmed by the US Supreme Court in May 2001, after a two-decades-long dispute.

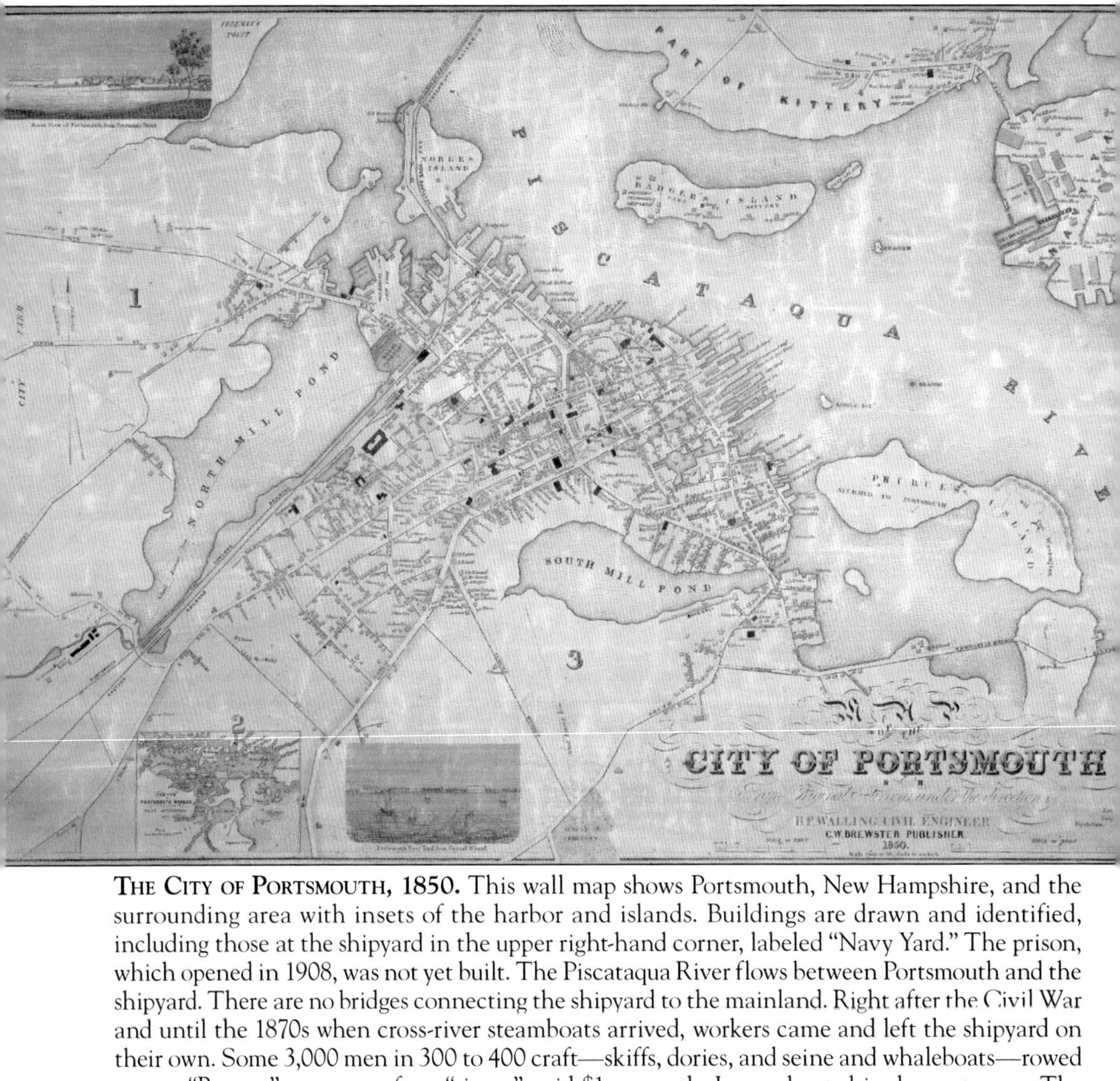

The City of Portsmouth, 1850. This wall map shows Portsmouth, New Hampshire, and the surrounding area with insets of the harbor and islands. Buildings are drawn and identified, including those at the shipyard in the upper right-hand corner, labeled "Navy Yard." The prison, which opened in 1908, was not yet built. The Piscataqua River flows between Portsmouth and the shipyard. There are no bridges connecting the shipyard to the mainland. Right after the Civil War and until the 1870s when cross-river steamboats arrived, workers came and left the shipyard on their own. Some 3,000 men in 300 to 400 craft—skiffs, dories, and seine and whaleboats—rowed across. "Rowers" went over free; "sitters" paid $1 a month. Larger boats hired men to row. The morning trip over was peaceful. The trip back at the end of the day was a free-for-all. Boats raced each other to the shore, with the larger ones usually winning. Townspeople gathered on the shore to watch, wager, and root for their favorites. It was a fierce competition with frequent collisions and exchanges of choice words. (CMHS.)

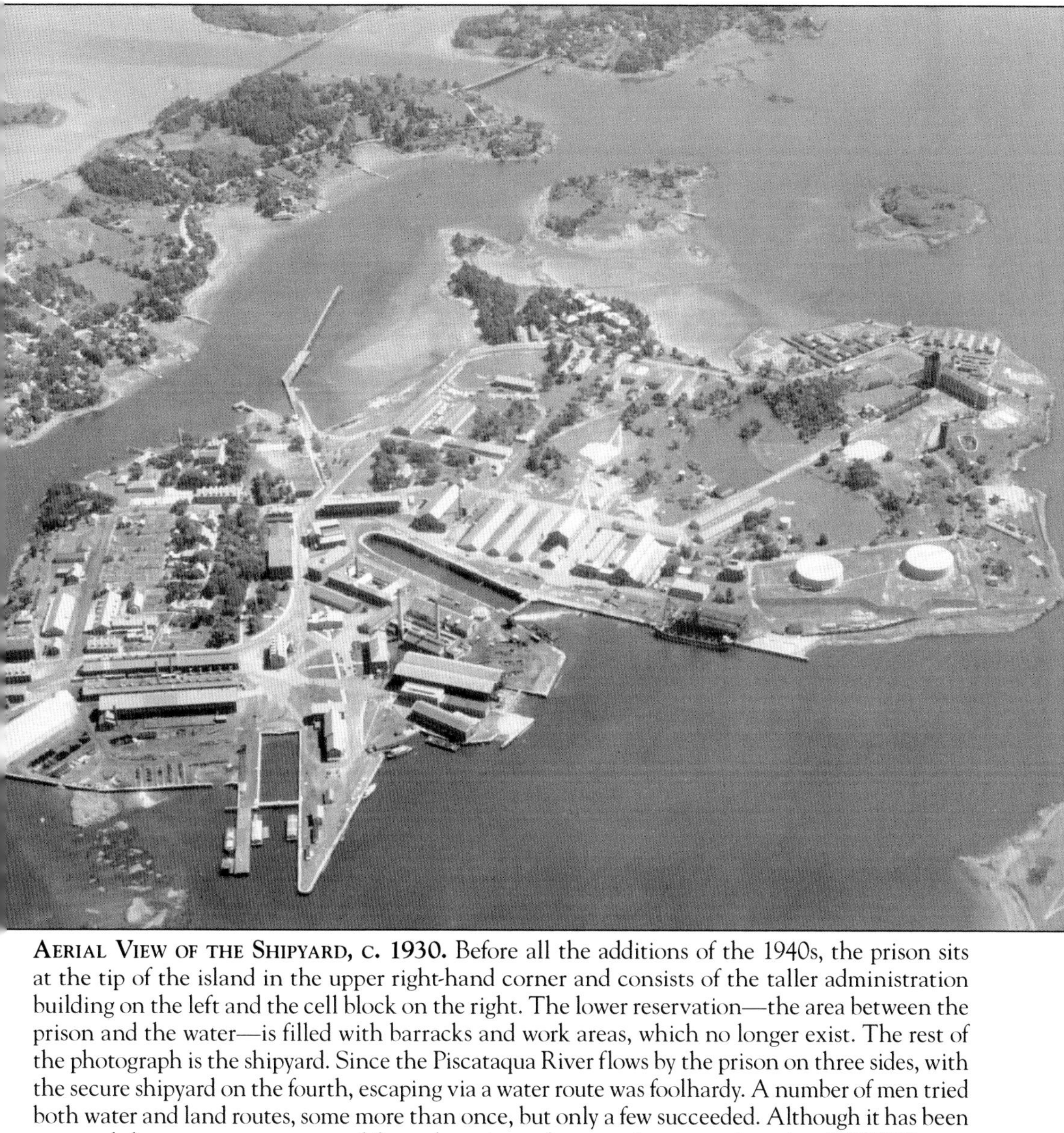

Aerial View of the Shipyard, c. 1930. Before all the additions of the 1940s, the prison sits at the tip of the island in the upper right-hand corner and consists of the taller administration building on the left and the cell block on the right. The lower reservation—the area between the prison and the water—is filled with barracks and work areas, which no longer exist. The rest of the photograph is the shipyard. Since the Piscataqua River flows by the prison on three sides, with the secure shipyard on the fourth, escaping via a water route was foolhardy. A number of men tried both water and land routes, some more than once, but only a few succeeded. Although it has been rumored that no one ever escaped from the prison, the record proves otherwise. (NHHC.)

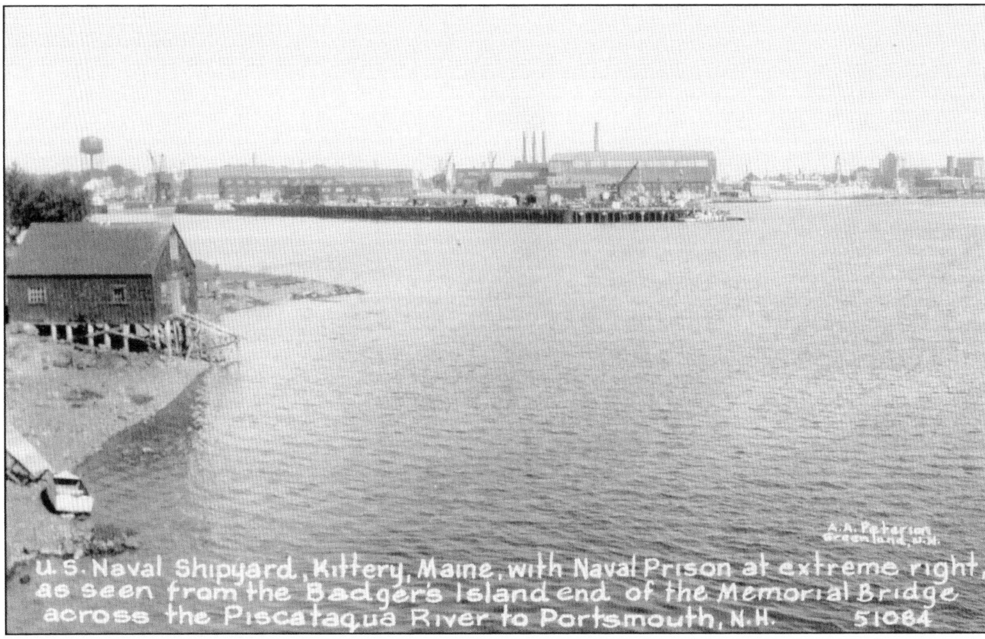

THE PORTSMOUTH NAVAL SHIPYARD. This photograph was taken between 1940 and 1960. The history of the prison is intertwined with history of the shipyard, whose fortunes waxed and waned, influenced by politics, economics, and the country's relationship with its neighbors. It was the War of 1812, once again with England, which finally illuminated the dire need for armed sailing ships, called men-of-war, as well as for skilled shipbuilders and seamen. (PAC.)

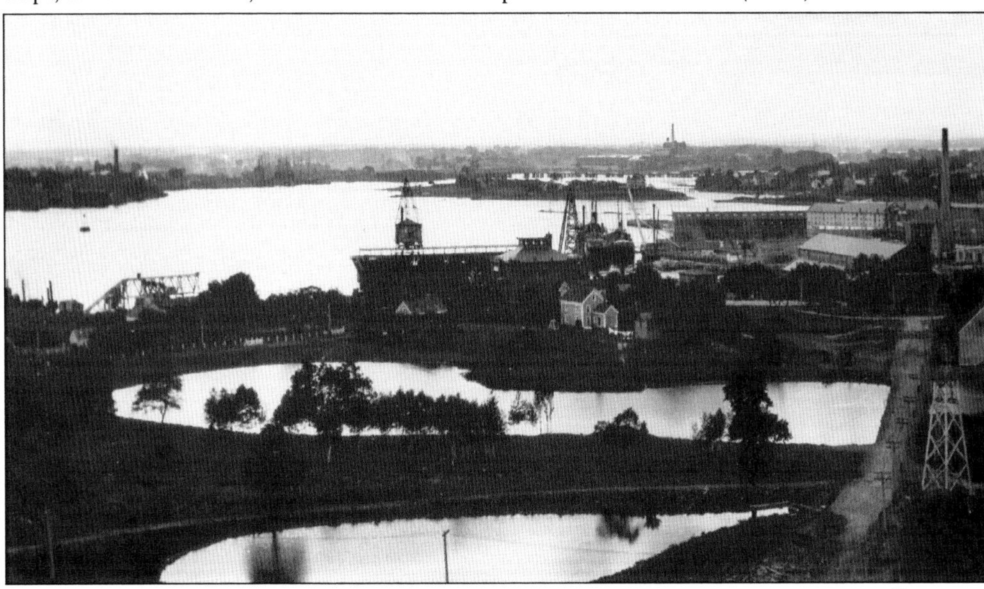

PRISON VIEW OF SHIPYARD. With the United States tired of other countries, principally France and England, violating American territorial waters and seizing ships, crews, and cargo, shipyards up and down the eastern seaboard sprang to life—Portsmouth, Boston, New York, Philadelphia, Washington, DC, and Norfolk, Virginia. Established between 1800 and 1801 by the Navy Department, itself created in 1798, the six yards were built to defend American shores and shipping from Great Britain. (NHHC.)

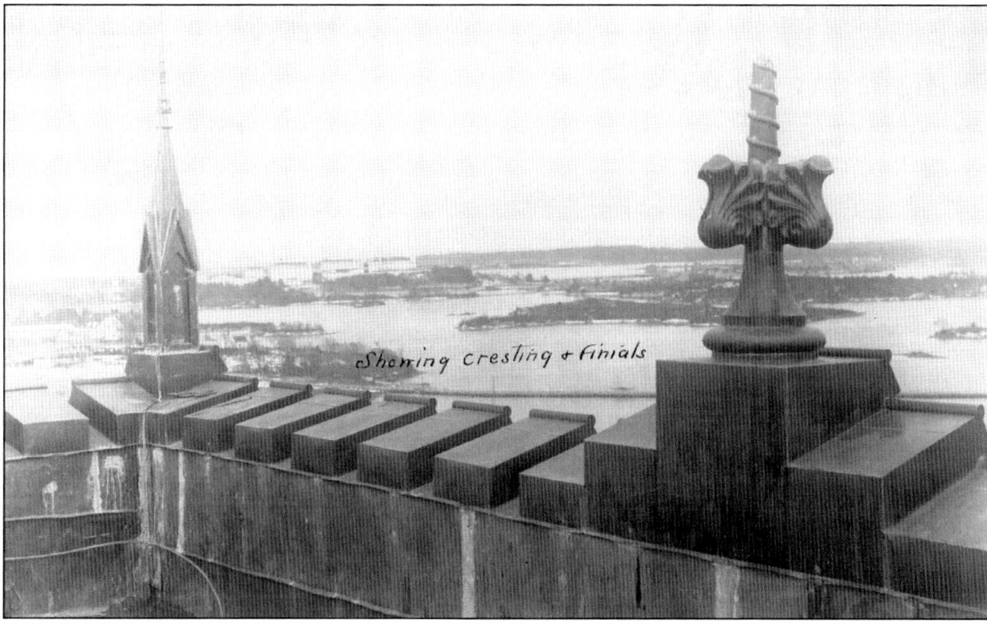

VIEW FROM THE ROOF, 1906. Taken from the top of the administration tower in January 1906, this view shows not only the ornamental features—cresting and finials—but also the islands and opposite shore. It was said that when newly court-martialed men arrived at the prison and looked out across the river, they saw Wentworth-by-the-Sea in New Castle, a big white hotel with mansard towers, the color and shape not unlike their own accommodations, and thought it was another prison. (NARACP.)

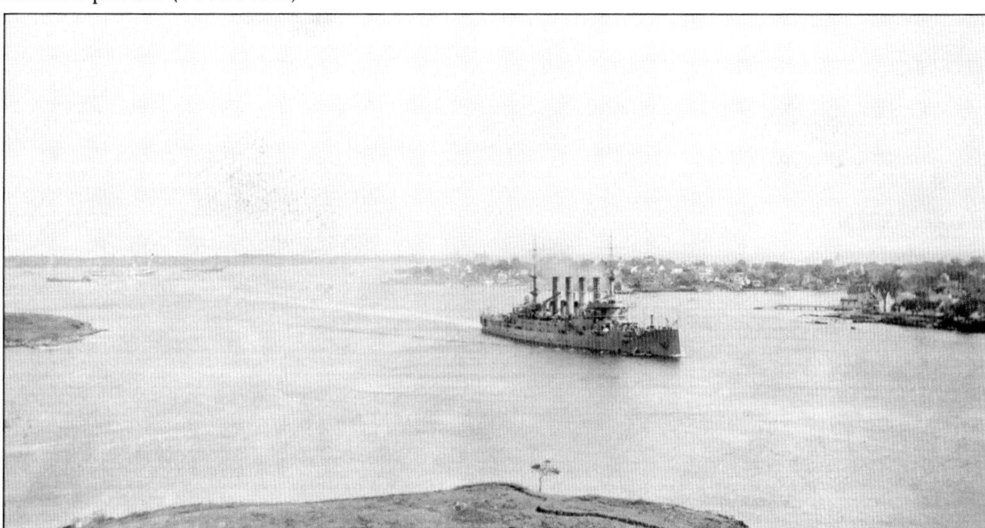

PORTSMOUTH HARBOR, USS *NORTH CAROLINA*, 1911. The lodgers in the New Castle hotel, looking out and seeing the off-white prison, thought it was another hotel. Notable guests at the elegant Wentworth included the Japanese and Russian delegations that stayed at the hotel for 30 days without charge. Traveling from their respective countries to the shipyard to negotiate, the delegation drafted the Treaty of Portsmouth, which was signed in 1905, ending the Russo-Japanese War, a fight for control of Korea and Manchuria. Visitors are still attracted to the shipyard site. (LMCQ, Fitzgerald Collection.)

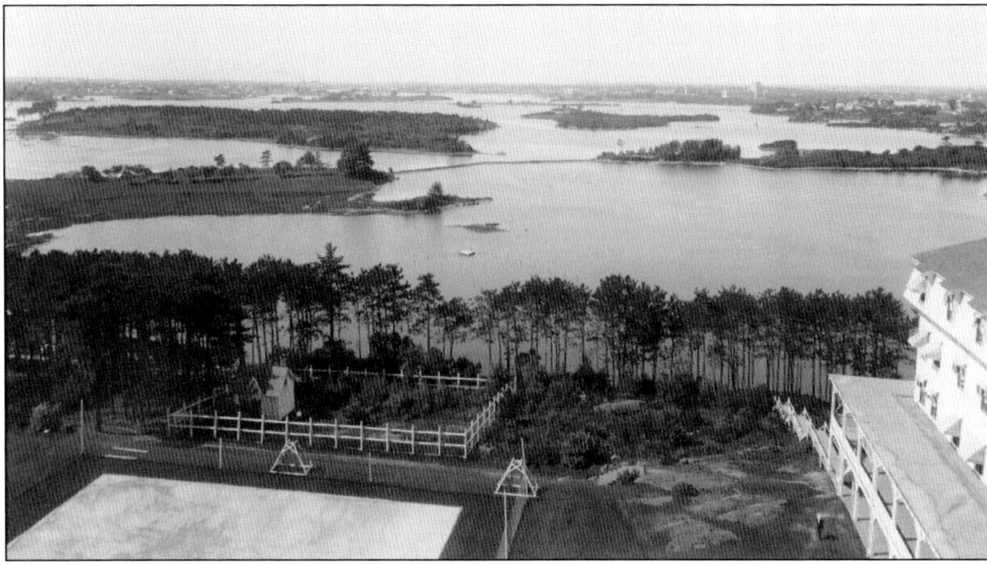

View from Wentworth Hotel, Undated. Guests at the Wentworth Hotel in New Castle—which is still open for business—could see the prison in the distance. In this photograph, the prison is barely visible; it is the only tall building on the horizon at the right. From the prison's opening in 1908 until its decommissioning in 1974, no man managed to escape by swimming. (PAC.)

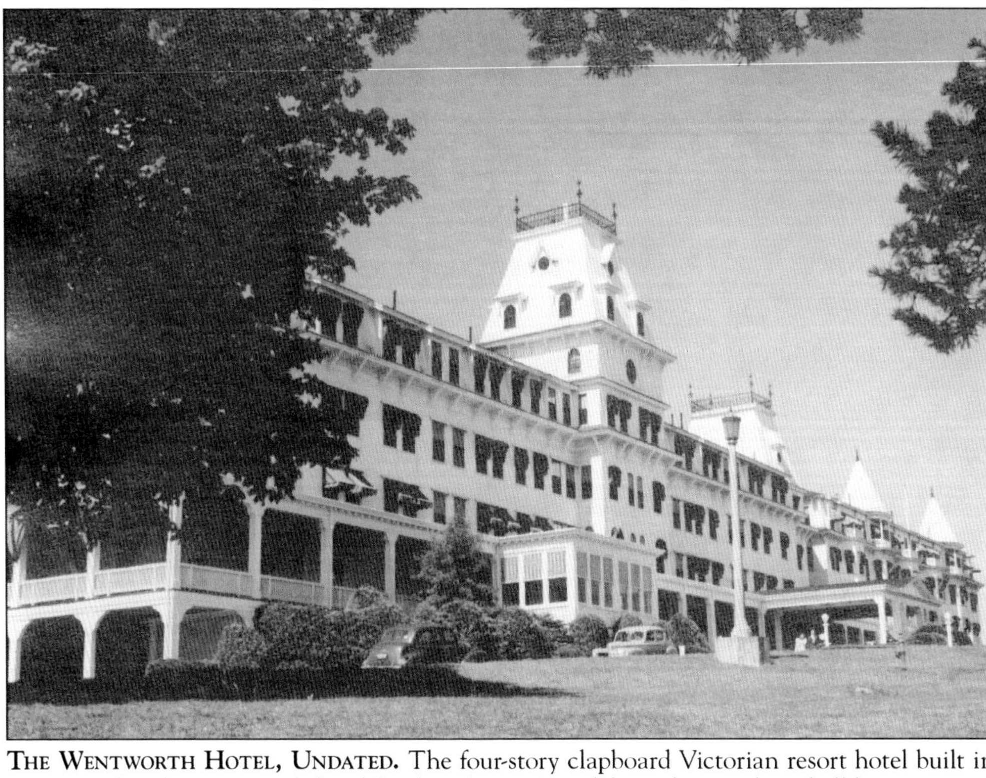

The Wentworth Hotel, Undated. The four-story clapboard Victorian resort hotel built in 1874 was closed in 1980 and slated for demolition. Saved from the wrecking ball by concerned citizens, it reopened in 1997. Its 1897 golf course was known for the ledge outcropping, which consistently deflected golf balls into the ocean. (NCHS.)

Two

THE FIRST PRISONERS IN 1898

Despite the prison's fearsome reputation, the first prisoners on Seavey's Island were well treated. Built to house 1,562 enlisted men and noncommissioned officers taken captive during the Spanish-American War, Camp Long was reportedly erected in 48 hours, starting in early July 1898. Men were held captive and also nursed back to health before returning to Spain two months later. Named for then Secretary of the Navy John D. Long, a Maine native, the camp became a tourist attraction for the staid New Englanders. Thousands of people on the shore and in boats watched the unloading of the ships, respectfully quiet as the prisoners—many wounded, sick, and threadbare—streamed from barges to the island. The prison camp remained a popular attraction that summer.

Part of this beneficence toward the Spanish prisoners was the result of a nationally heralded incident. In an attempt to bottle the Spanish fleet inside Havana Harbor, Lt. Richmond Pearson Hobson and a handful of seamen refitted the *Merrimac*, a collier (coal ship) and, though under constant fire, entered the channel to explode their vessel and block the exit. Heavily damaged, the *Merrimac* sank but only partially blocked the harbor entrance. The seamen, clinging to a raft, were rescued by none other than Adm. Pascual Cervera y Topete, commander of the Spanish fleet, who, instead of shooting them, remarked on their valor. The Americans were brought to Castle Morro as prisoners; Cervera notified the American admiral William T. Sampson that the men were safe. Subsequently, the Spanish fleet, under orders to engage the enemy, was forced to exit the harbor in single file around the *Merrimac*, an easy target for the American fleet that awaited them. The entire Spanish squadron was destroyed.

In a subsequent prisoner swap, Hobson and his men were returned unharmed and spoke of their good treatment. Newsmen quickly wrote about the exploit and both Hobson and Admiral Cervera were lauded for their actions. Both became national news, which helped to exonerate Cervera when he returned to Spain with his men in September and afforded the Spanish prisoners at Portsmouth excellent treatment in return.

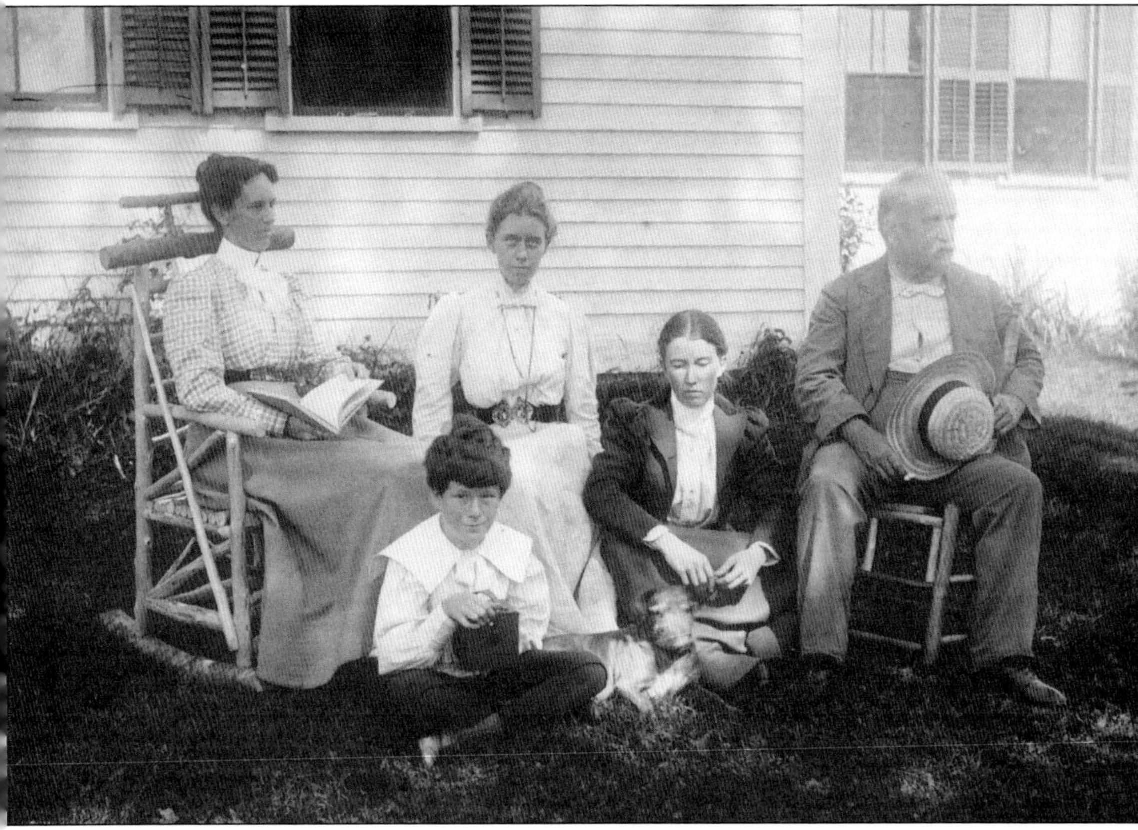

John D. Long and Family, 1899. In front of Long's ancestral home in Buckfield, Maine, from left to right, are Agnes (Peirce) Long; daughters Helen and Margaret; John D. Long, with his hat; and his son Peirce Long, on the ground holding a box camera. John Davis Long (1838–1915) was secretary of the Navy when over a thousand prisoners from the Spanish-American War were shipped up the Eastern Seaboard to Seavey's Island. A graduate of Hebron Academy, Harvard College, and Harvard Law School, John was lieutenant governor and then governor of Massachusetts, and served three terms in the US House of Representatives before being appointed secretary of the Navy from 1897 to 1902. The prisoners had departed for Spain when this photograph was taken, but Camp Long has remained a touchstone when recounting the history of the Portsmouth Naval Prison. (CMHS, Stanley Museum.)

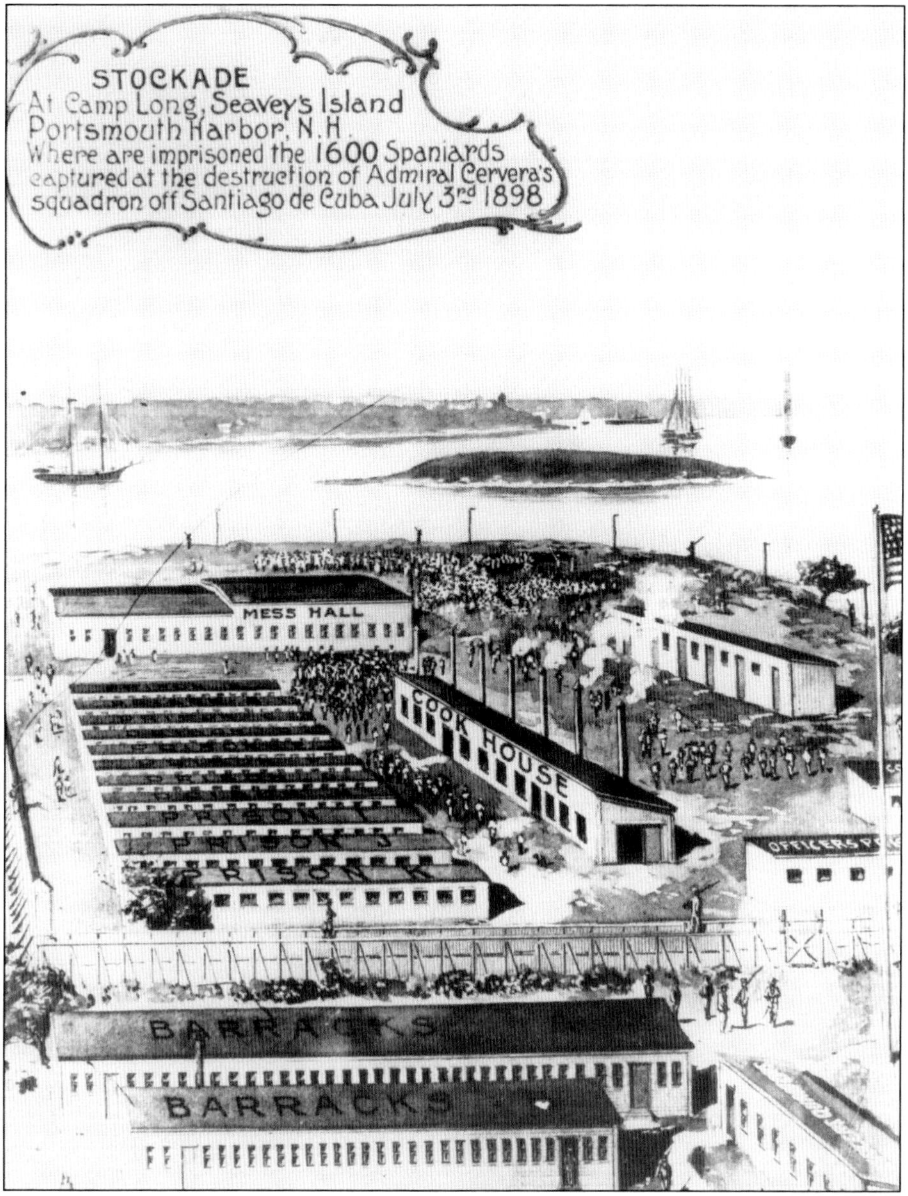

CAMP LONG, JULY 3, 1898. This popular postcard shows the completed Camp Long, which was reportedly erected in 48 hours. Several US ships, among them the USS *St. Louis* and the USS *Harvard*, arrived here carrying prisoners at the behest of Secretary John D. Long. Officers were later transported to Annapolis, Maryland. By the time the Navy Department designated Seavey's Island as the site of the prison, ships were already headed north. Capt. Benjamin Crowninshield, chief of the Navigation Bureau, and a swarm of carpenters hastily constructed the New England prison camp, which consisted of row upon row of tents, 13 barracks (two for the Marine guards), a hospital, mess hall, cookhouse, electric lights, quarters for officers and physicians, and a complete water and sewage system. A high stockade with a plank walk enclosed the facility. Gatling guns dotted the area. The facility stood essentially where the prison sits today. Secretary Long paroled Spanish chaplains and doctors who were then at liberty in Portsmouth and on Seavey's Island to attend to the men. (UNHL.)

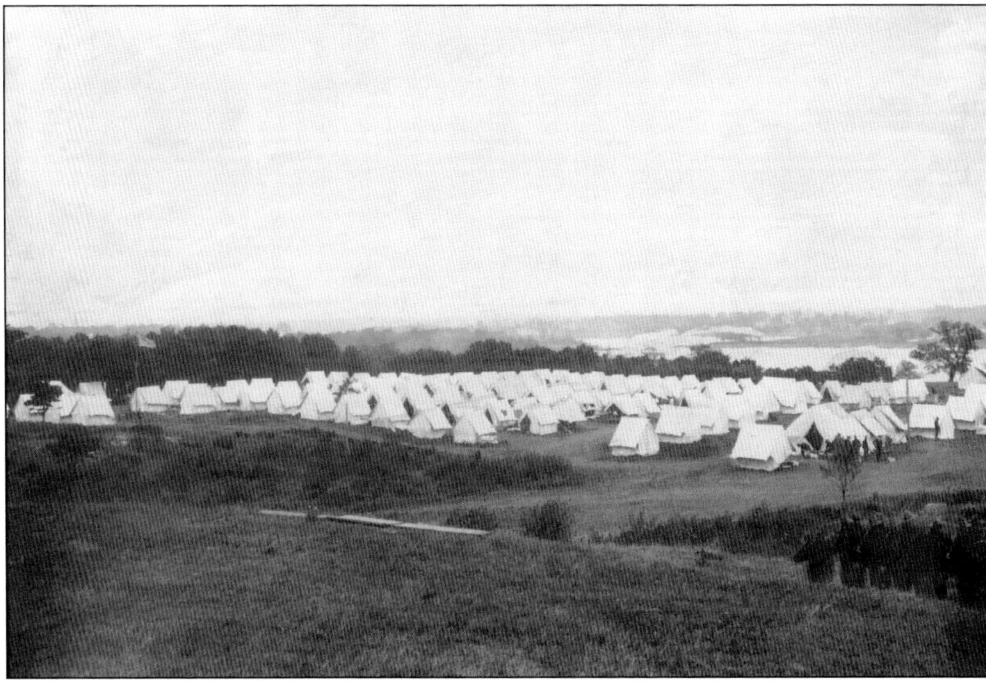

First Marine Battalion, 1898. The Marines, as they would continue to do for the next several decades, guarded the prisoners at the stockade and were largely billeted in tents, as this photograph depicts. The first group of Marines to guard the camp was a contingent from the Boston (Charlestown) Navy Yard. (LMCQ, Little Collection.)

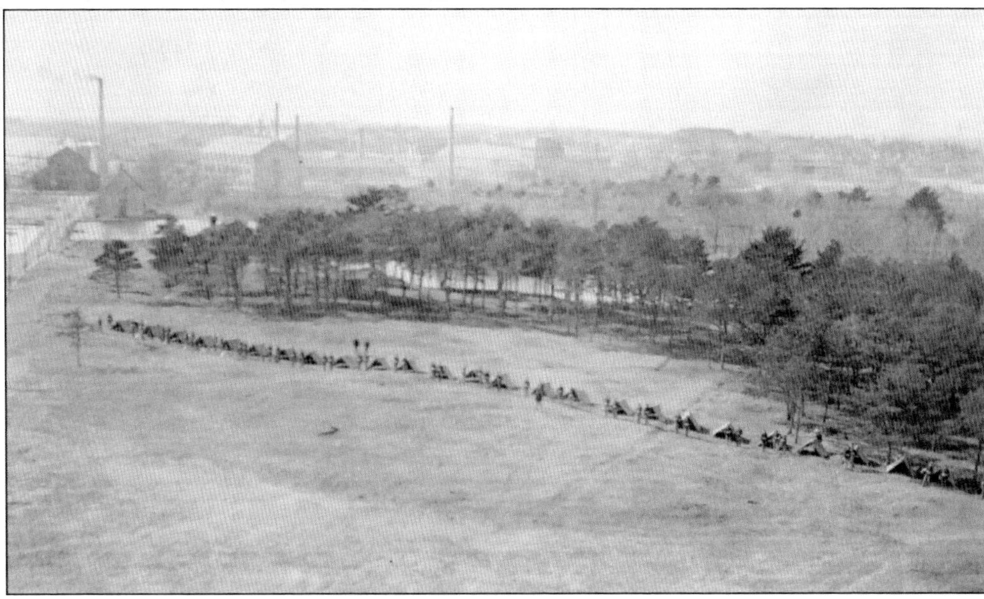

Guard Inspection, Tents Up. The quarters were named Camp Heywood after Waterville, Maine, native Charles C. Heywood (1839–1915), who had been in command in Cuba. He would be the first Marine to hold the rank of major general. The First Marine Battalion under Heywood was commanded by Robert W. Huntington (1849–1917). These men had arrived in August aboard the *Resolute* also to guard the stockade. (LMCQ, Fitzgerald Collection.)

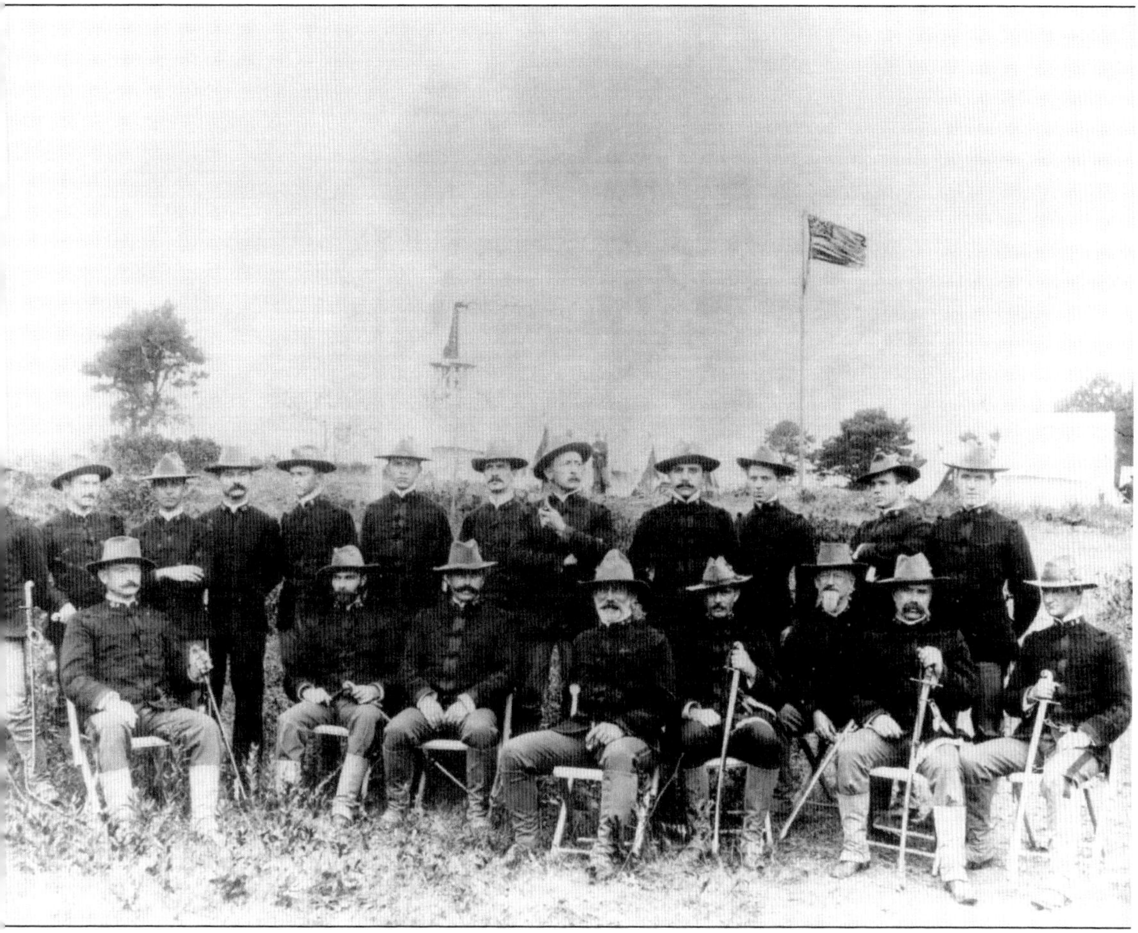

COLONEL HUNTINGTON AND MARINES, 1898. In this image taken in Portsmouth following their participation in the Spanish-American War are several Marines who went on to make names for themselves. Among them are 2nd Lt. Smedley D. Butler (1881–1940), second row, third from the right, who became one of the most decorated major generals in US history; and 1st Lt. Wendell C. Neville, first row at the right end, later commandant of the Marine Corps. Pictured are, from left to right, (first row, sitting) 1st Lt. James E. Mahoney; 1st Lt. Lewis C. Lucas; 1st Lt. Herbert L. Draper; Col. Robert W. Huntington; Capt. Charles L. McCawley, AQM; Capt. Francis H. Harrington; Capt. William F. Spicer; and Neville; (second row, standing) 2nd Lt. George C. Reid; 1st Lt. Charles G. Long; 2nd Lt. Edwin A. Jonas; Lt. John M. Edgar, MC, US Navy; 2nd Lt. Newt H. Hall; 1st Lt. Clarence L.A. Ingate; 1st Lt. William N. McKelvey; Capt. George F. Elliott; 2nd Lt. Louis J. Magill; Butler; 2nd Lt. Philip M. Bannon; and 2nd Lt. Melville J. Shaw. (UNHL.)

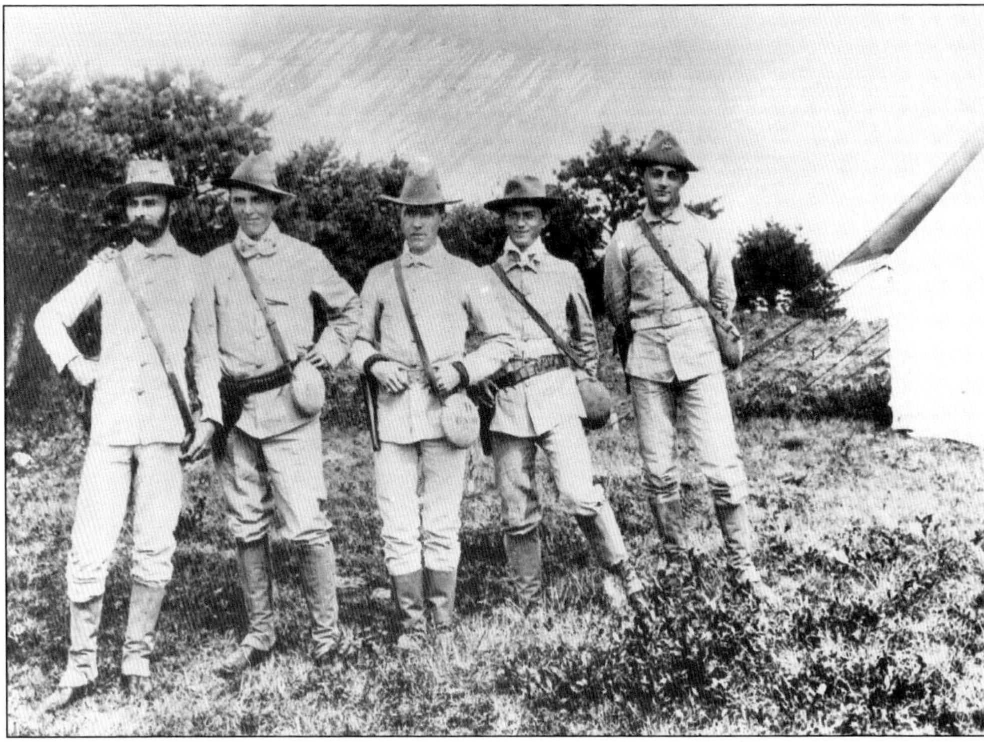

Officers, First Battalion Marines, 1898. These are officers who have also returned from Cuba. They are, from left to right, 1st Lt. Lewis C. Lucas, 1st Lt. Clarence L.A. Ingate, 2nd Lt. Melville J. Shaw, 2nd Lt. Newt H. Hall, and 2nd Lt. George C. Reid, who would become a brigadier general and recipient of the Medal of Honor. (UNHL.)

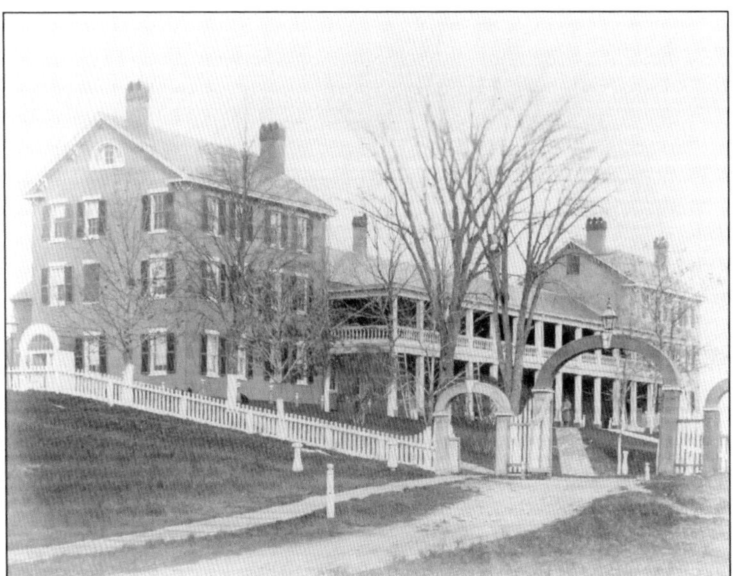

Shipyard Marine Barracks, 1901. Although this barracks, built in 1828, usually housed shipyard Marine guards, prison guards later stayed here as well. This was taken before the third story was added. (UNHL.)

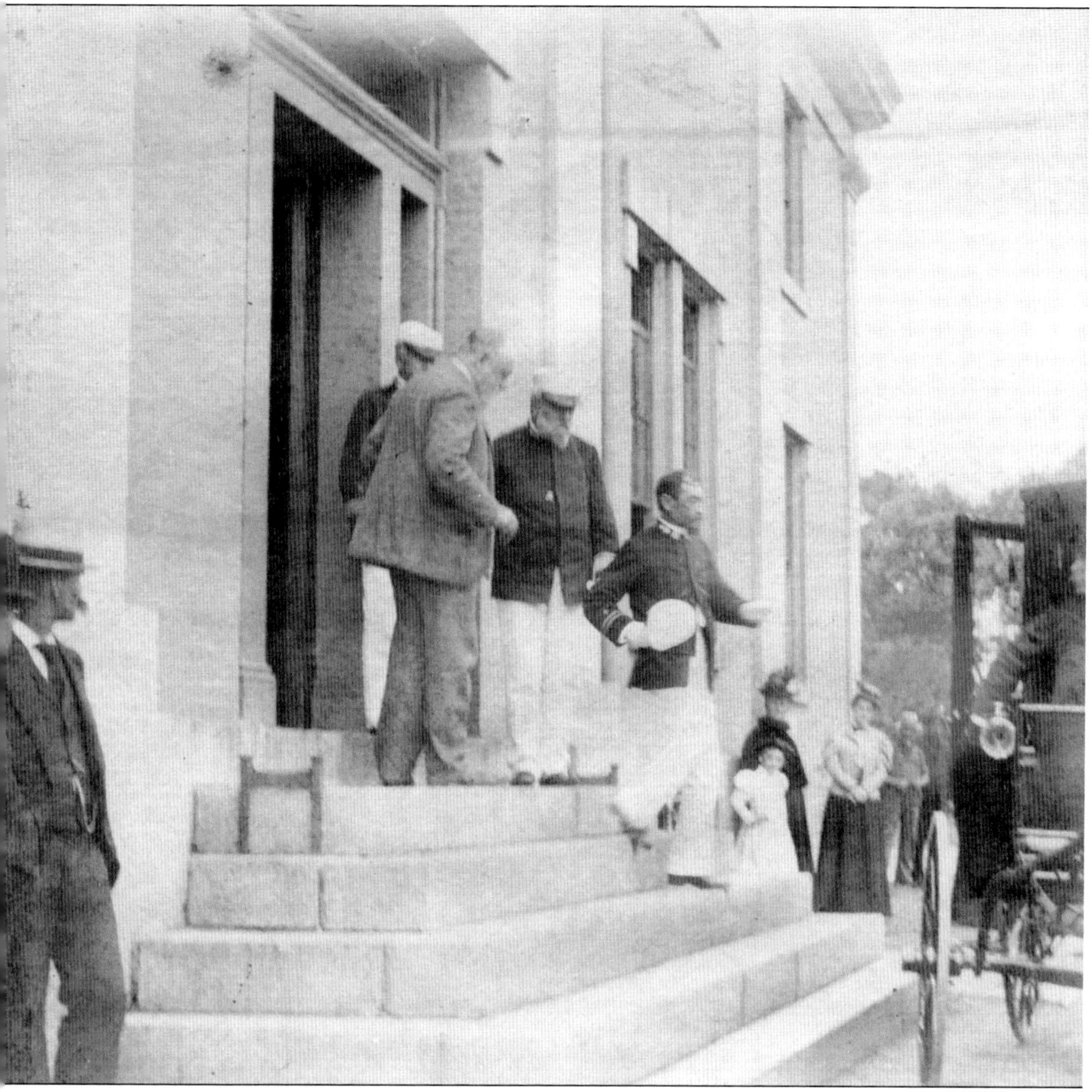

ADMIRALS CERVERA AND CARPENTER, 1898. Spanish admiral Pascual Cervera y Topete (1839–1909) (in front, holding his hat) and American admiral Charles C. Carpenter (just behind him, to the right, with a beard), are descending the steps of the administration building at the shipyard. Allowed to go on his own recognizance, Cervera stayed in the Rockingham Hotel. Admiral Carpenter was a lieutenant commander in the Union navy and commandant at Portsmouth Naval Shipyard from 1890 to 1896, when he retired. He was called back to active duty from April 1898 to August 1898 when the Spanish prisoners were held on Seavey's Island. Tragically, Carpenter was dead a year later of a self-inflicted gunshot wound and is buried in Portsmouth. (CMHS.)

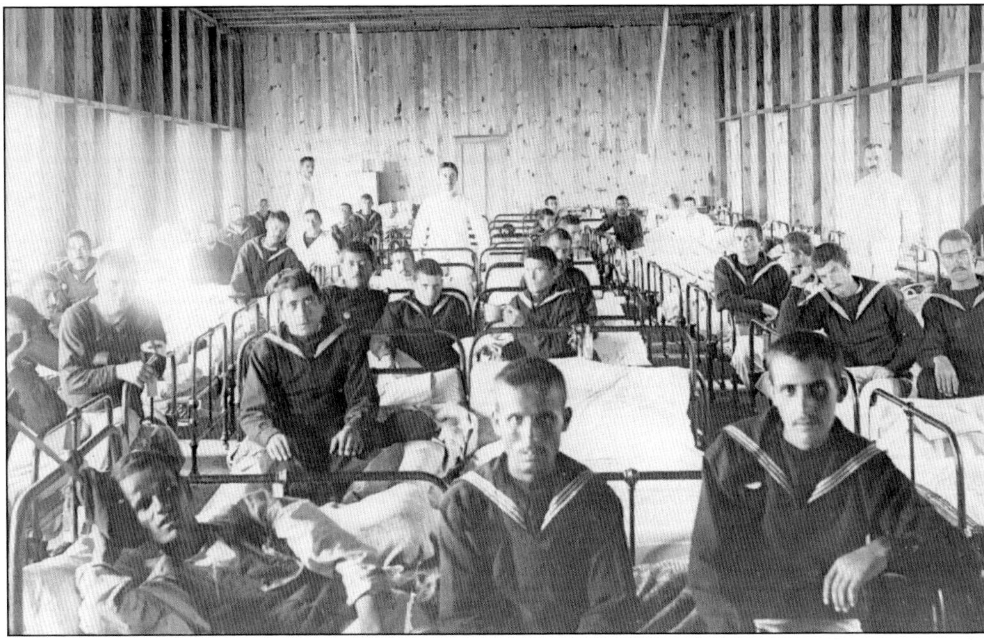

SPANISH PRISONERS, CAMP HOSPITAL, 1898. Male nurses from the American Red Cross attended the sick and wounded. Several dozen Spaniards died while in captivity, some en route who were buried at sea and 31 who died on the island. The rest left after two months. At 12:15 p.m. on September 12, 1898, the steamer *City of Rome* carrying Admiral Cervera—who had made farewell visits to the Navy Yard officers—boarded 1,700 prisoners and officers, 104 of them from the hospital. (PNSYM.)

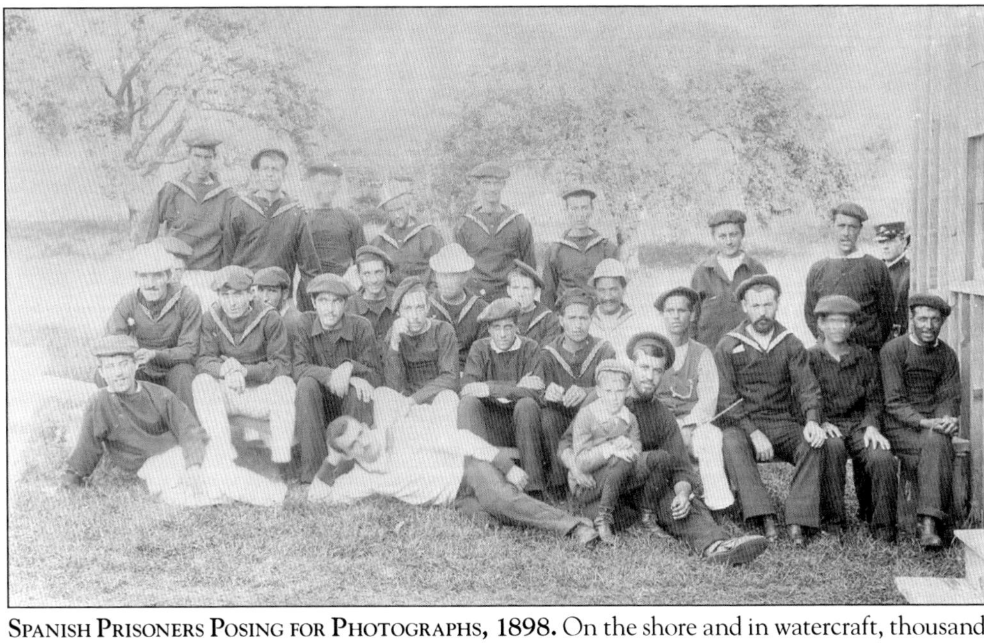

SPANISH PRISONERS POSING FOR PHOTOGRAPHS, 1898. On the shore and in watercraft, thousands of Americans turned out to bid the prisoners farewell before they returned to Santander, Spain. Newspapers reported that they were in far better shape when they left than when they arrived. After the prisoners returned to Spain, the stockade was decommissioned. (UNHL.)

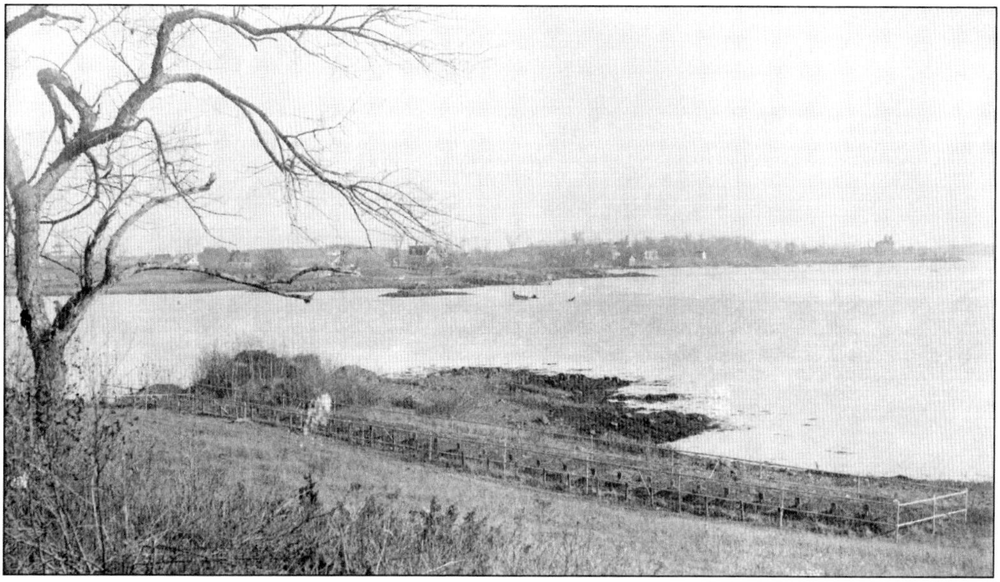

Graves of the Spanish Prisoners, 1899. Thirty-one Spanish prisoners remained buried in a cemetery on a grassy knoll north of the camp, which was dismantled after settlement terms with Spain had been reached. In 1916, a Spanish man-of-war picked up the remains and returned them to their homeland. This is the plot of land where the men who died here were buried. The 1899 Yards and Docks Department annual report lists the expenditure for maintaining the Spanish prisoners at $24,840.15. (NARACP.)

Spanish-American Marker and Walkway. The inscription on the monument reads, "Within a stockade built on the grounds now occupied by the naval prison were confined 1612 officers and men of the Spanish squadron which was destroyed by the American fleet at the battle of Santiago, July 3, 1898. These prisoners of war were guarded by a battalion of U.S. Marines." (NHHC.)

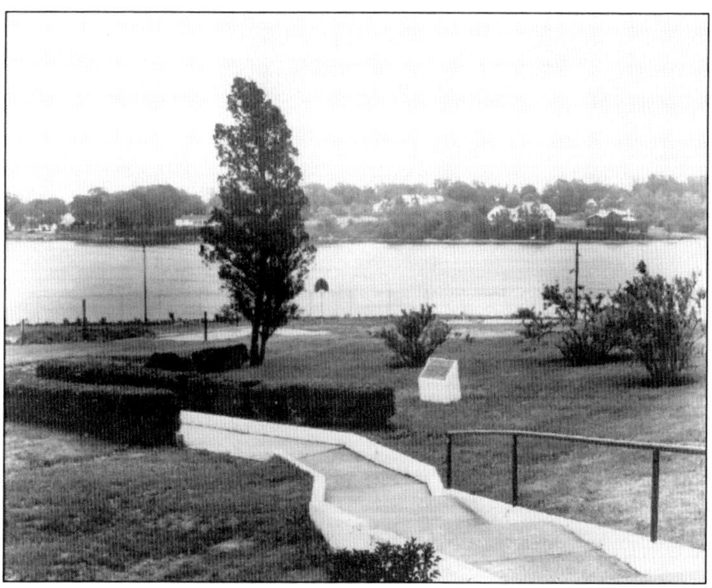

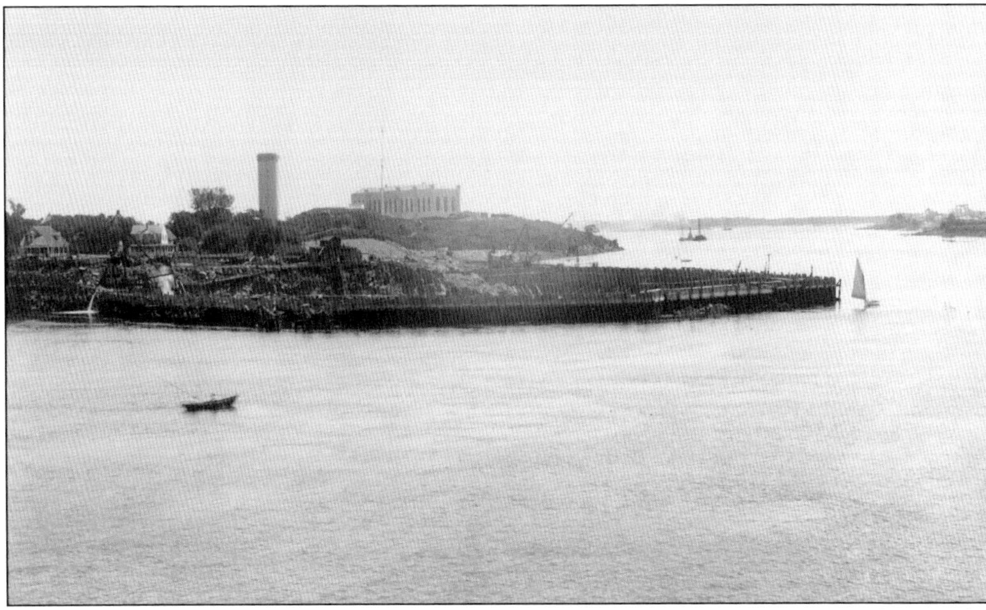

Henderson Point, 1905. Taken five hours before the Saturday, July 22 1905, explosion, this photograph shows the previously dug cofferdam on Henderson's Point (to the left of the sailboat) at the south side of Seavey's Island. Also known as Pull and Be Damned Point, it jutted 500 feet into the Piscataqua River, narrowing the channel and creating a swift tidal current that made large-ship navigation difficult. (PAC.)

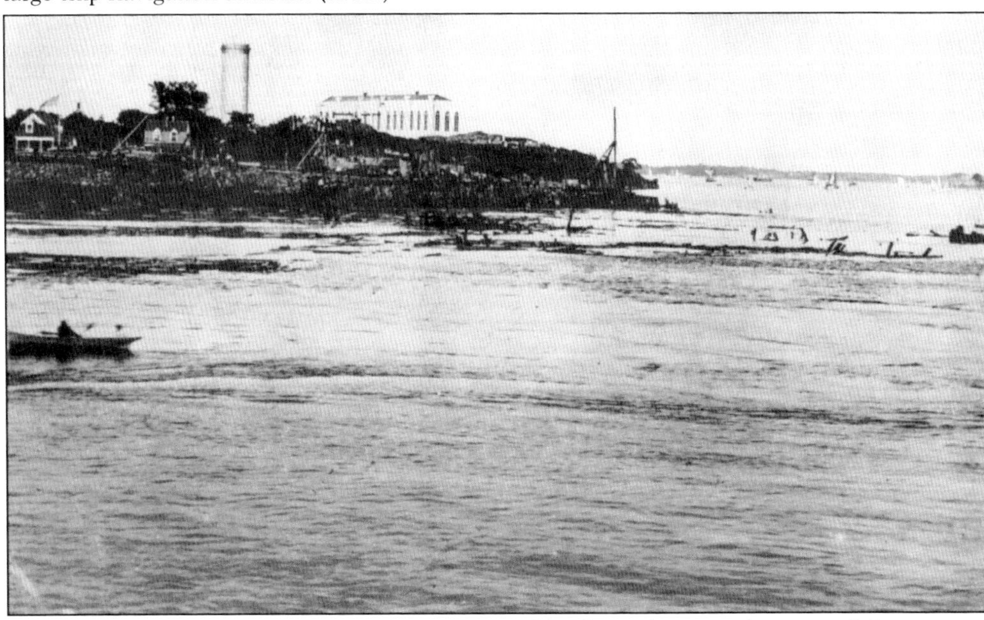

After Explosion, 1905. The blast became a worldwide media event because of the quantity of explosives—46 tons of dynamite—and planning. The project began in August 1902, and the Massachusetts Contracting Company charged $749,000 for the job. Seventy thousand tons of rock were removed and the explosion threw water 100 feet in the air. A wave flooded bridges and the shore, lined with spectators with complimentary tickets. As planned, no one was drenched or injured. It took two more years to dredge the rock from the channel. (PAC.)

Three

USS *Topeka* and USS *Southery*

So great was the need to eliminate overcrowding in the other facilities—ships at sea brigs, guardhouses, and barracks—that prison ships were used to house the overflow. Both the USS *Topeka* and the USS *Southery* had storied pasts. The USS *Southery* was originally built as a steamer in England in 1889. The Navy bought the ship a decade later, converted it to a collier (coal ship), and sent her where she was needed up and down the East Coast. That transformation lasted a year before it was sent to the Norfolk Navy Yard in Virginia to be refitted as a prison ship. Next, it was sent to Boston to house men while that prison was expanded. Then, in 1902, it was briefly in Charleston, South Carolina, and finally, in July 1903, full of prisoners, she was brought back to New England and anchored at the back-channel pier adjacent to the Portsmouth prison, where she remained until 1918.

Another ship, the USS *Topeka*, was used at Portsmouth from 1905 to 1916. Prisoners first arriving at the prison were processed there, inspected, given uniforms and supplies, and then quarantined. They were then routed to either the USS *Southery* or the prison. The USS *Topeka*, built in 1881 in Kiel, Germany, was not put into service until the Navy bought it in 1898 and converted it into a gunboat. Used in the Havana harbor blockade during the Spanish-American War, she remained in active duty primarily in the Caribbean and West Indies until brought to the shipyard. As World War I broke out, both the USS *Topeka* and USS *Southery* were re-designated: The USS *Topeka* went to New York in 1916 as a receiving ship and later to active duty; it was scrapped in 1930 in Baltimore, Maryland. With the construction of new barracks on the lower reservation, the USS *Southery*, no longer needed for detention, overflow, or discharge, was moved back to Boston in the 1920s and scrapped in 1933.

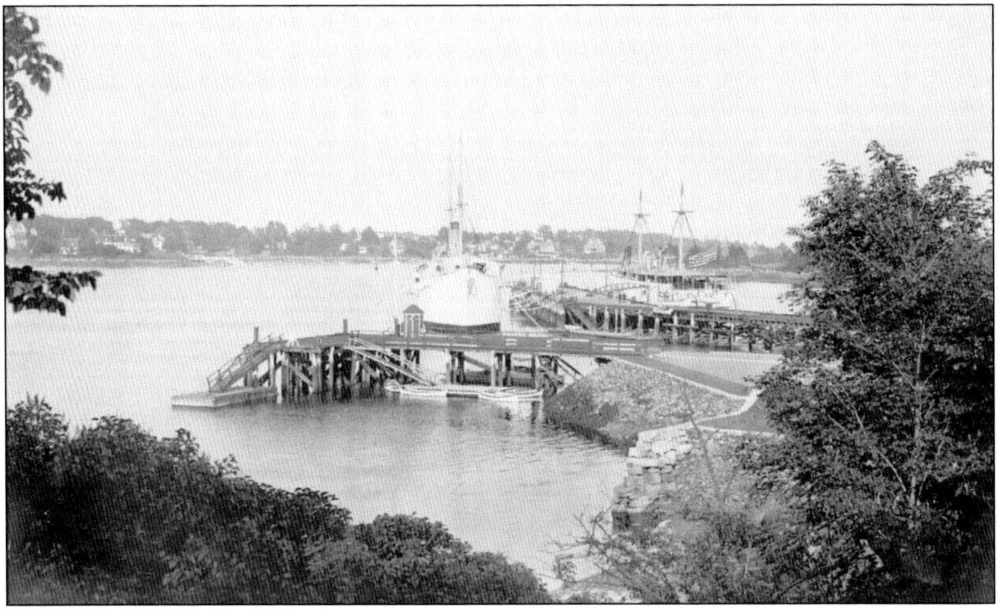

USS *Southery* and USS *Topeka*, Portsmouth, 1914. At the turn of the century, as the prison was being completed, a reform movement swept the country with adherents, known as "progressives," bent on addressing the inequities created by America's industrialization—the change from farms to factories. Among them were prison reformers. They cast a wide net that included naval prisons. Thinking, with some justification, that first-time offenders should not be willy-nilly thrown in with returnees or hardened criminals, progressive policy makers created the naval detention system. (LMCQ, White Collection.)

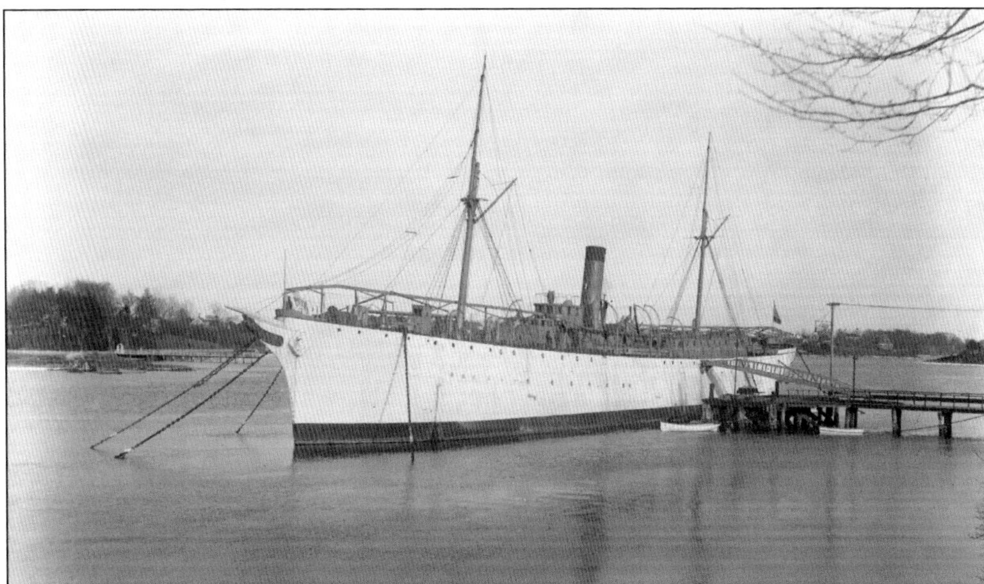

USS *Southery*. Young, first-time offenders, deserters who turned themselves in, and older men with exemplary conduct were funneled into detention and slated for return to the fleet. At Portsmouth, they were placed on the USS *Southery*. These men were retrained and allowed to work at the shipyard proper with minimal supervision. (PAC.)

YARD WORKING FORCE LEAVING USS *SOUTHERY*, 1915. The detention system was eliminated in 1917 under General Order 110 and replaced by the establishment of the probation system. This allowed men to remain in the service with reduced pay and restoration with good behavior. (UNHL.)

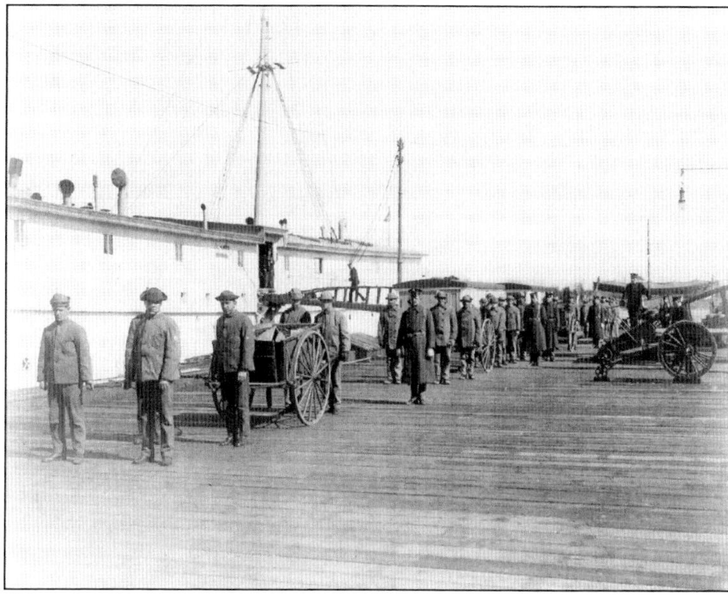

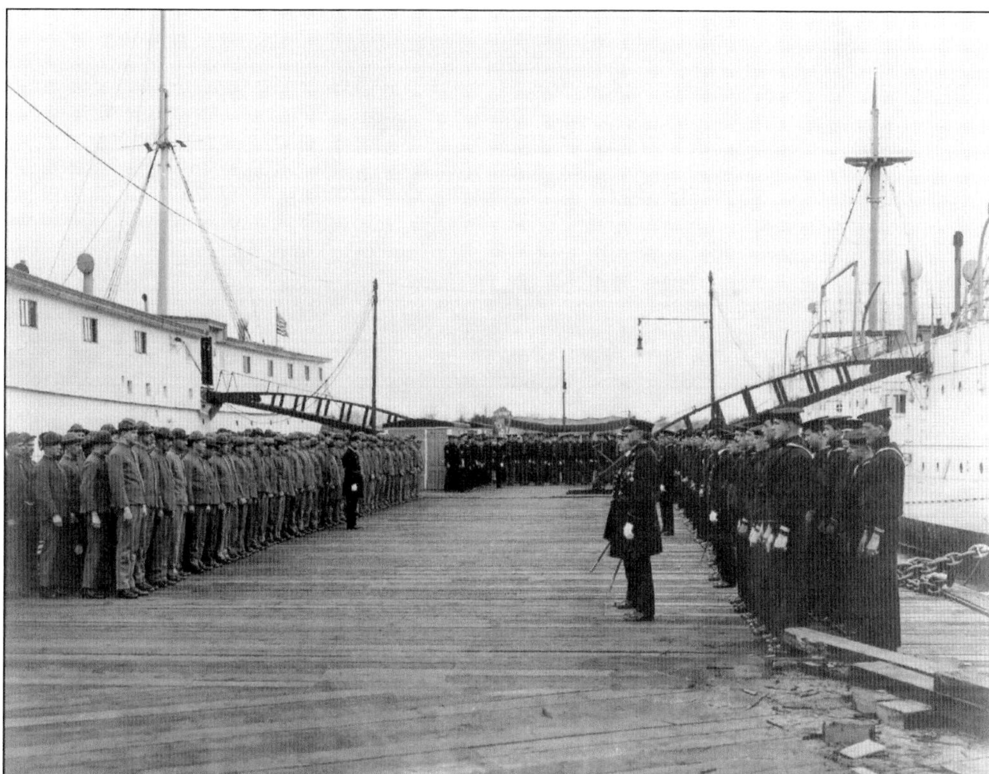

COURT-MARTIALED PRISONERS BY USS *TOPEKA*, UNDATED. Originally filled with court-martialed prisoners from Boston, the USS *Southery* (right) served as center for receiving and discharging prisoners from the opening of the prison in April 1908 until 1918. (UNHL.)

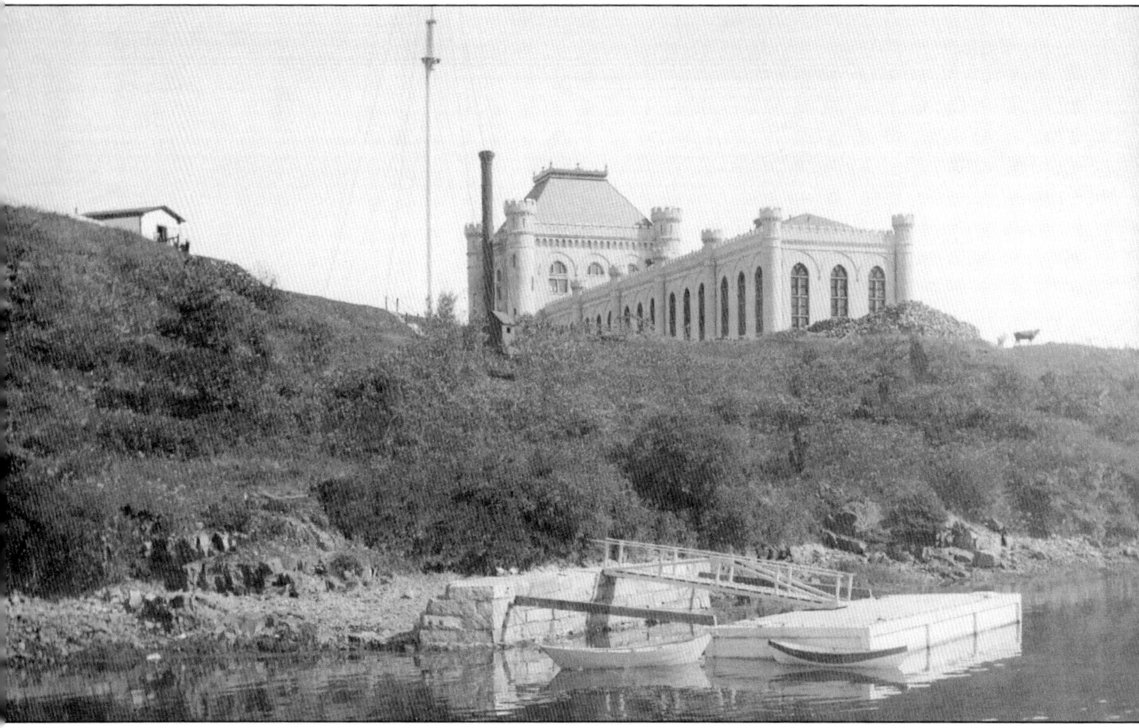

WORKMAN'S LANDING, OCTOBER 2, 1907. The first documented escape attempt was from the USS *Southery*, one of two prison ships moored at the shipyard before the prison itself was completed. On Tuesday, May 8, 1906, the *Portsmouth Herald* headline proclaimed "Daring Attempt." The story goes on to note that "one of the most desperate attempts to escape on record was made by two prisoners of the United States receiving ship *Southery* at the navy yard at about eleven o'clock this (Tuesday) forenoon." The three prisoners were engaged in a work detail when the escape plan was hatched. "It appeared that the three men had talked over a plan to escape, but one of them would not agree to it. This left it to the other two named Dutton and Myers, to carry out the desperate deed." The two took shovels, knocked down the guard, took his revolver, and sprinted to an old boat landing. Another guard, Sergeant O'Leary, hearing the disturbance gave chase, capturing them at the water's edge after a tussle with the gun. (NARACP.)

Four

BUILDING "THE ROCK"

Drawings for the prison by architects and engineers from the US Navy Bureau of Yards and Docks were completed in 1903. However, construction of the prison—Building 93 as part of the Portsmouth Navy Shipyard—came in stages: as Congress appropriated money, further work was completed. When the facility formally opened in 1908, workmen as well as prisoners occupied the building but only the prisoners were forced to stay.

Construction began in 1904. Despite the positive publicity generated by the Spanish-American War experience, rancor had already surfaced of the "not in my backyard" variety. Captain Goodrich, Navy Yard commandant, submitted a formal protest to Washington on behalf of naval officers and the residents of Portsmouth. An article to that effect appears in the October 18, 1903, *Boston Daily Globe*. But by then, Congress had already appropriated $95,000 for the project and the Bureau of Yards and Docks was soliciting bids.

Plans originally called for two long identical wings—north and south cell blocks—joined by an administration building, which would have been, nationally, the largest structure of its kind; by 1904, however, only the south cell block had been contracted for. By 1906, all of the appropriation had been spent, yet a quarter of the work was still to be completed. In fits and starts, Congress would release money—finally enough to fully operate the prison by 1912, after the opening and commissioning. Lack of resources would cause the first few prison commandants headaches, which were eloquently stated in their annual reports to the secretary of the Navy. Commandants were probably well informed of the challenges of a prison but were perhaps caught unaware by the challenges of Washington.

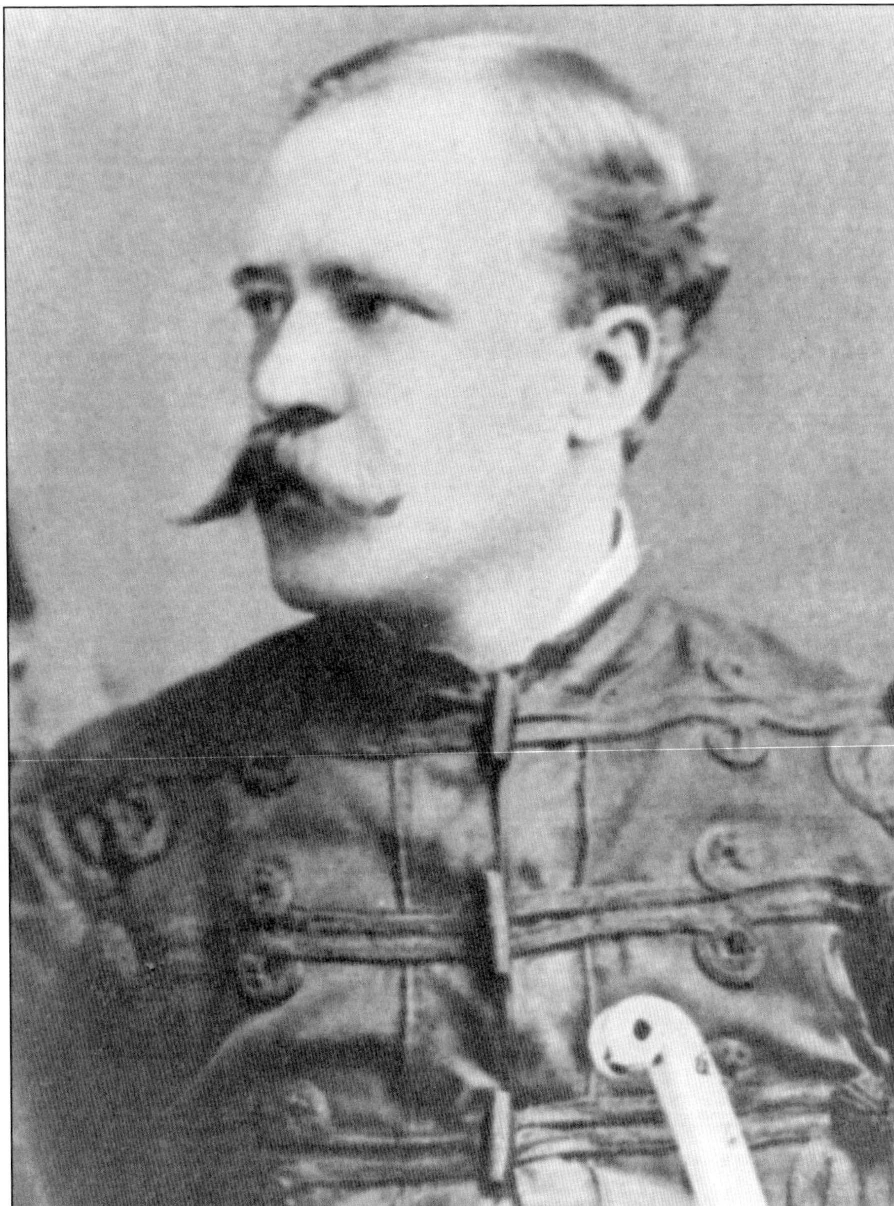

Lt. Col. Allan C. Kelton, 1908. Lieutenant Colonel Kelton, USMC, was in charge of construction of the prison and in command when it opened on April 11, 1908, still incomplete. He had fought at Guantanamo, Cuba, and returned a hero to Camp Haywood with the First Marine Battalion, having received the rare Brevet Medal for "distinguished conduct." When Kelton became commandant, he was 62 and would retire shortly after his stint at the prison. But as early as January 1908, Kelton had recommended training of the Marine guards and employment for the prisoners, suggesting that prisoner-made buckets, swabs, mattresses, and boat fenders would not only give them something to do, but also reduce costs. He had recently attended the Congress of the National Prison Association as the official Navy Department delegate. Experts there indicated that employment was necessary to prevent insanity. Kelton retired from the military in January 15, 1909, having served more than 40 years. (NHHC.)

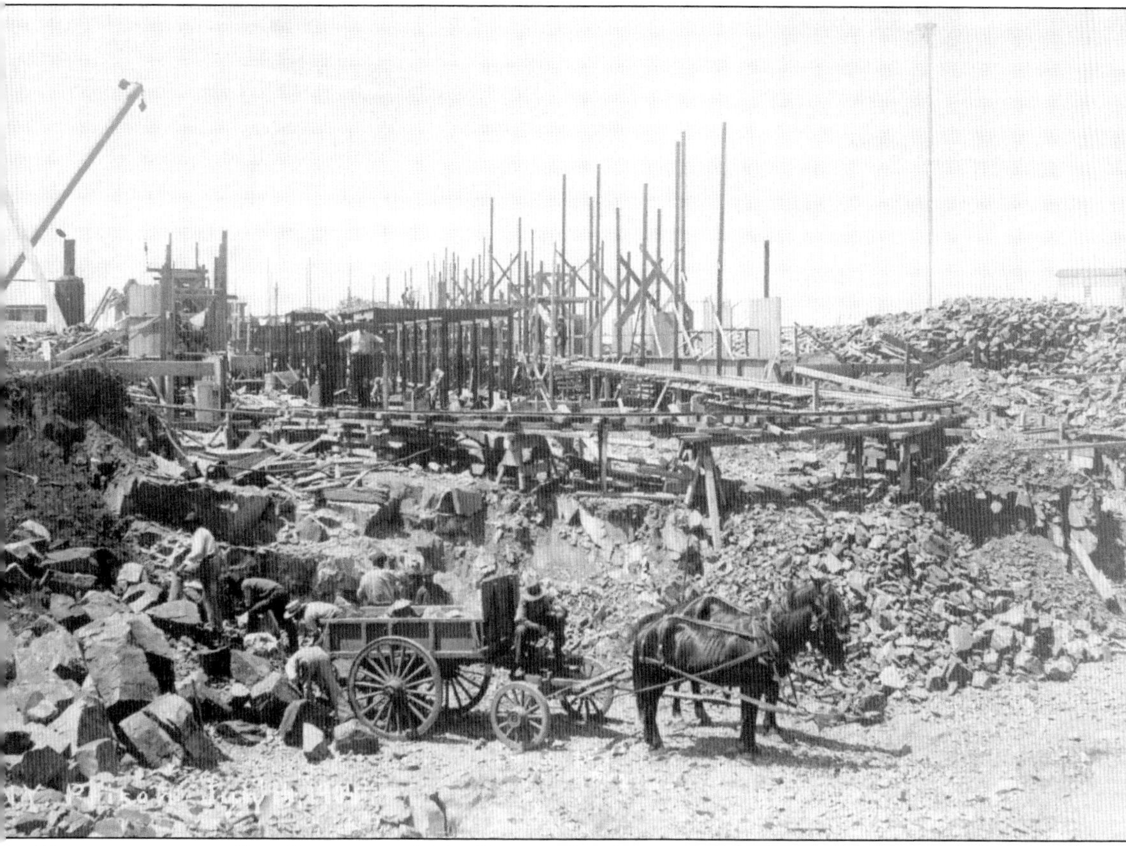

CONSTRUCTION OF CELL BLOCK, C. 1904. The initial architects and builders of the prison, which was first envisioned in 1903, were the US Navy Bureau of Yards and Docks and the Snare & Triest Company. Snare & Triest, out of New York, was responsible for much of the outside concrete ornamentation detail that characterizes the prison as well as the door, column, and ceiling details inside. A large and well-known company in its day, it also helped to construct the Rip Van Winkle and Triborough Bridges. Later, the firm split up to form two separate companies. In 1939, the Frederick Snare Company won the $34 million federal government contract to enlarge the US military base at Guantanamo, Cuba. Contrary to myth, the prison design was not inspired by Hollywood. (NARACP.)

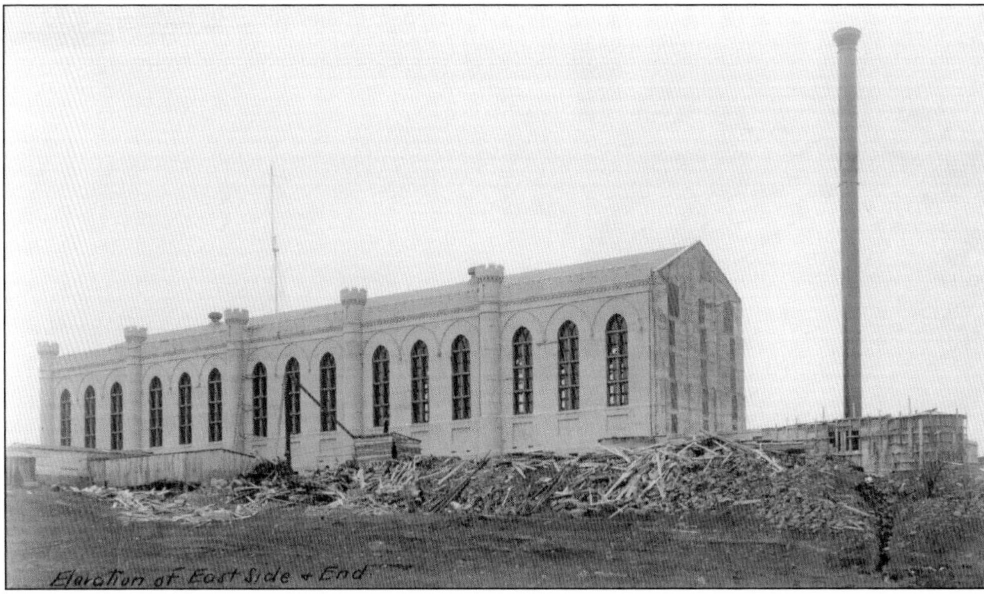

The Cell Block, January 1906. The cell block design is based on the Auburn Plan, named after the Auburn Prison still located in the town of the same name in central New York. Designed in 1821 by William Britton, a master carpenter, the plan puts prisoners in individual cells that are stacked back to back in four tiers. (NARACP.)

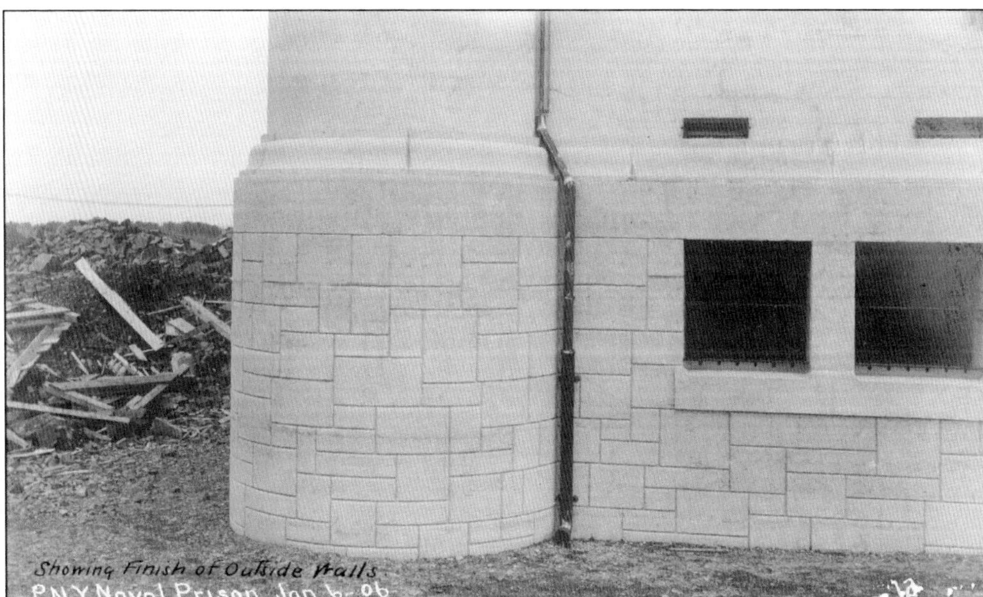

Outside Wall Finish, 1906. Initial Auburn cells measured seven feet long and high and three and a half feet wide, the smallest dimensions a person could both stand and sleep in. The individual-cell, stacked-tier design, if not the cell dimensions, became the model for many subsequent prisons, including Portsmouth. One newspaper account notes that the outside finish was ashlar, which contained cement and finely crushed granite from the mountains near Conway. It was, however, scored concrete. (NARACP.)

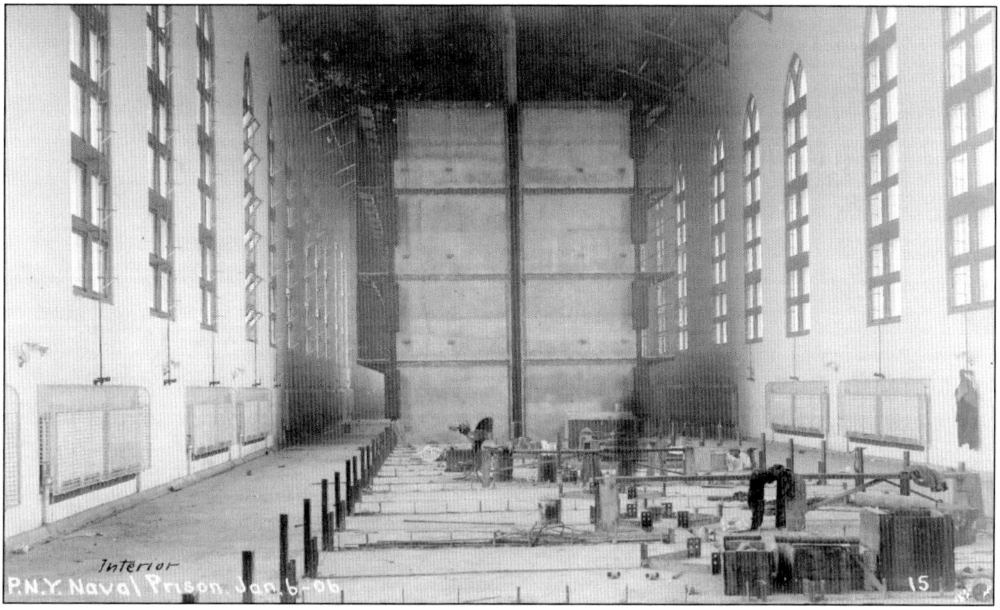

INTERIOR OF CELL BLOCK WITHOUT CELLS, 1906. The four tiers of cells were freestanding, back to back—a steel island—with access by metal staircases at each end and iron walkways encircling at each level. The inside of the cell block was painted white and sections of the large cell block windows could be opened for light and ventilation. Approximately 40 cells were on each side of a tier, 80 to a tier, with a total cell block capacity of 320. (NARACP.)

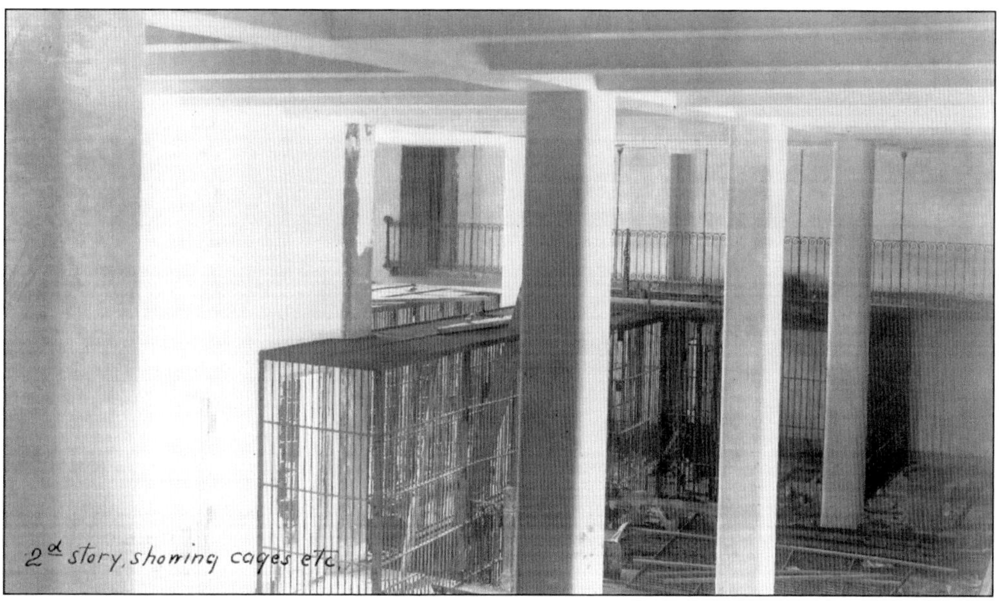

SECOND-STORY CAGES, JANUARY 1906. Even in 1916, the medical officer would report: "Winters are cold . . . and winds are usually of more velocity than comfortable. The ventilation is adequate. The chief trouble is too much air unheated in the winter." While these cells were being installed, prisoners were housed aboard the USS *Southery*. (NARACP.)

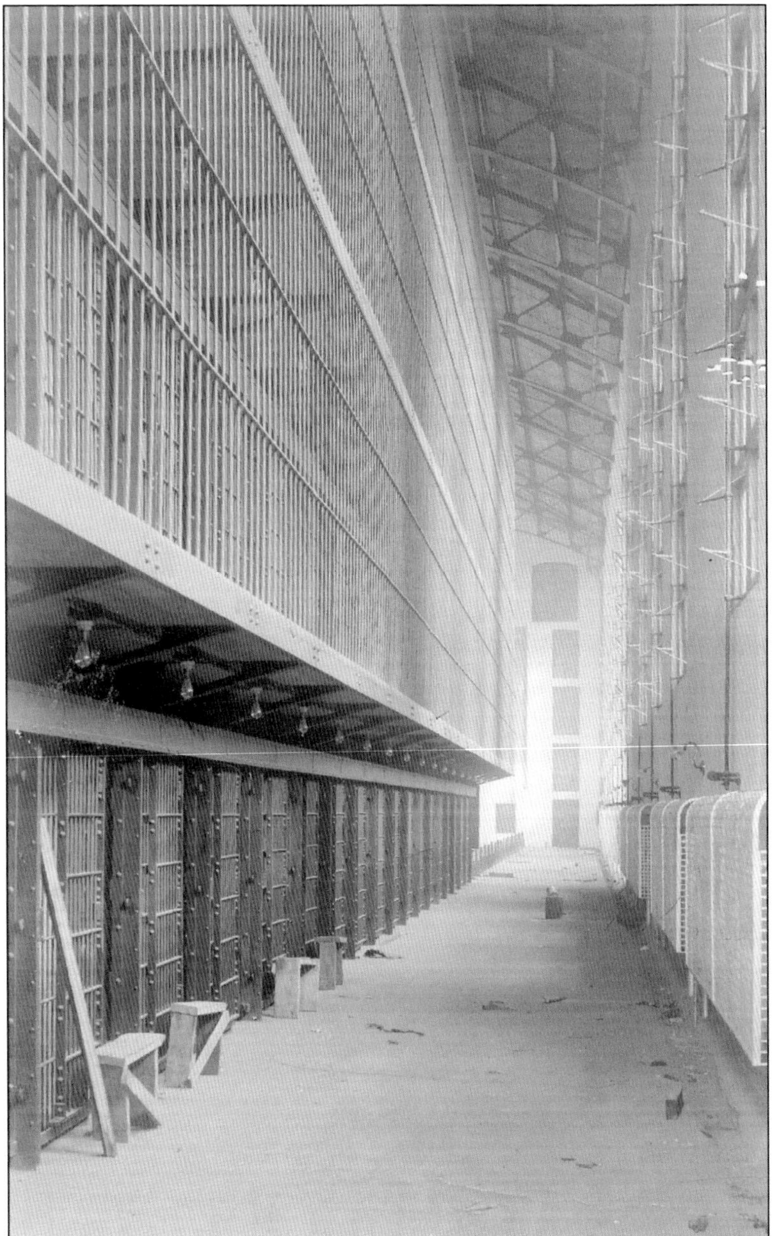

Cell Installation, 1906. Cells were six by eleven feet. Bunks, which were located adjacent to the cell door and raised and lowered by chains, were made for tall, slender prisoners: two feet, two inches by six feet, four inches. The toilet, with adjacent sink with running water, was in one corner; a chair, shelves, and sometimes a table, in the other. Count—the tallying of every prisoner four times a day—began as prisoners left the cell block each morning and was recorded on the sergeant of the guard's slate. Although other descriptions of this period indicate that men's heads were shaved, Kelton's annual report indicates that the men had their hair trimmed once a month. They were shaved two or three times a week. Men polished their own shoes at the end of the day and changed out of their work uniforms. Underwear was changed weekly, unless the weather was hot, when it was given an extra wash. Kelton was advocating for three washes. (NARACP.)

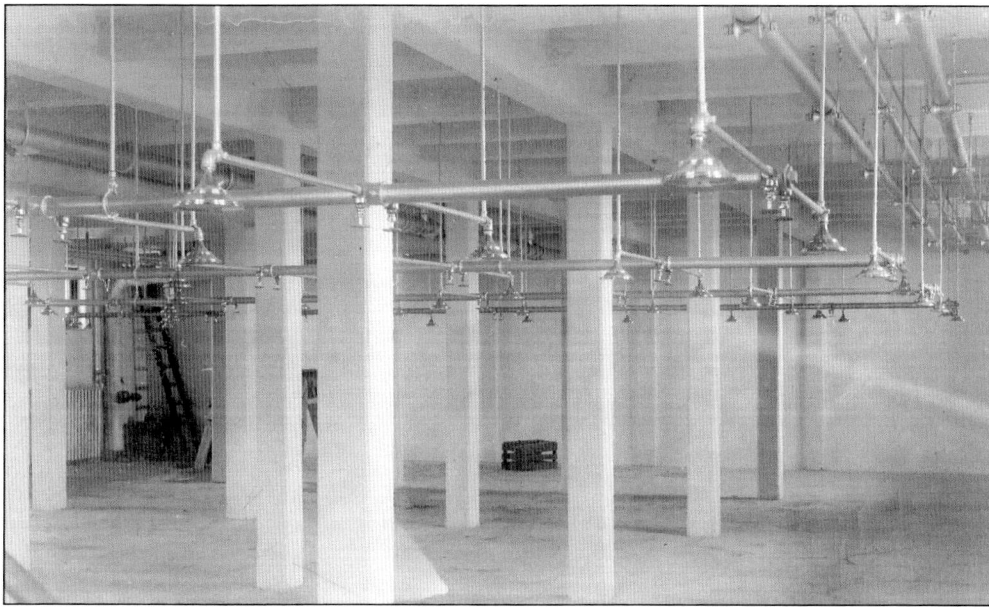

SHOWER ROOM, JANUARY 1906. The south wing cell block was finished in 1906, and work on the adjoining administration building began as the cells were being installed. The cell block contained three levels: a basement, four tiers of cells, and an attic. The basement included a shower room, sickroom, laundry, "provisions and storage," large kitchen and bakery, and three iron staircases leading upstairs. (NARACP.)

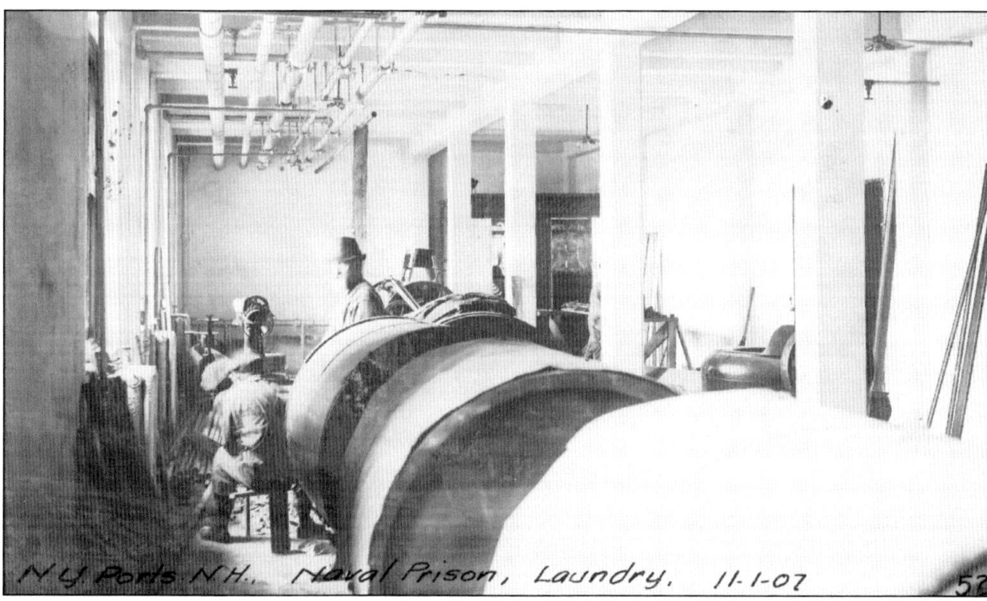

WORKMEN IN LAUNDRY, NOVEMBER 1907. Here, workmen labor in the cell block basement before the opening, but many were still on hand several years after the prison's commissioning. The uneven funding and the unfinished work, however, provided a way to keep prisoners occupied, a decided advantage. (NARACP.)

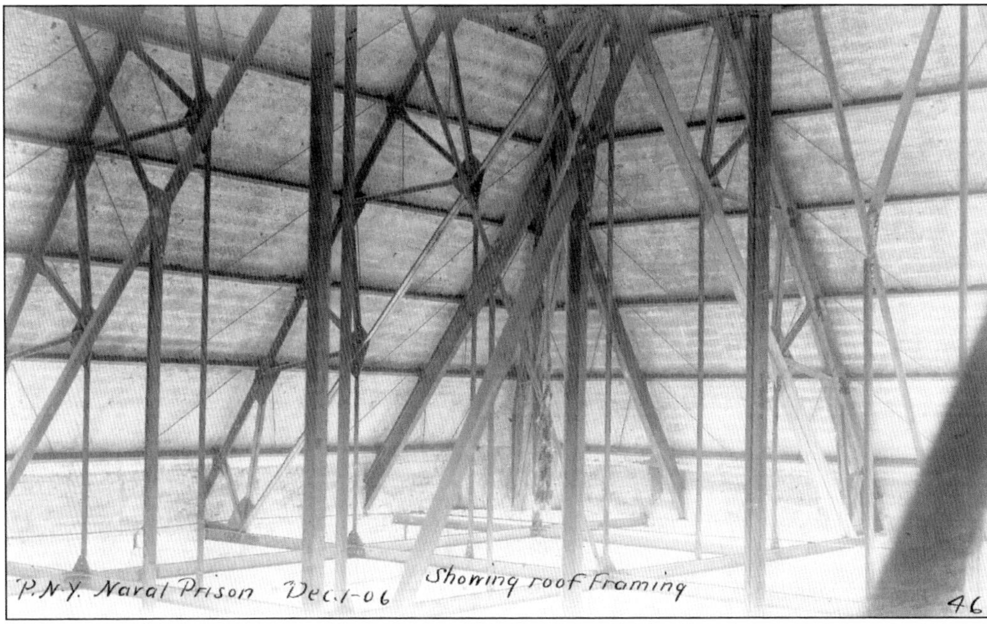

Roof Framing, December 1906. The attic above the cell block, later named the "Bull Pen," was similar in construction to this roof framing. It would be used for many years to alleviate overcrowding but was initially open with exposed trusses. (NARACP.)

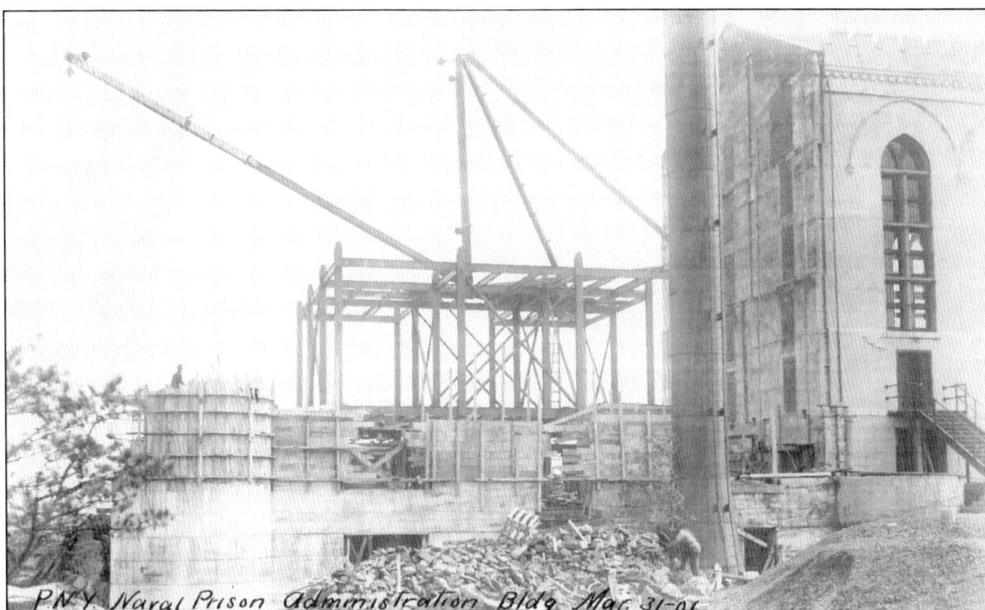

Construction of Administration Building. Construction on the administration building began in 1906, even as cell block work continued. Concrete footings and a concrete slab floor built over ledge rock, reinforced concrete columns, and beams characterized the design. The administration building was more ornate than the cell block, with four distinctive towers on each corner about 120 feet high and 13 feet in diameter. One contained an elevator, another a spiral staircase to the fourth floor. (NARACP.)

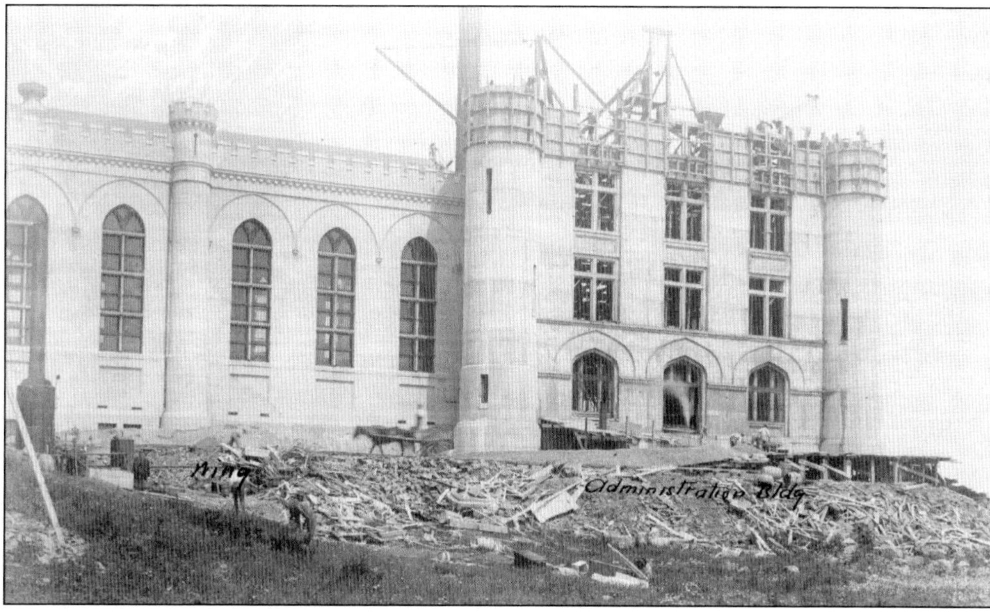

SEASIDE VIEW, JULY 1906. Long staircases with mahogany railings and ornate metal scrolling, conceived by Snare & Triest, were prominent in the administration building. On the first floor, the officer in charge, and the recorder and secretary were on the left and right respectively. On the second floor was a receiving room with five cells, a waiting room and two visitors' cages, the clothing department, and surgeon's office. The third floor contained the quartermaster, guardrooms, and stairs to the cell block. (NARACP.)

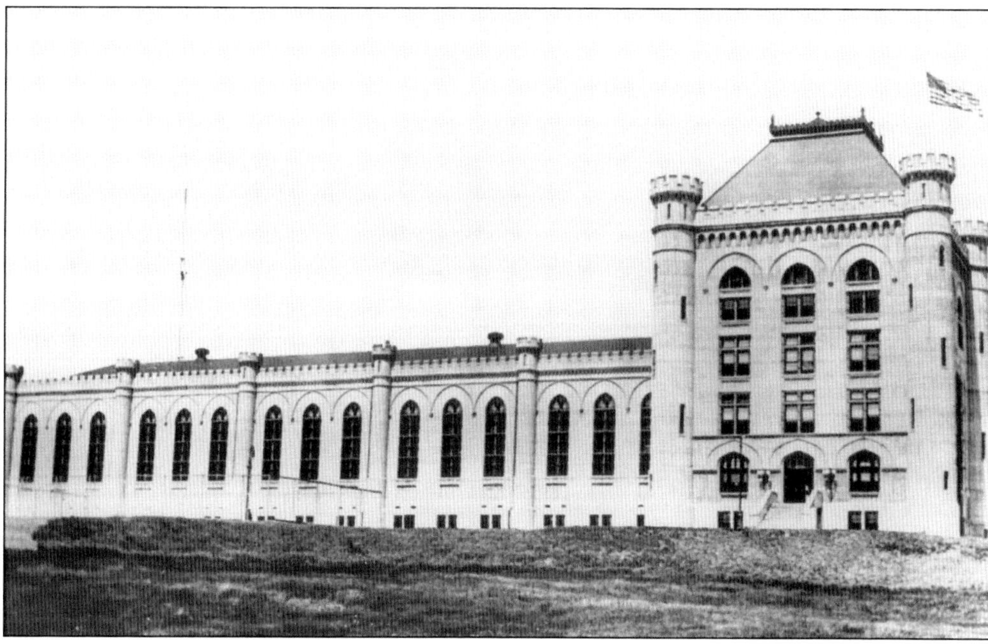

THE PRISON FACING SEAWARD, 1910. The distinctive architecture of the prison is Gothic Revival, a style popular among the 19th-century prison and church architects for its ability to inspire awe and fear: architecture was thought to shape the morality of those who entered. More frequently known as the "Castle" or "Rock," it was also called "the Stone Frigate." (UNHL.)

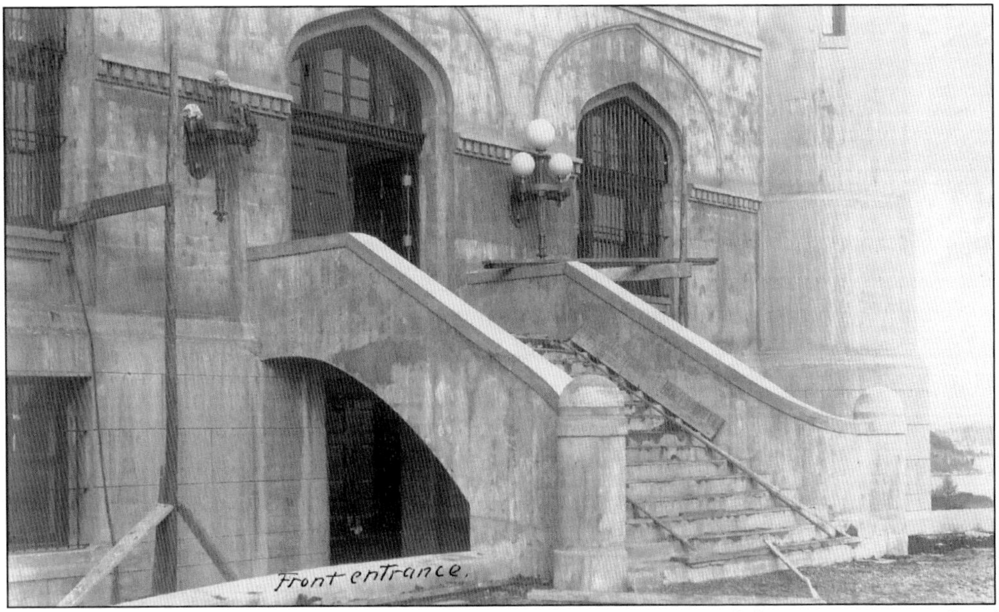

Seaside Main Entrance, January 1907. The massive entrance of the prison was made of concrete and flared, with stairs stretching first 18 feet wide and narrowing to 10 feet in front of an imposing 14-by-8-foot wooden double door. The stairs had concrete sides, known as balustrades, with rounded cement newels at the ground level. Flanking the entrance at the top were two five-globe brass electroliers, or chandeliers lit electrically, if the visitors needed one last imposing sight. (NARACP.)

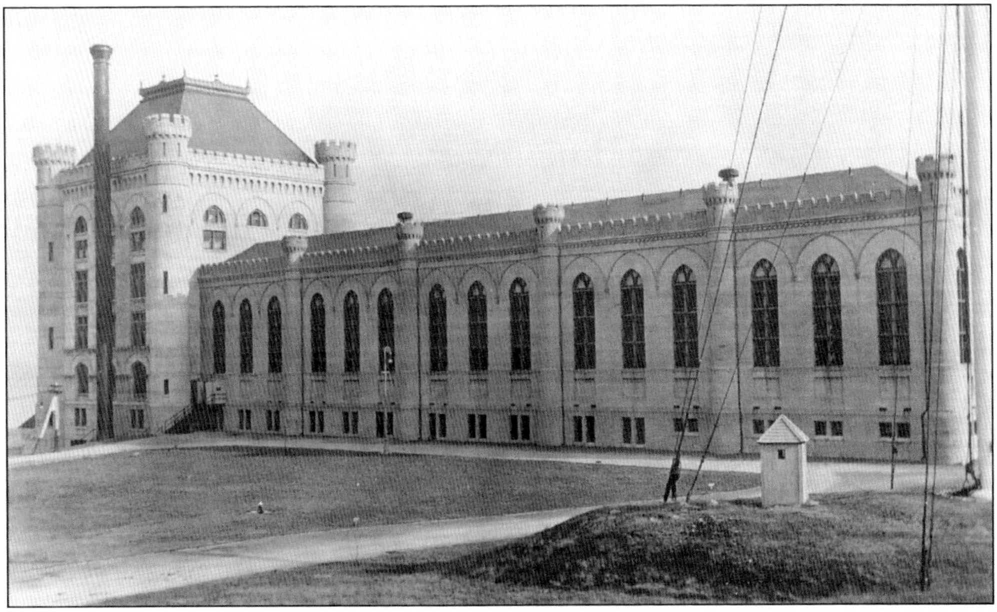

Back View Showing Parade Grounds, c. 1910. The building's crenellated parapets, decorative moldings, ornamented corbel, and pointed arch windows and entryways were meant to symbolize the virtues of the Christian medieval past. The long cell block has a six-inch concrete basement floor built on rock. (LMCQ, Fitzgerald Collection.)

Five

The First Hard Years

The prison was not ready for Col. Allan C. Kelton, USMC, until 1907 and was finally officially accepted for the "detention of court-martialed prisoners" on April 11, 1908. For several months only, a small group of working prisoners stayed in the few finished cells. Finally, on July 3, 1908, Kelton reported that he had received 151 prisoners from the USS *Southery*, less one who was discharged and one restored to duty. Of the 151 men, 126 were from the Navy and 25 were Marines. At that time, only that many of the 320 planned cells were finished, with no housing for the 43 Marine guards assigned there. Further, with a shortage of Marines, as many were being sent to Panama and other foreign hot spots, prisoners were forced to remain in their cells more than Kelton thought desirable, a fact notes in his report—the first annual—to the Navy Department.

He had established a daily routine with cooks called at 3:00 a.m., the mess gang at 4:45, and reveille at 5:10. Shaping up exercises began at 5:50 with breakfast at 6:10. Working gangs were engaged from 7:15 to 11:15 and from 1:00 to 4:15. Everyone showered at 4:25, had supper at 5:00, and got his mail at 6:15. The smoking lamp—designating when smoking was permitted—was turned out at 7:00. Interestingly, the daily routine in the annual report is not written in military time, which had not yet been adopted by the Navy. And, despite Kelton's despair over the lack of prisoner activity, much was accomplished the first year. Prisoners were repairing and grading roads, cleaning buildings, drilling and breaking rock, cooking, baking, and painting. As well, they were engaged as clerks, shoemakers, tailors, blacksmiths, mechanics, and officer assistants. The average cost for each prisoner yearly was thus far $70.84.

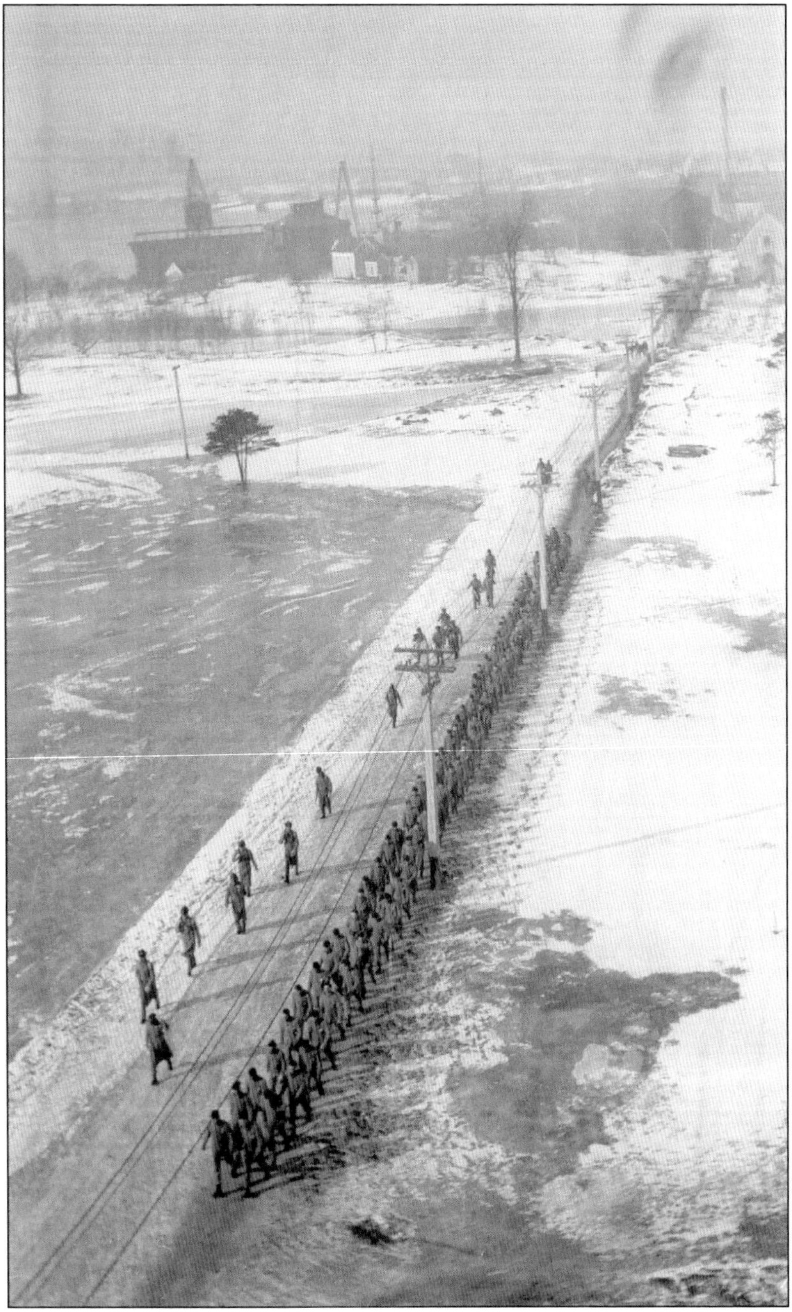

Prisoners Returning from Work at Shipyard, 1908. As part of the program, talking and all communication between prisoners was forbidden. This included inside the prison proper as well as outside while on work detail. Any prisoner wanting to hand something to another had to do so through a "sentinel" who would first inspect it. In vogue at the time, and thought to be a significant reform, was this no-talking Auburn system of prisoner control—the same Auburn system that had been the model for the four-tiered cell block. Portsmouth was, compared to Boston or Mare Island (California) where Navy, Marine and Coast Guard prisoners were also sent, a harsher and more demanding facility. (UNHL.)

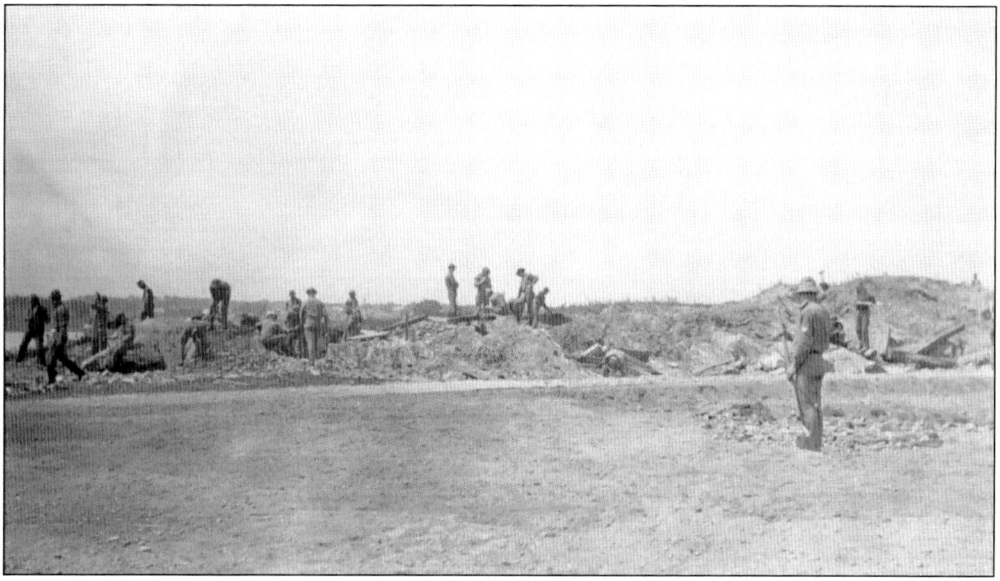

Prisoners at Work, 1911. On file at the National Archives at Boston are summaries of the early court-martial proceedings. Men ended up at the prison for a variety of reasons, a punishment that today may seem harsh. For example, John J. Murphy, ship's cook, second class, US Naval Reserve Force, was tried by general court-martial on July 11, 1918, at the Navy Yard, Boston, Massachusetts, and found guilty of "absence from station and duty without leave." (LMCQ, Fitzgerald Collection.)

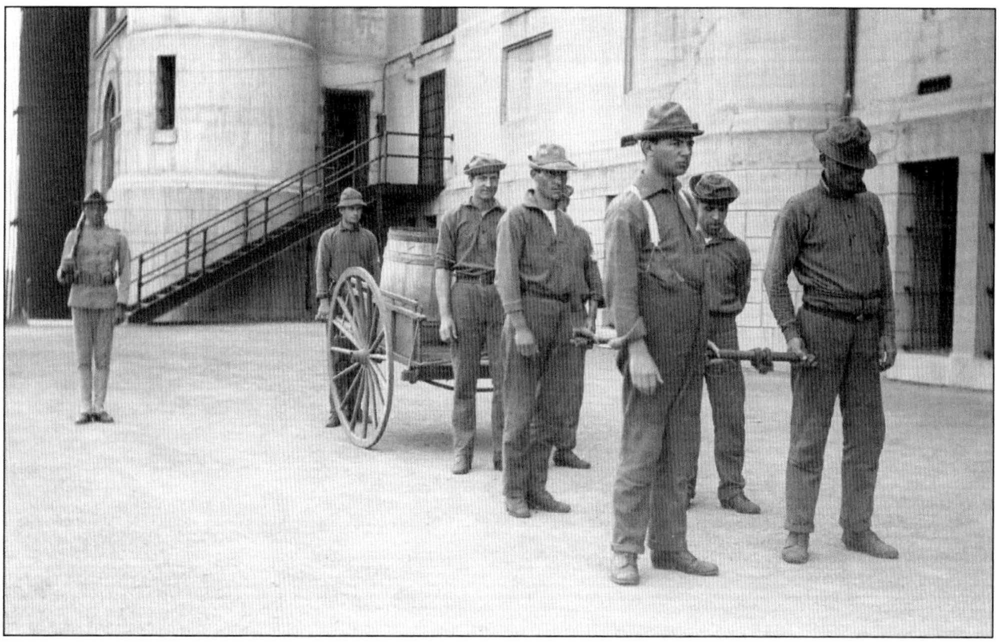

Prisoners Hauling a Cask, 1908. Murphy's sentence included a reduction in rating to ship's cook, third class and "confinement for a period of two (2) years at the Naval Prison at the Navy Yard, Portsmouth, New Hampshire." Stanley Philip Laundeck, fireman, third class, US Navy, received a similar sentence for stealing a $50 Liberty Bond. Both were also dishonorably discharged. (UNHL.)

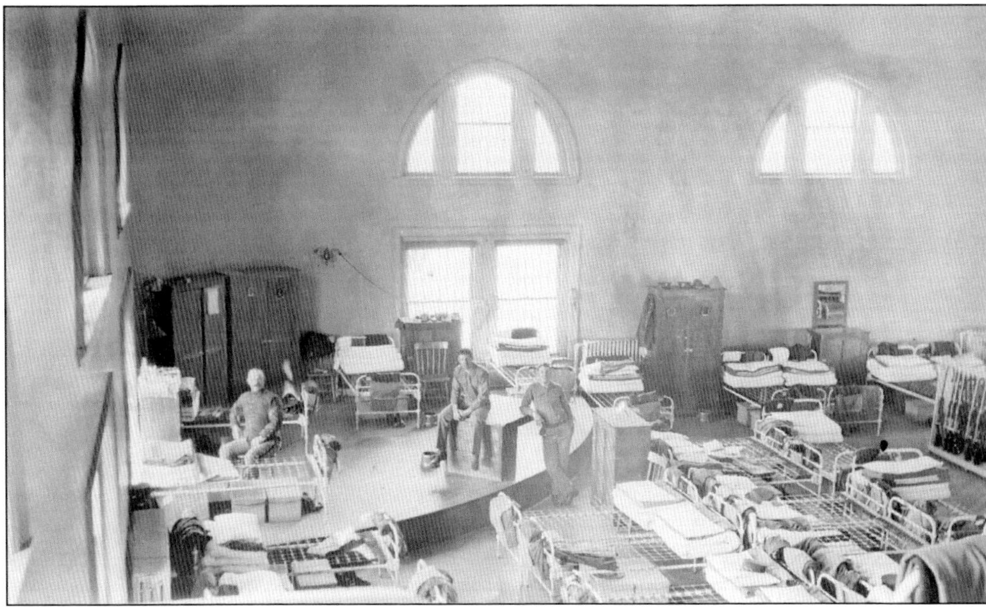

Marine Quarters, c. 1911. When the prison opened, there were no quarters for the Marine guards who, by necessity, would take over the fourth and most of the third floors of the administration building. (LMCQ, Fitzgerald Collection.)

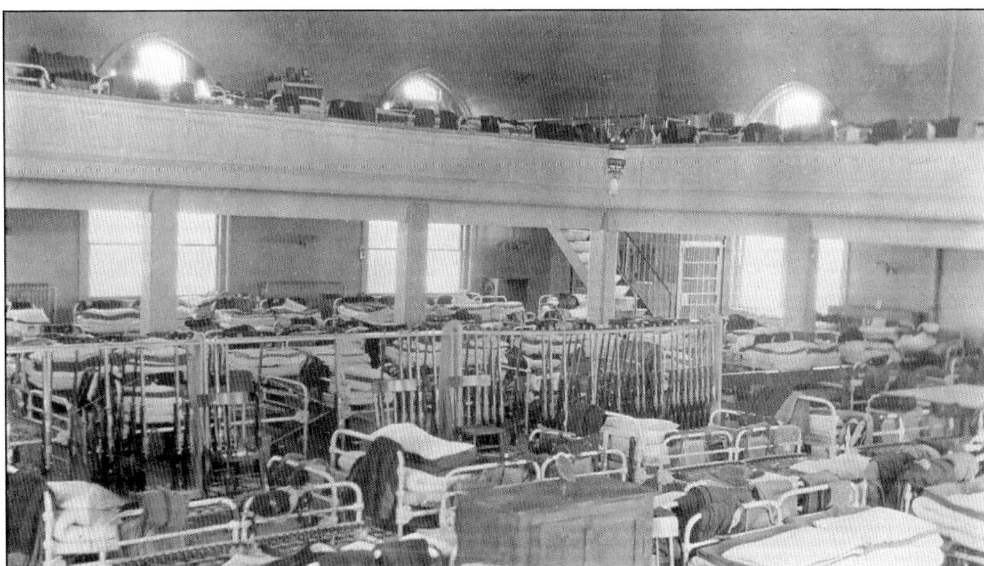

Marine Quarters, Administration Building. Although space was at a premium, there was still room for rifles, standing in a row in the middle of the photograph, parallel to the balcony. (NHHC.)

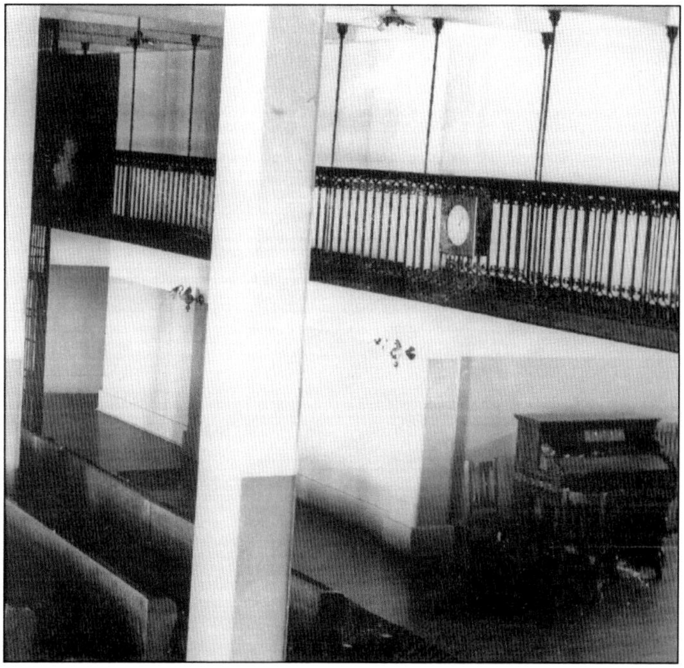

First-Floor Chapel, 1910. The chapel at this time was on the first floor. The mahogany railings and ornate metal scrolling in the mezzanine are characteristic of the Snare & Triest Company. (NHHC.)

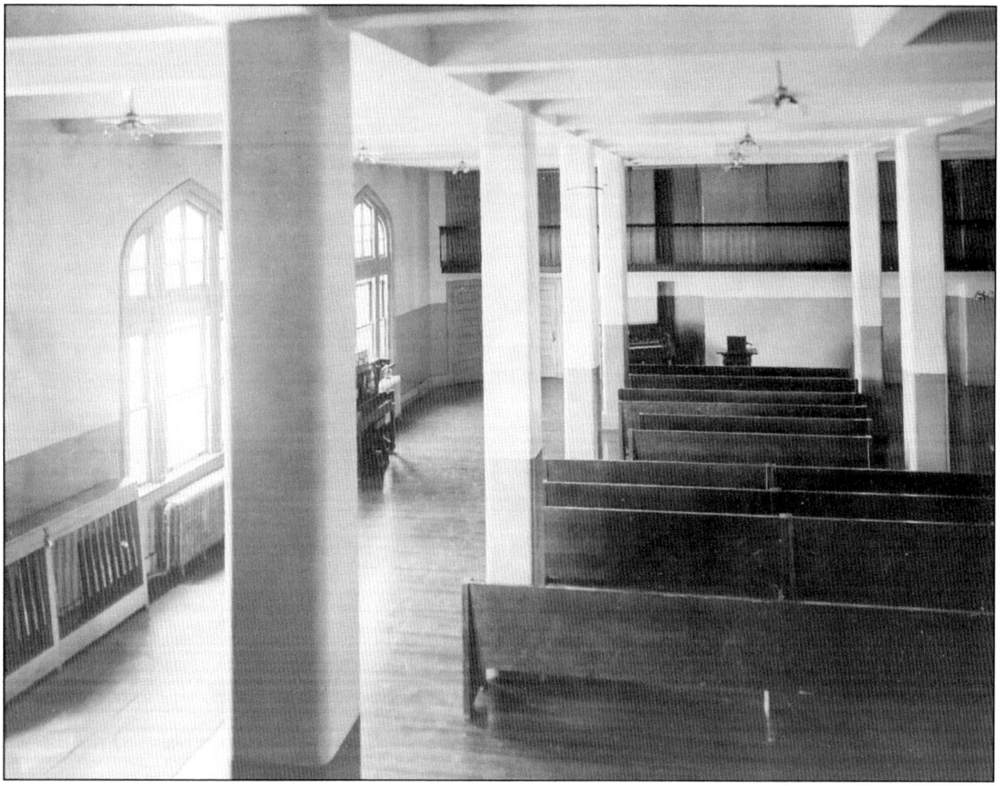

Administration First Floor, 1910. After the prison's commissioning in 1908, "divine services" were held Sunday morning and afternoon for a few Christian denominations. Only later would the annual report discuss services for Jewish prisoners. (NHHC.)

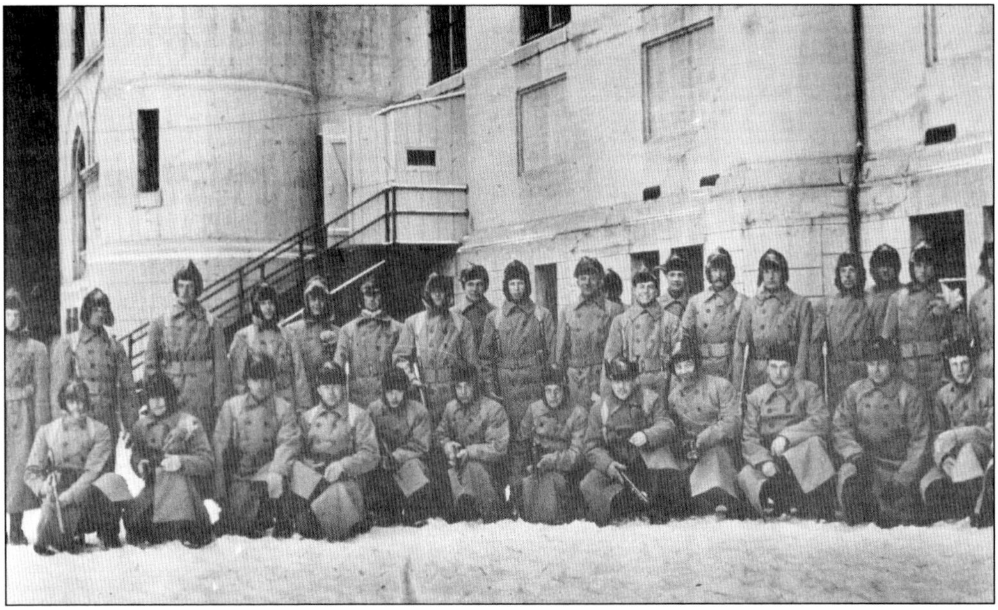

MARINE GUARD IN WINTER GEAR, C. 1910. At this time, all security was provided by the Marines. The detachment was divided into exterior perimeter security and "chasers" inside with the prisoners to guard their movements and control activity. The Marine Guard was usually headed by the Marine captain who would be designated as officer of the guard. He would report to the commandant, the prison's commanding officer. (PAC.)

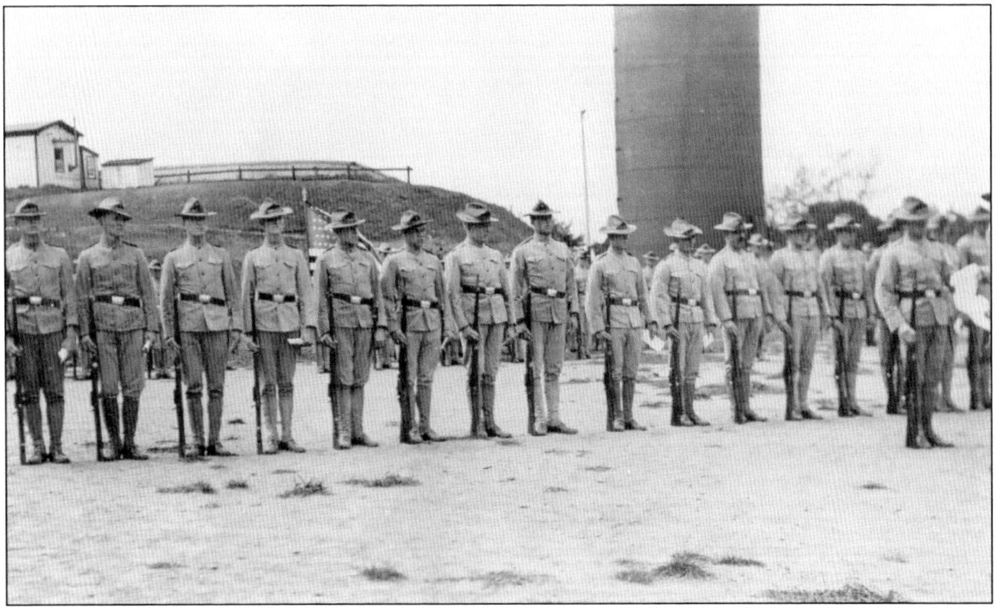

MARINE GUARD INSPECTION, 1908. As well as guarding prisoners, the Marines engaged in daily drills and exercises, reported for instruction and inspection, known as guard mount, which is shown here. The large steel standpipe in the background is prominent in a number of the early photographs of the prison. It was constructed around the turn of the century along with a central power and lighting system for the shipyard. At the time, standpipes were used to hold and distribute water. (NHHC.)

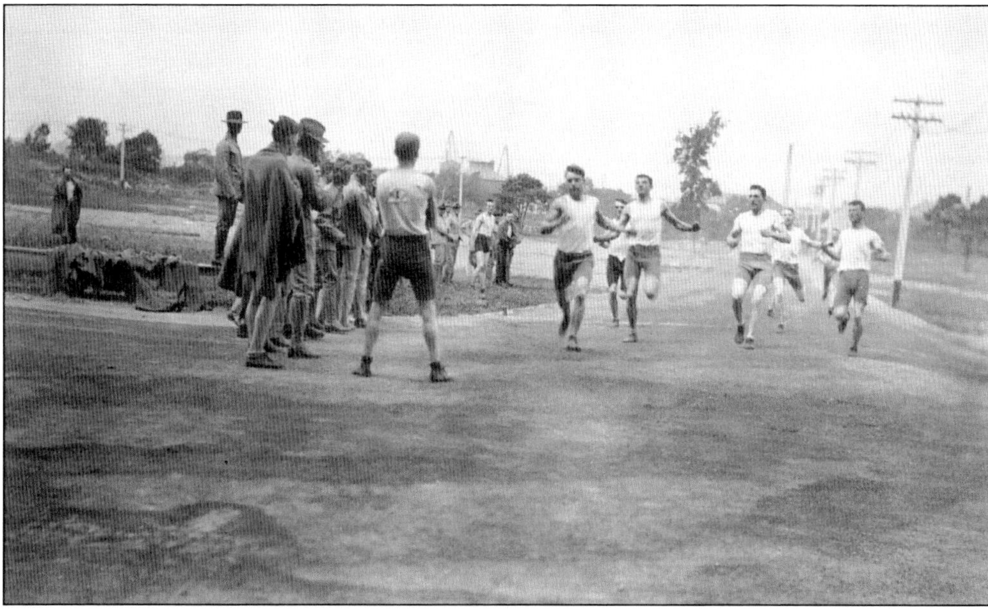

THE 440-YARD DASH, 1910. This is the finish of the race won by Corporal Newton, standing with his arms folded. Many photographs show the Marines at work; few show them at play. The fields around the prison and the long road to the shipyard seem to have inspired a number of diversions, some of the few in the early years. Although it is clear that the Marines participated in the race, it is doubtful that the prisoners did as well. (LMCQ, Fitzgerald Collection.)

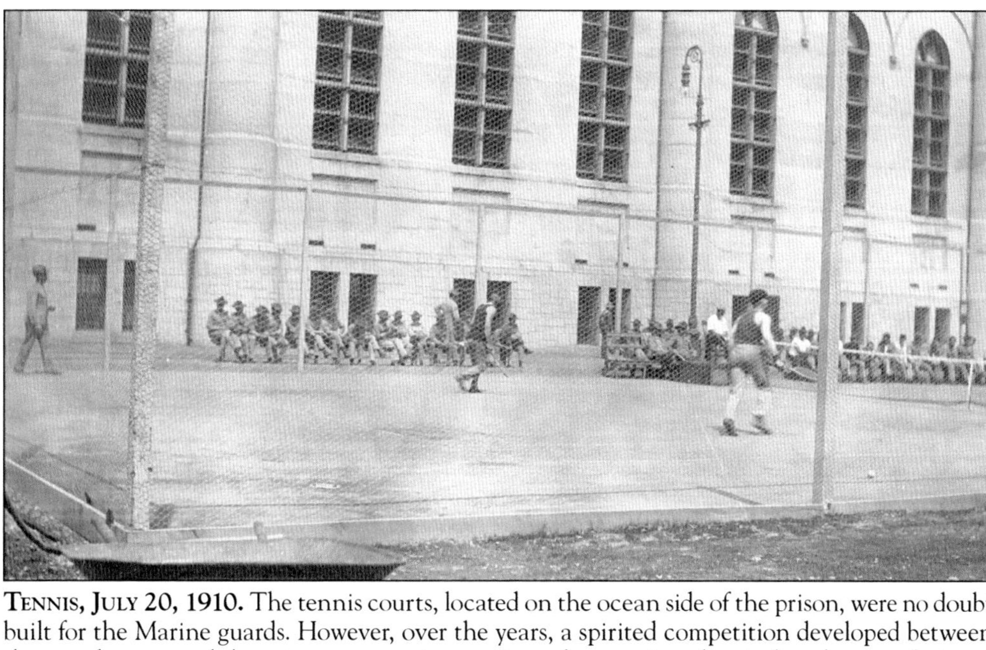

TENNIS, JULY 20, 1910. The tennis courts, located on the ocean side of the prison, were no doubt built for the Marine guards. However, over the years, a spirited competition developed between the guard teams and the prisoner teams in a variety of sports. Lore has it that the more heinous the crime, the better the athlete. (LMCQ, Fitzgerald Collection.)

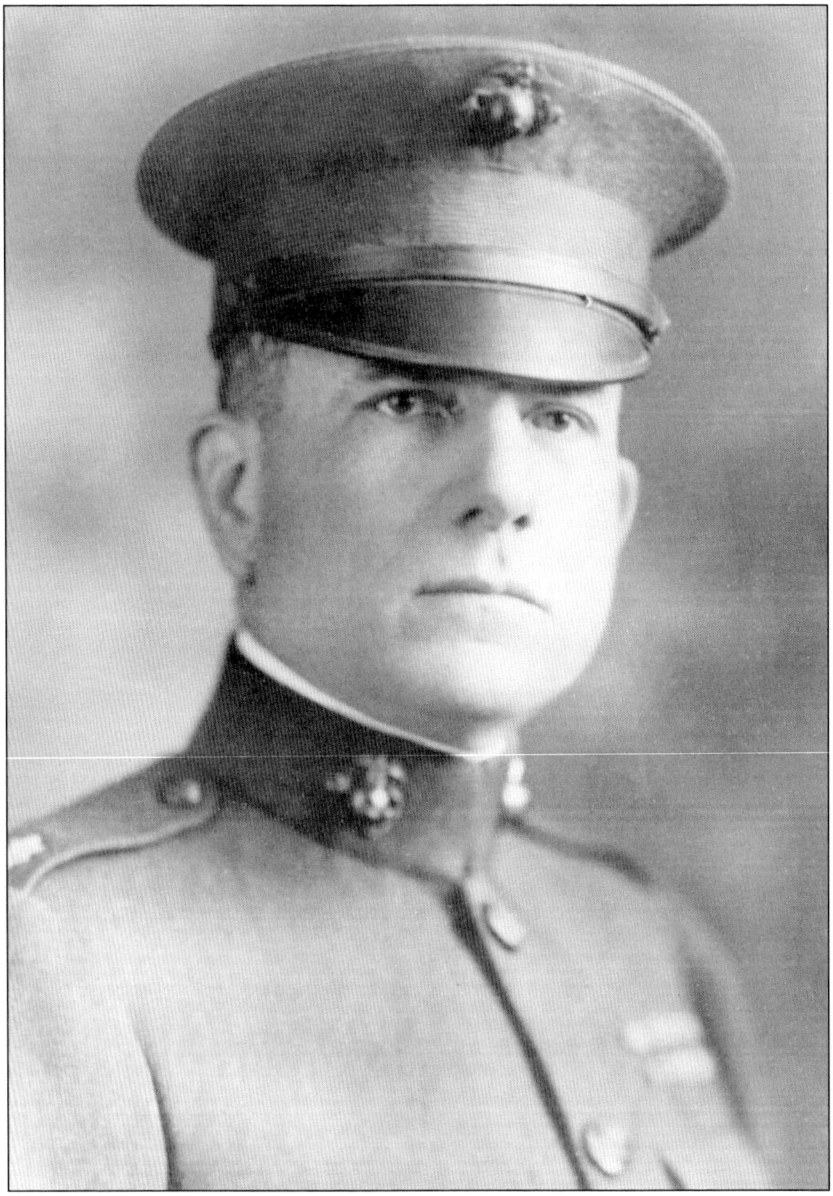

Maj. Henry Leonard, USMC. When Maj. Henry Leonard arrived on September 10, 1908, to replace Col. Allan C. Kelton, he inherited many of Kelton's problems. Too few Marines were on hand and they were still quartered in the administration building; the cell block locking system proved defective, and the undergrowth on prison grounds was a perfect hiding place for escapees. Like Colonel Kelton, Major Leonard pressed for separate barracks for the prison guards and quarters for the officers. He was, however, less generous with the prisoners. Leonard felt that the amount of meat eaten and the coffee drunk contributed to men's disciplinary problems, so he reduced meat servings and eliminated coffee altogether. Leonard, who had lost an arm in the Battle of Tientsin in 1900, would later become a lieutenant colonel and a prominent Washington, DC, lawyer. He would successfully defend his old friend Maj. Gen. Smedley Butler in 1931, when Butler was court-martialed over remarks he made about Italian premier Benito Mussolini. Leonard died in Colorado Springs in 1945. (NHHC.)

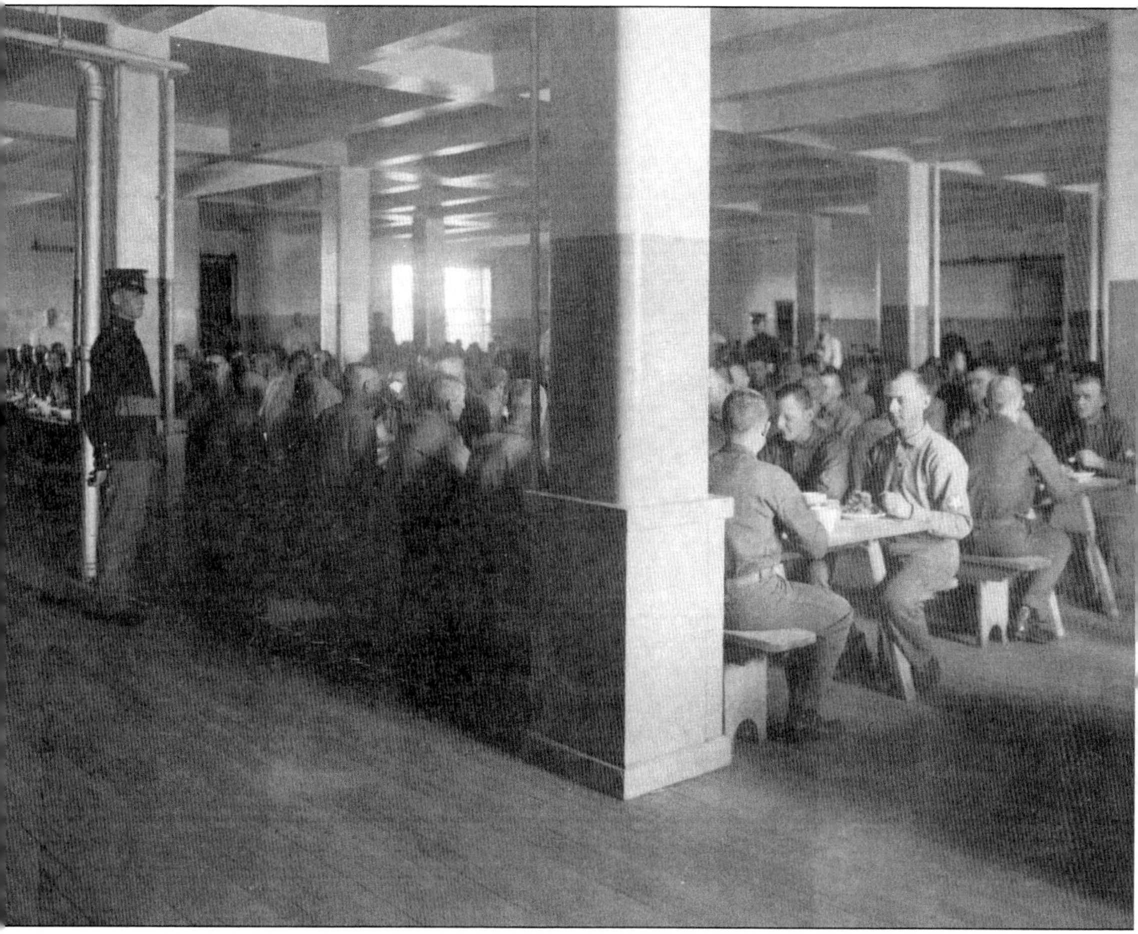

PRISONERS AT MESS, MARCH 1915. For prisoners, the menu was nutritious but uninspiring. Breakfast for the week in 1913 was pork and beans and bread, cornmeal mush and bread, or oatmeal mush and bread. Dinner, the main meal of the day, consisted largely of beef—roast, corned, or boiled—gravy, potatoes, bread, and a vegetable, generally beans of some kind or vegetable soup. The evening meal was always bread with pea or bean soup, macaroni, and pork and beans. If there was dessert or sugar of any kind, it does not appear on this menu. (PAC.)

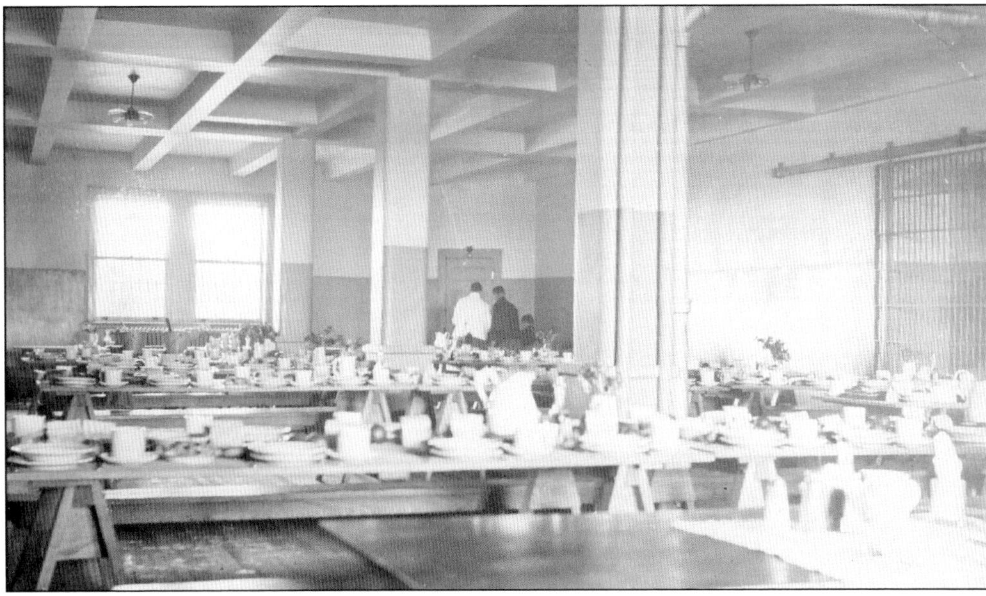

MARINE MESS HALL, THANKSGIVING 1911. The mess hall was first located in the basement of the administration building, with separate dining facilities for prisoners and guards and a common kitchen. Prisoners were still not permitted to talk to each other and sat according to their behavioral status. However, a school, run daily with two prisoners detailed as schoolmasters, was established. (LMCQ, Fitzgerald Collection.)

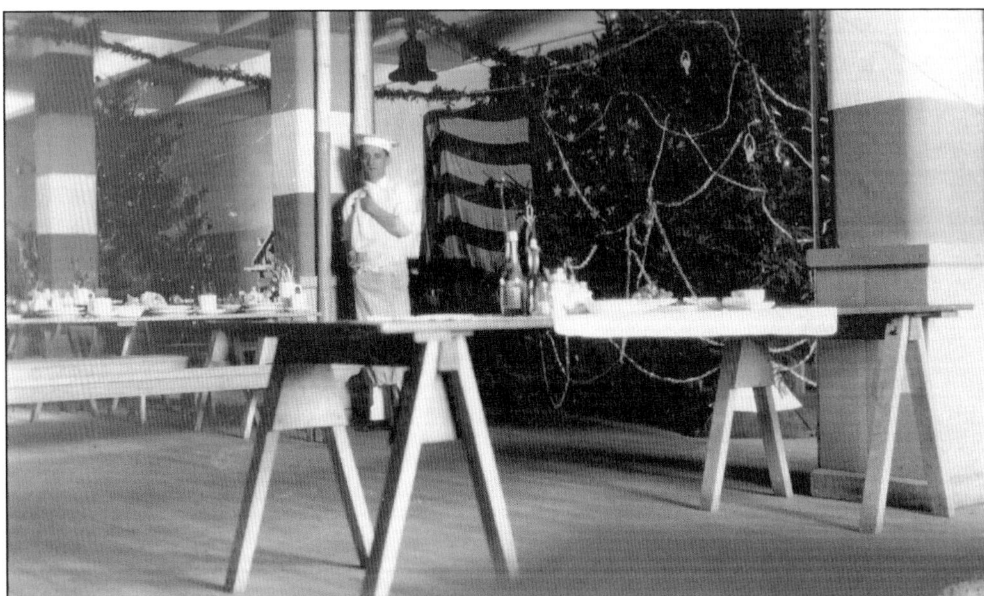

MARINE MESS HALL, CHRISTMAS 1912. Like Kelton, Leonard kept the men busy. They graded the road, lined sewers, cleared snow, stored ice, reinforced the seawall, and contributed to the general maintenance of the prison. With the installation of new equipment, whole departments were now run by prison labor: laundry, carpentry, painting, and prison printing, as well as work done by blacksmiths, tailors, cobblers, and barbers. (LMCQ, Fitzgerald Collection.)

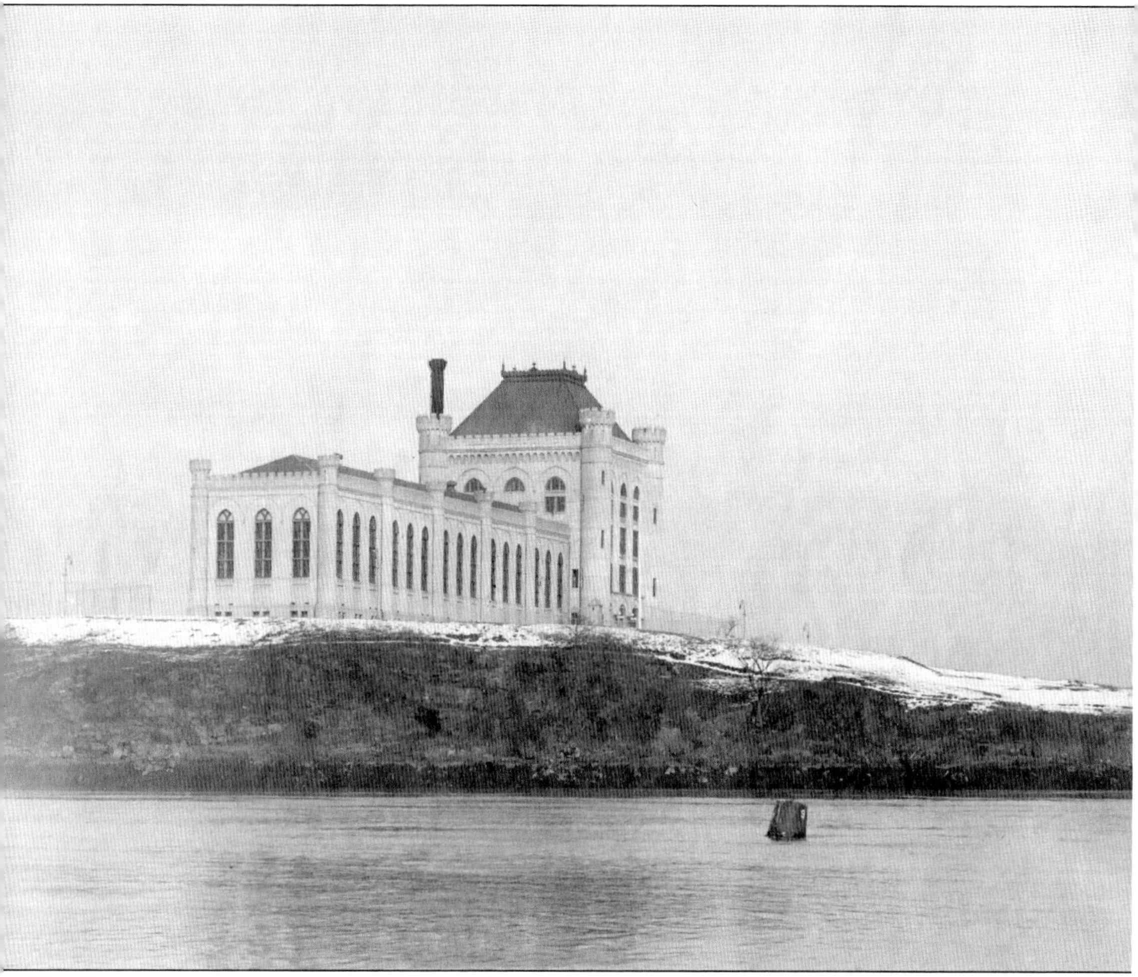

The Prison from the Piscataqua. One of the few winter escape attempts made all the local as well as many national newspapers. "Shot Down by Guards" headlines the January 29, 1910, *Boston Daily Globe*. After their noon meal, Raymond F. Spurling, Harry McGarvey, and Albert J. Montgomery were walking, under guard, back to their work detail. Near the water's edge, the three suddenly broke away and sprinted toward a workman's idle boat and rowed toward New Castle, New Hampshire, on the opposite shore. "The guard blew the whistle for help and a general alarm was sounded and soon other guards arrived and firing, with rifles loaded with buckshot, began." Spurling was wounded in the chest and died an hour later. McGarvey was wounded in the left arm; Montgomery, the left leg and right arm. "The boat drifted helplessly about the river with its wounded crew for some time before the guards could put out and tow it back," reported the *New York Times*. "The wounded men were sent at once to the Naval Hospital [in the navy yard] for treatment." (NARACP.)

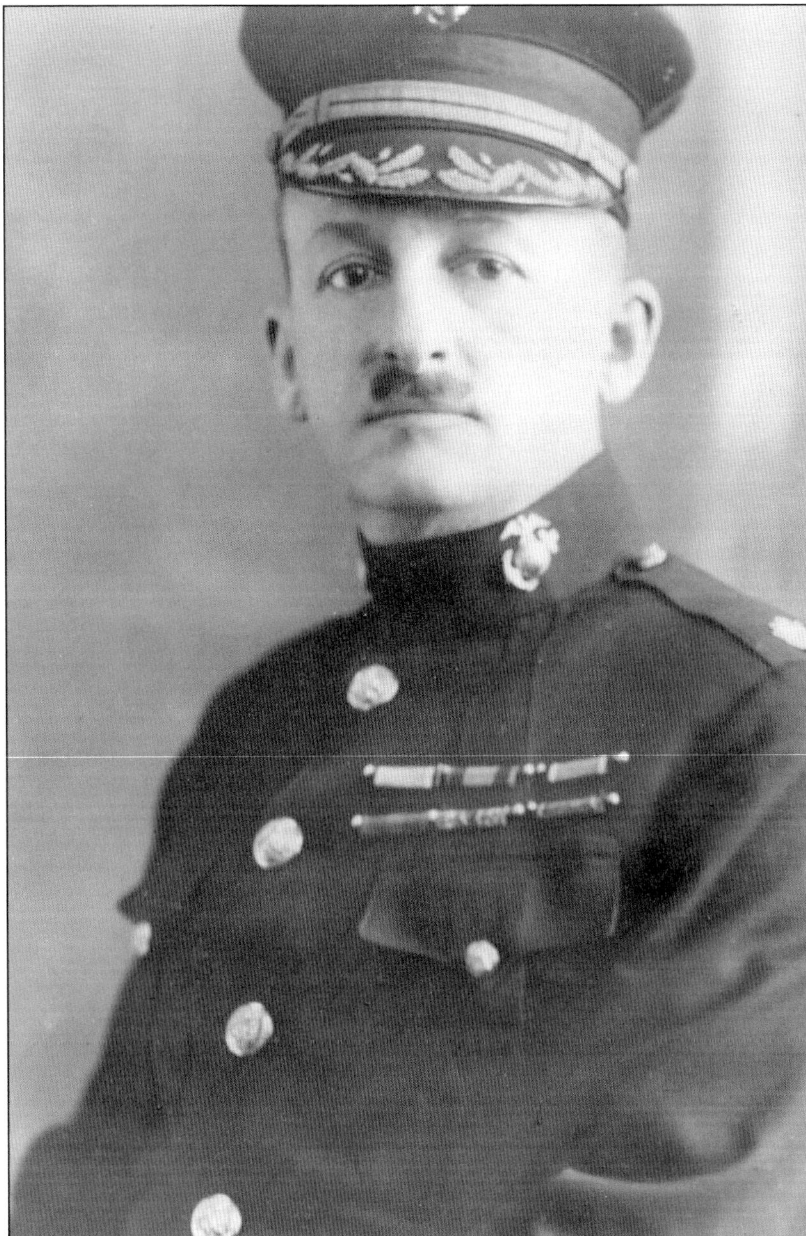

Capt. Julius S. Turrill, USMC. Prior to Maj. George C. Thorpe assuming command of the prison in September 1911, Capt. Julius S. Turrill had the briefest command—from August 19 to September 13, 1911. Before coming to the prison, he had been on the battleship *Missouri* when Pres. Teddy Roosevelt sent the United States' fleet around the world, which gave rise to a record number of deserters, many of whom ended up at Portsmouth. With the United States expanding into the Philippines and the West Indies, part of the difficulty in keeping Marines at the prison was due to their being billeted elsewhere. This seemed to include Turrill. By June 1912, he was the commander of Company D in the First Provincial Regiment at Guantanamo, Cuba. A native of Shelburne, Vermont, Turrill retired in 1932 as brigadier general after 34 years in the service. A much decorated Marine, he died in 1943. (NHHC.)

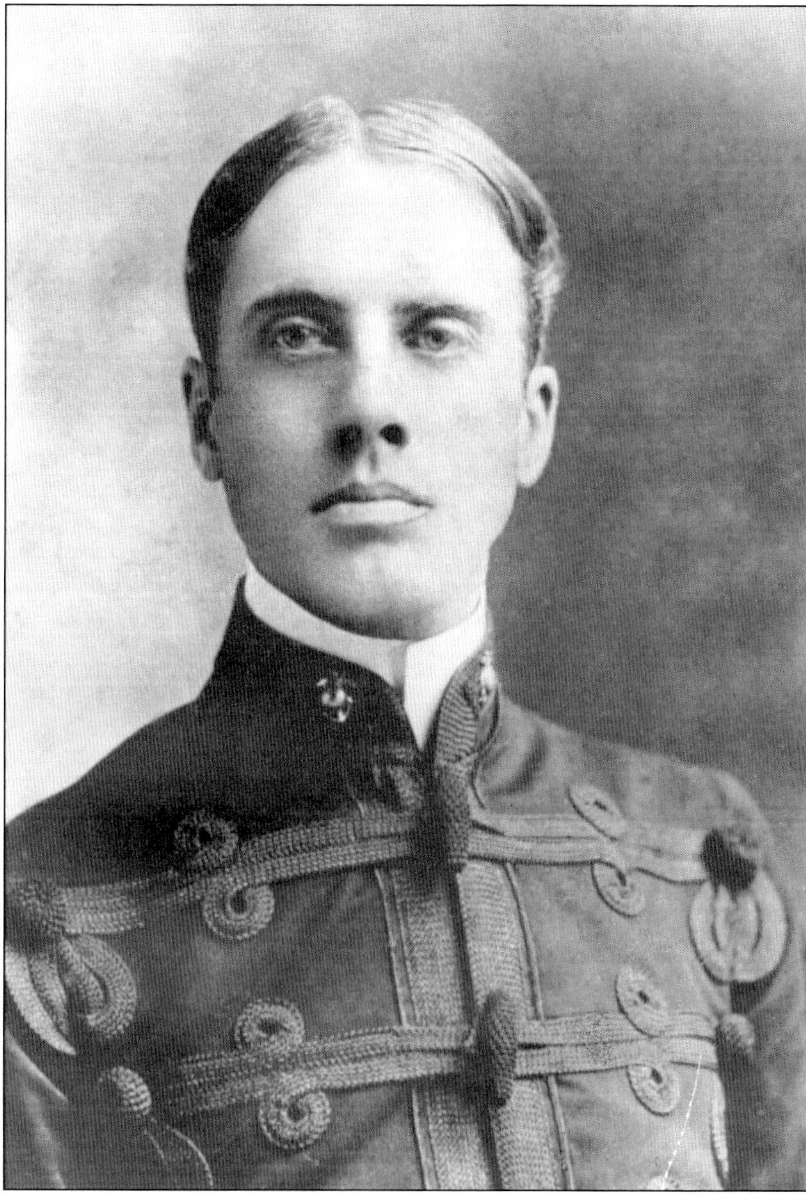

CAPT. GEORGE CYRUS THORPE. With a college degree from New York University, Thorpe assumed command of the prison in September 1911. Prior to arriving at the prison, he had participated in the Spanish-American War, the insurrection in the Philippines, and was with American forces in Cuba. Like Kelton, he was a recipient of the rare Brevet Medal. Perhaps influenced by the Elmira Reformatory system, Thorpe institutionalized the classification and separation system—a hallmark of the prison—that Zebulon Brockway had used with youthful offenders in Elmira, New York. Although previous commanders had tried to restore men to service, Thorpe's systematic methods yielded better results. With extensive intake and exit interviews and using some of the newer ability and personality tests, Thorpe was able to inventory his men by age, religion, health, educational level, temperament, and background. He then developed a tiered system that provided increasing privileges to those who showed exemplary behavior. In a trend that would increase as World War I grew near, Thorpe restored four men to service. (NHHC.)

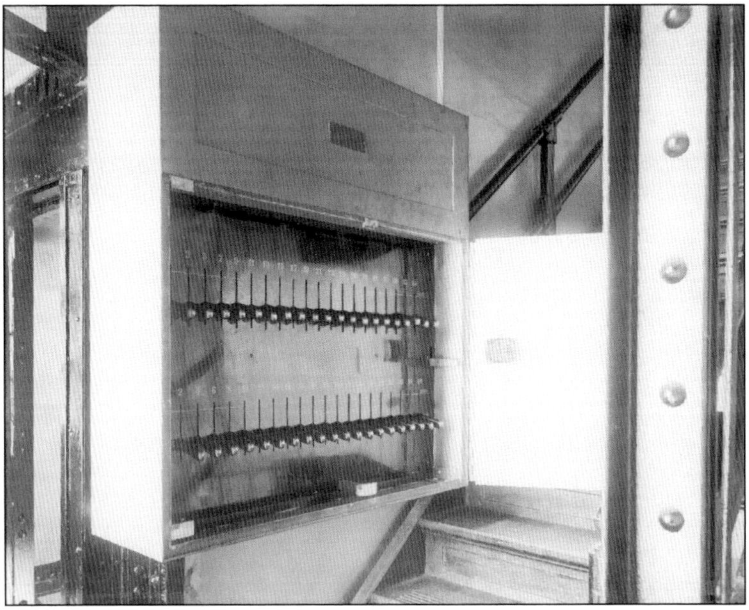

New Locking System, 1911. Installation of the new locks required dismantling the cell block tier by tier, temporarily reducing the number of prisoners housed there by about 40. The old cranking system was replaced by a lever block that could open a row or individual cells. (NARACP.)

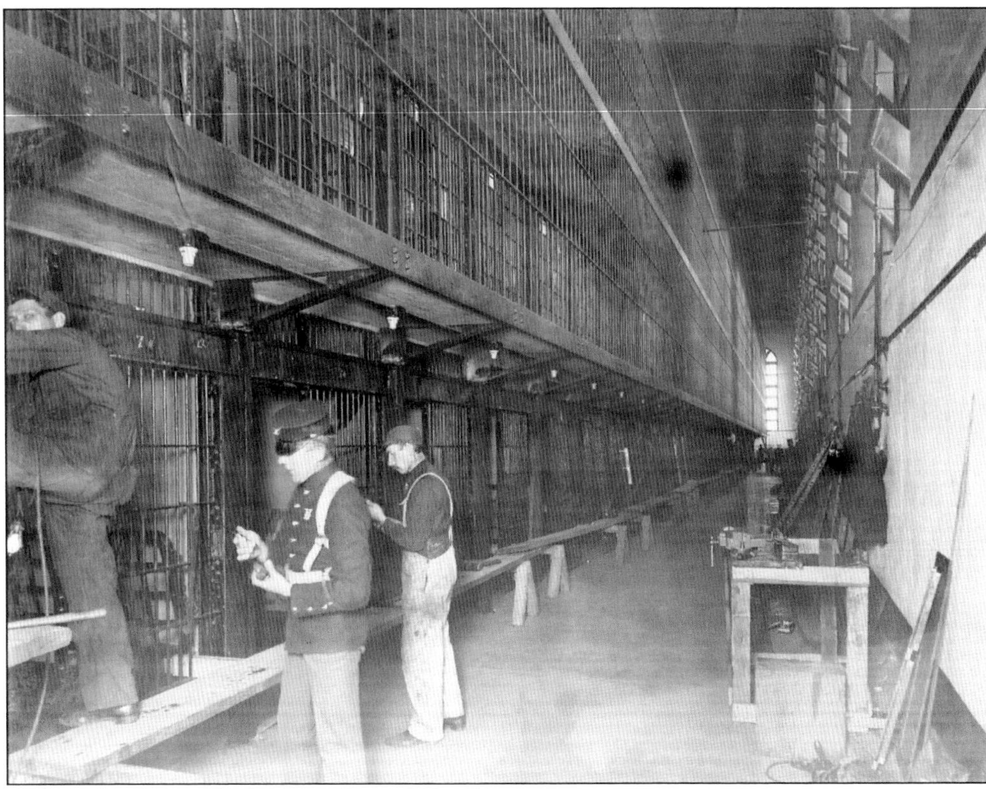

Installation of New Locking Device, October 1911. Although installing the new system displaced men for a time and was a significant inconvenience, the new locks were easier to operate and more secure. Pictured from bottom to top are Able, Baker, and Charlie tiers. Several solitary confinement cells would be built into the cell block, just below Able. (NARACP.)

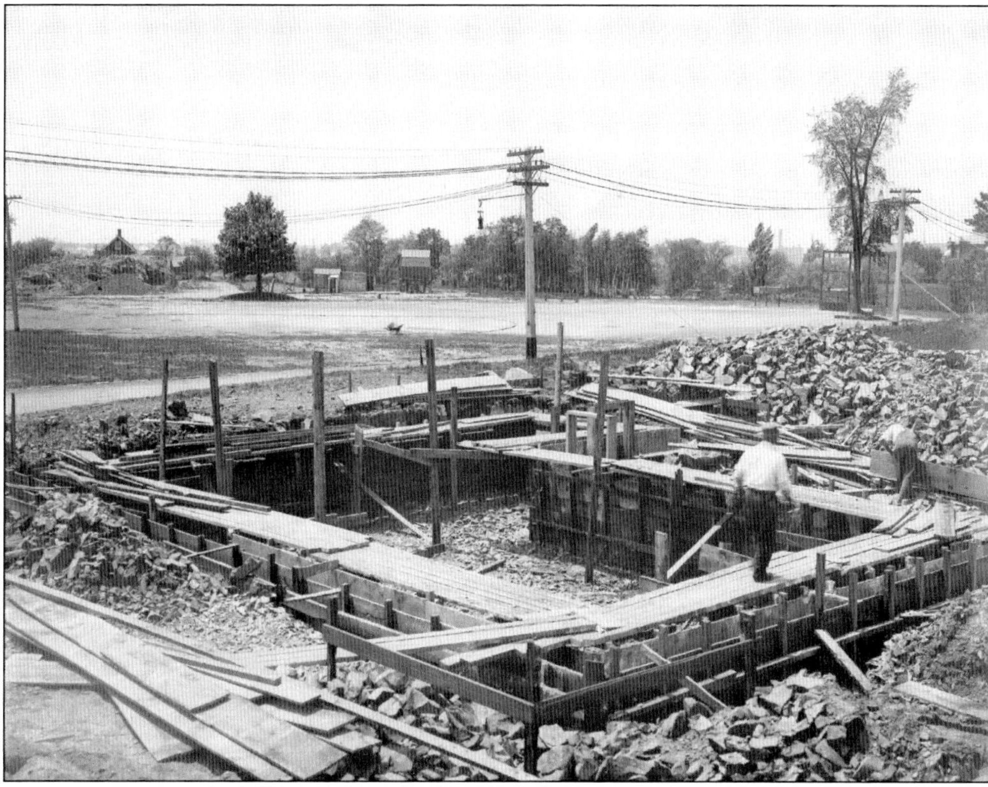

FOUNDATION OF QUARTERS Q, 1913. In the spring of 1913, construction began on Quarters Q, a residence for the prison commander, located just down the road from the prison. Construction continued into the winter. It was not as grand as Quarters A, the home of the shipyard commander, but no doubt a welcome addition. There seems to be little record of where the prison commander stayed from its opening in 1908 until the completion of Quarters Q in the winter of 1913. (NARACP.)

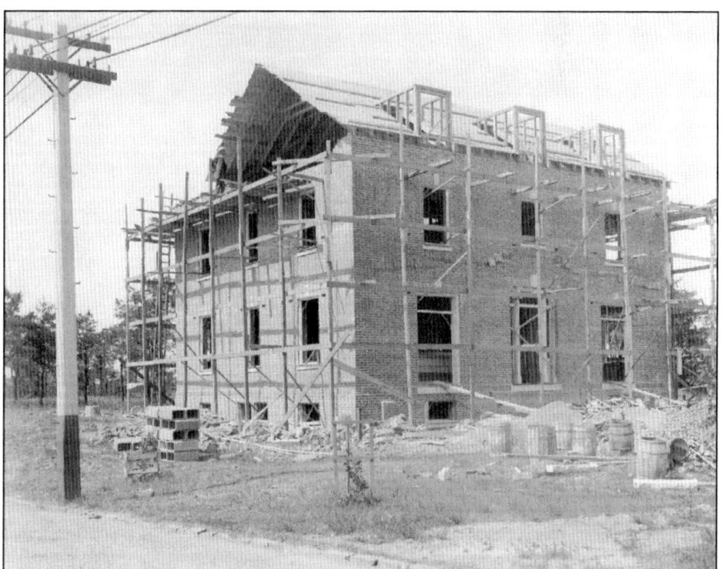

FRAME OF QUARTERS Q, 1913. Most commanding officers stayed from one to four years. The only one to stay longer was Col. Joseph A. Rossell, who had two separate four-year stints: one in the 1930s and another in the 1940s. (NARACP.)

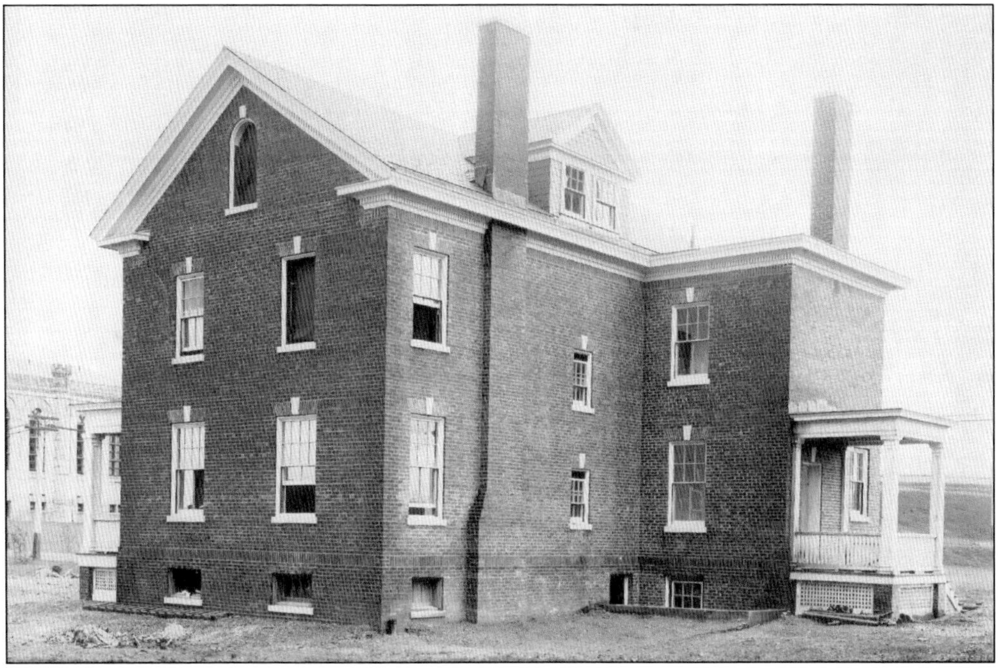

REAR VIEW, QUARTERS Q. The management structure of the prison varied with the times, but, with two exceptions, the commandant or commanding officer (CO) was a Marine colonel or lieutenant colonel. He had final decision-making authority. The Navy executive was the administrative head, managing departments and controlling the purse strings. He reported to either—or both—the Navy director of corrections and the secretary of the Navy in Washington, DC, depending on the philosophy and mandates at the time. (NARACP.)

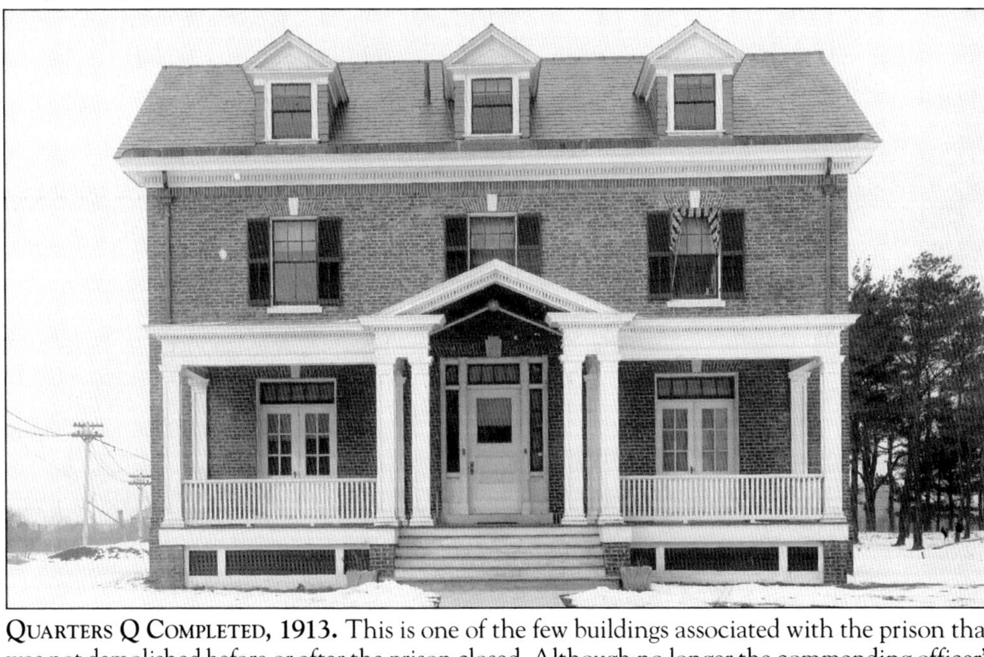

QUARTERS Q COMPLETED, 1913. This is one of the few buildings associated with the prison that was not demolished before or after the prison closed. Although no longer the commanding officer's quarters, it is still in use. (NARACP.)

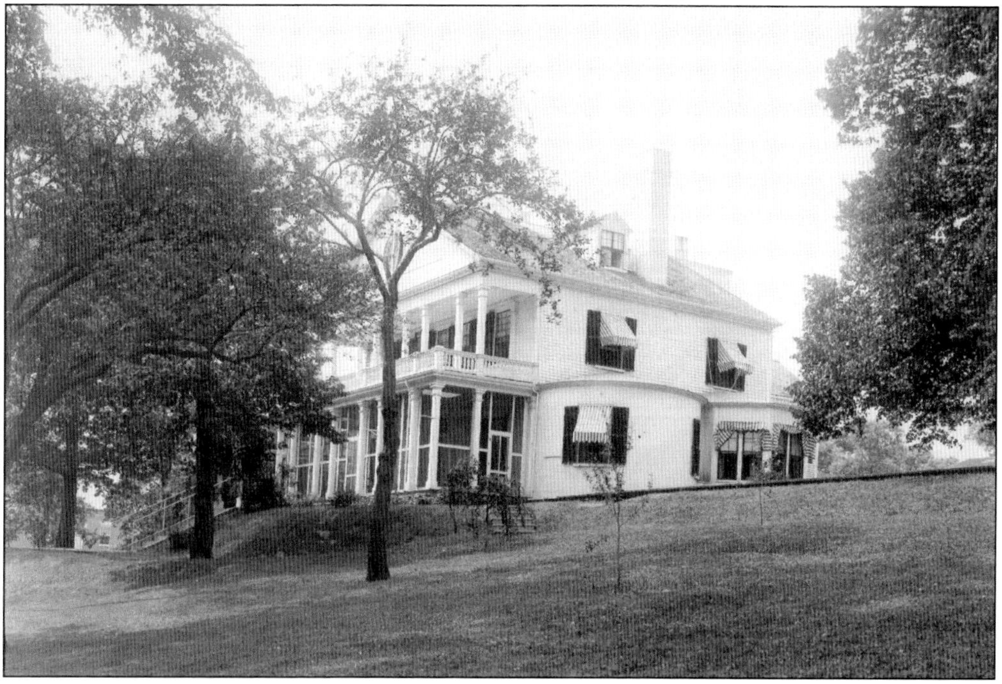

QUARTERS A. This is the Navy Yard commander's residence, built between 1813 and 1815 by local joiner John Locke for the shipyard's first commander, Capt. Isaac Hull, the former captain of the USS *Constitution*. In the National Register of Historic Places, as are several dozen buildings in the shipyard, it is the oldest shipyard building still in use and is a bit grander than Quarters Q, the accommodations for the prison commandant, built a century later. (NARACP.)

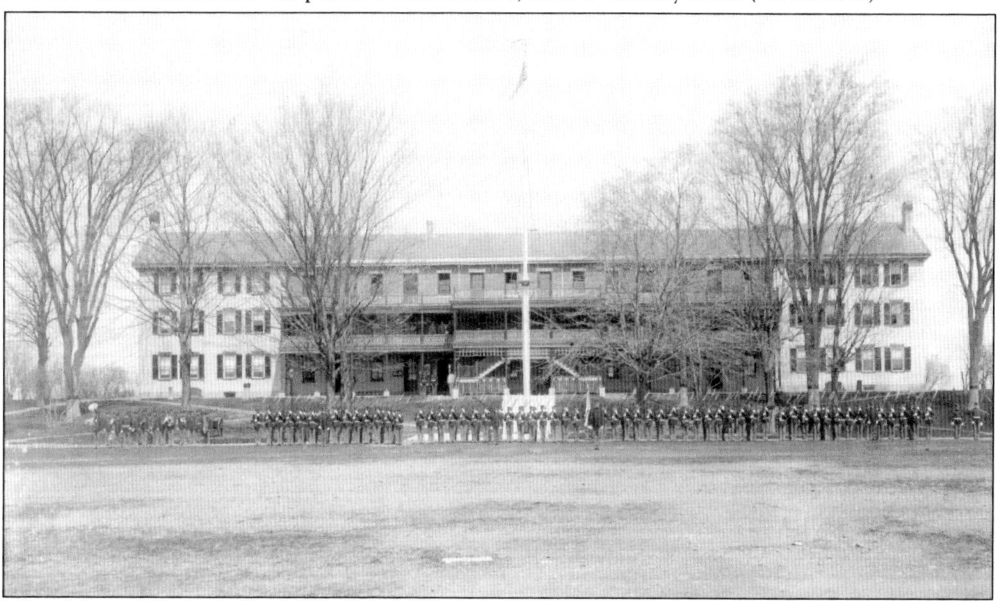

MARINE QUARTERS. First Constructed in 1828, the Marine Barracks at the Portsmouth Naval Shipyard originally consisted of two three-story Gothic Revival buildings connected by a two-story veranda. The structure was enlarged in both the 19th and 20th centuries, when a third story was added and then whitewashed, as shown in this photograph. (LMCQ.)

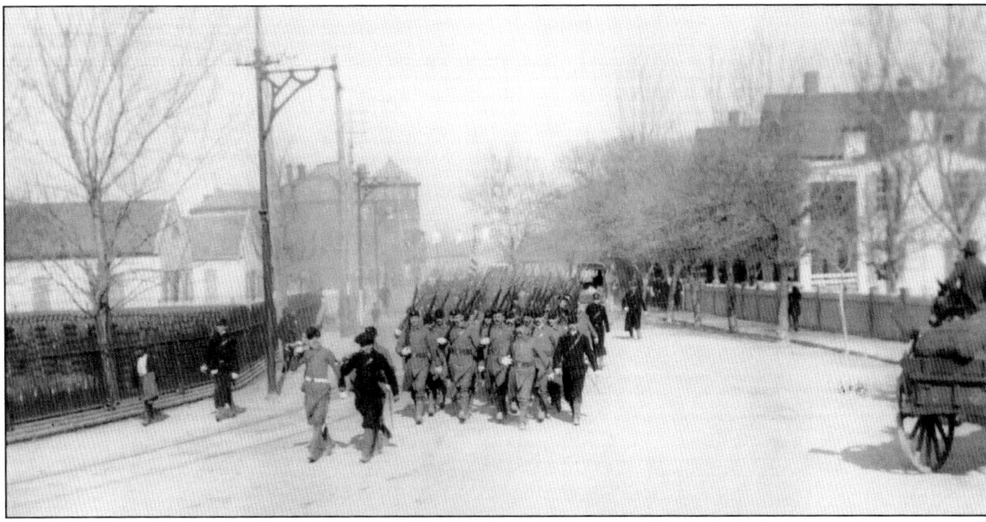

MARINES ON PARADE, c. 1895, PORTSMOUTH. This is a photograph of the Marine detachment of the USS *Maine* ashore. (LMCQ.)

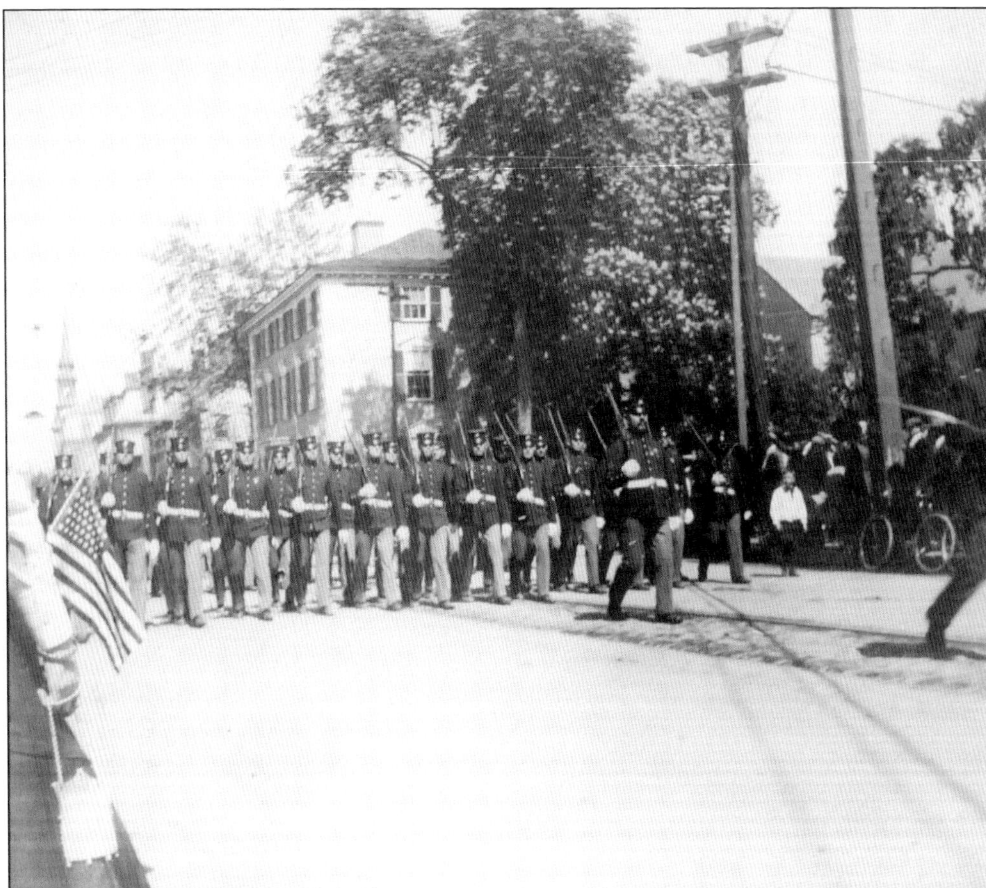

MARINES ON DECORATION DAY, PORTSMOUTH, 1911. The prison had opened just three years prior to this photograph. (LMCQ, Fitzgerald Collection)

Six

World War I–Era Redemption and Remodeling

When Thomas Mott Osborne, the new commandant, came to the Portsmouth Naval Prison in November 1917, he brought an array of revolutionary concepts and almost as much controversy. Prior to Portsmouth, Osborne had been an administrator at the Auburn Prison in Upstate New York and at Sing Sing Prison north of New York City. His modus operandi was to go undercover as a prisoner prior to assuming his position and institute reforms based on his experience. At Portsmouth, he spent a week aboard the USS *Southery,* disguised as a sailor. His recommendations were often sweeping. "With Commander Osborne's arrival as Commanding Officer, the prison underwent a sudden and radical change, since he immediately adapted his civilian idea of prison policy and reform to the Naval Prison," writes Robert Verge in his seminal 1946 book *A History of the U.S. Naval Prison*. "The system was new, in some aspects revolutionary, but it was a serious attempt to come closer to grips with a persistent problem, which the older methods of severe and harsh treatment had admittedly failed to solve."

Most noteworthy at all three prisons was the creation of the Mutual Welfare League—also known at Portsmouth as the Naval Welfare League—an organization run by the prisoners to manage and discipline themselves. Those with consistently good behavior could bunk in "honor squads" instead of their cells; most of the men in the cell block were moved out, and the Marine guard presence significantly reduced. The league was responsible for seeing that prison rules were enforced and from hearings could recommend punishments for violators.

A strong proponent of education instead of punishment, Osborne had ample men on whom to hone his theories. Deserters and other offenders from World War I's surge in military forces flooded the prison and increased the population from 350 when Osborne arrived to a peak of 2,295 just a year later. Thus began a building project that would significantly remodel the prison inside and also create new quarters outside in the space between the prison and the shoreline called the "lower reservation."

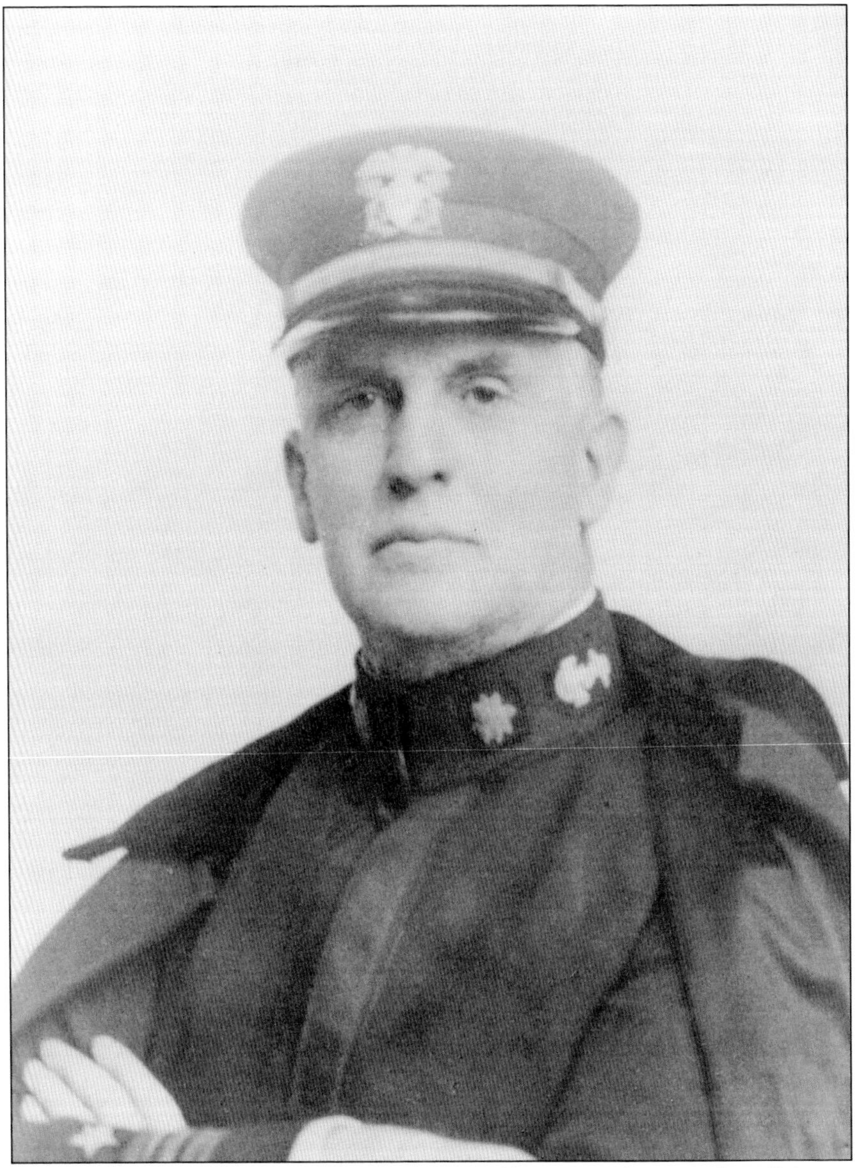

Thomas Mott Osborne. In that rare juxtaposition of history and personality, Osborne was at the right place at the right time. He grew up in Auburn, New York, in the shadow of the Auburn Prison. The son of a well-to-do businessman, Osborne had a lineage on his mother's side that included women's activist Lucretia Mott. When Osborne arrived at Portsmouth, the nation was riding the wave of the Progressive movement. These early-20th-century reforms included abolition of child labor, women's suffrage, Prohibition, and prison restructuring. Osborne, though lacking in military experience, was probably the only commanding officer with a Harvard education. Former chairman of the New York State Commission on Prison Reform, Osborne brought the blessing of a cadre of high-ranking government officials with him. All of these factors would no doubt have helped Osborne create a name for himself. But his personality and his reforms eventually ignited a firestorm. Yet the military, hungry for people to help fight the war, needed rehabilitated men. In 1917, to Osborne's great credit, 743 men were restored to service, with 1,563 restored the following year. (NHHS.)

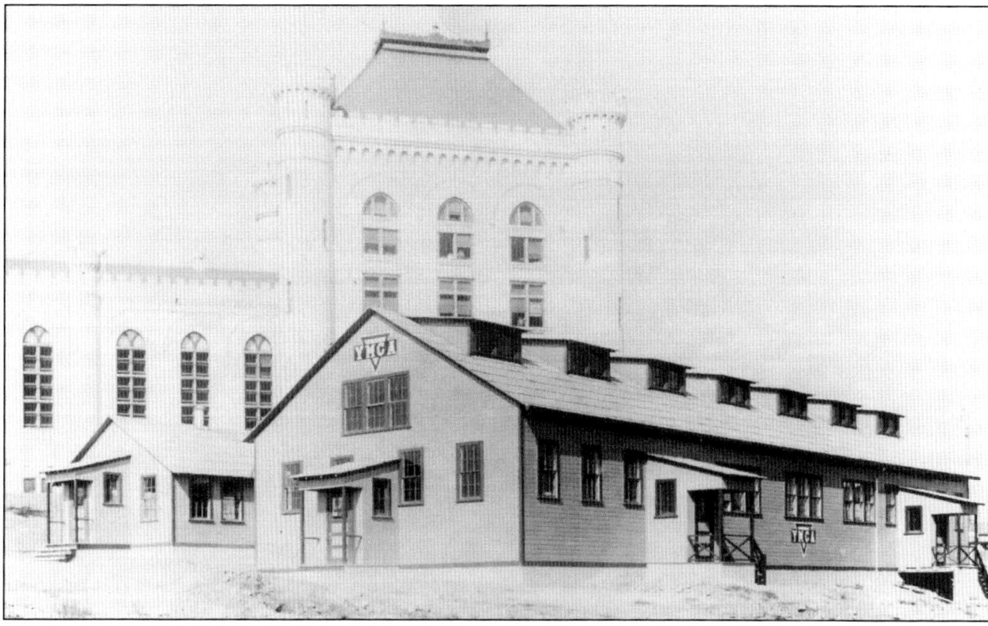

THE YMCA RECREATION HALL, 1918. Many viewed Osborne's new methods with skepticism, and the brass at the Navy Yard were incensed that he ignored their concerns. Rumors of "irregularities, immorality among the prisoners and laxity of officials" brought good friend Franklin D. Roosevelt, assistant secretary of the Navy, to the prison to investigate. Cleared of the charges, Osborne would nonetheless resign a short time later. To some, the recreation hall, pictured, here symbolized the transformation of the prison to a significantly less fearsome institution. (UNHL.)

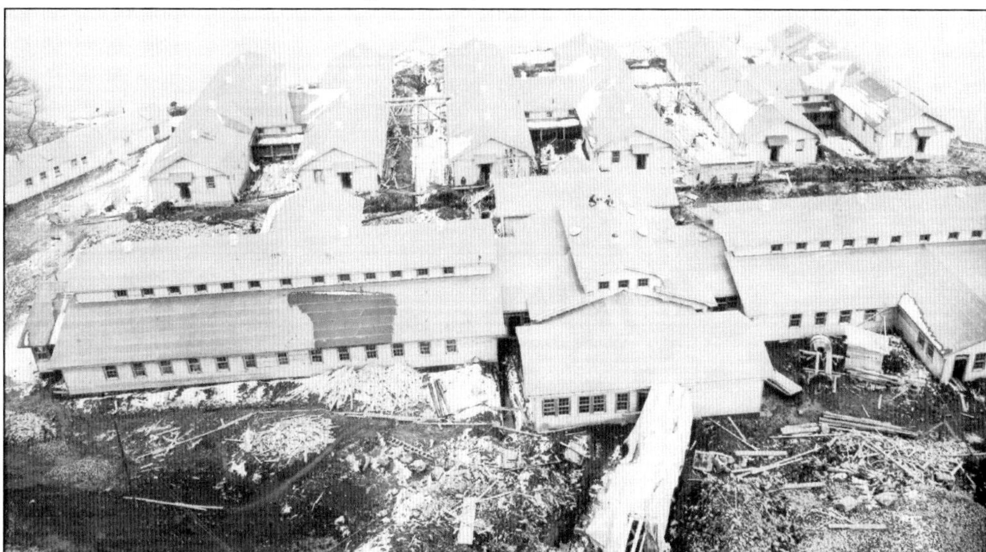

LOWER RESERVATION, FEBRUARY 25, 1918. By 1918, although the administration building and cell block were completed, the prison and the *Southery* were filled to overflowing. Near the shore, seven barracks, two large mess halls, a galley with a bake shop, and a recreation hall were built, increasing the prison's capacity by 800. Here, Building 121, the center building—made up of the mess halls and the galley—is connected to the prison. Behind it, near the water, are some of the new barracks. (NARACP.)

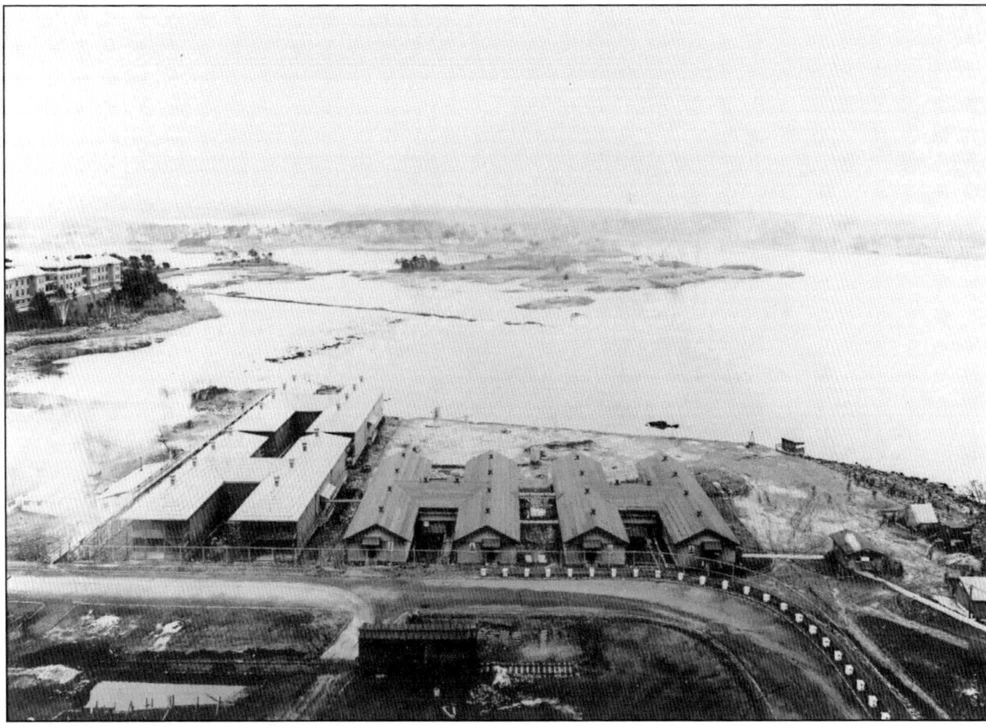

New Mess Halls and Barracks, March 1918. This photograph shows the additional four H-shaped barracks located to the left of the mess hall. The image below shows the tunnel to get to it. The new quarters relieved the overcrowding in the Bull Pen, the space between the cell block and the roof, eliminated the need for the *Southery* and moved the Marines from the administration building. The long building across the channel is the new shipyard hospital. (UNHL.)

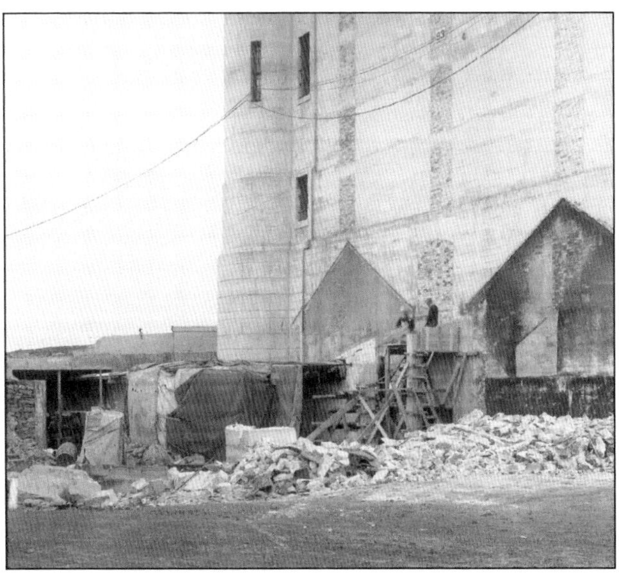

Concrete Tunnel to Mess, 1918. The second floor of the administration building was then largely dedicated to medical needs: a larger dispensary, examining room, seven-bed isolation ward, dentist's office, venereal treatment room, psychologist and medical officers' rooms. The third floor was converted into living quarters for 65 men plus a large washroom, a canteen, the Naval Welfare League office, and a schoolroom. Remains of the tunnel are still visible on the prison grounds today, although they are almost totally covered in weeds and vines. (NARACP.)

Building the Tunnel. To move men and material and install boiler steam lines between the mess hall and the lower level, the Turner Construction Company built a concrete tunnel with a wood frame by blasting 20 feet of solid rock. In the subbasement, a new furnace and boilers were installed, but the prison was still being heated by coal. (NARACP.)

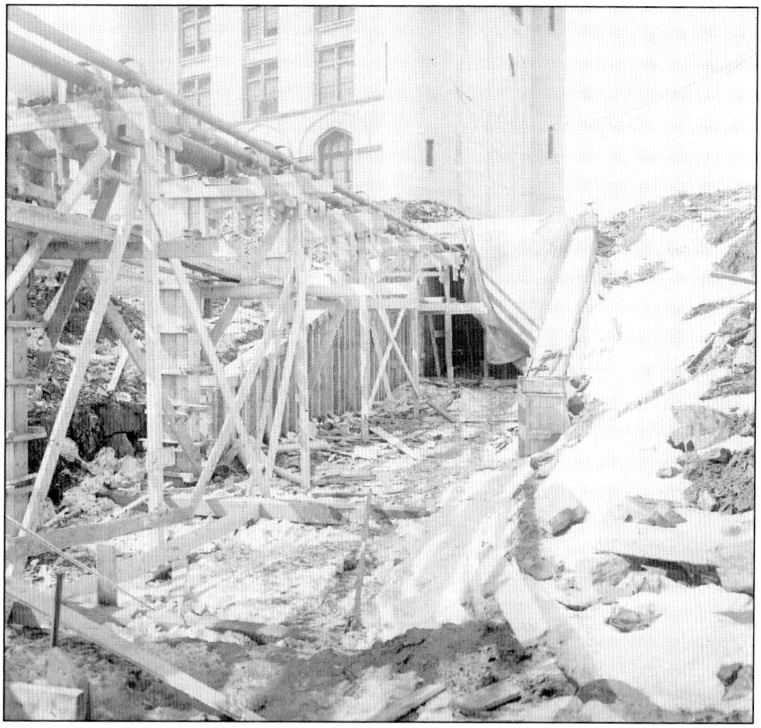

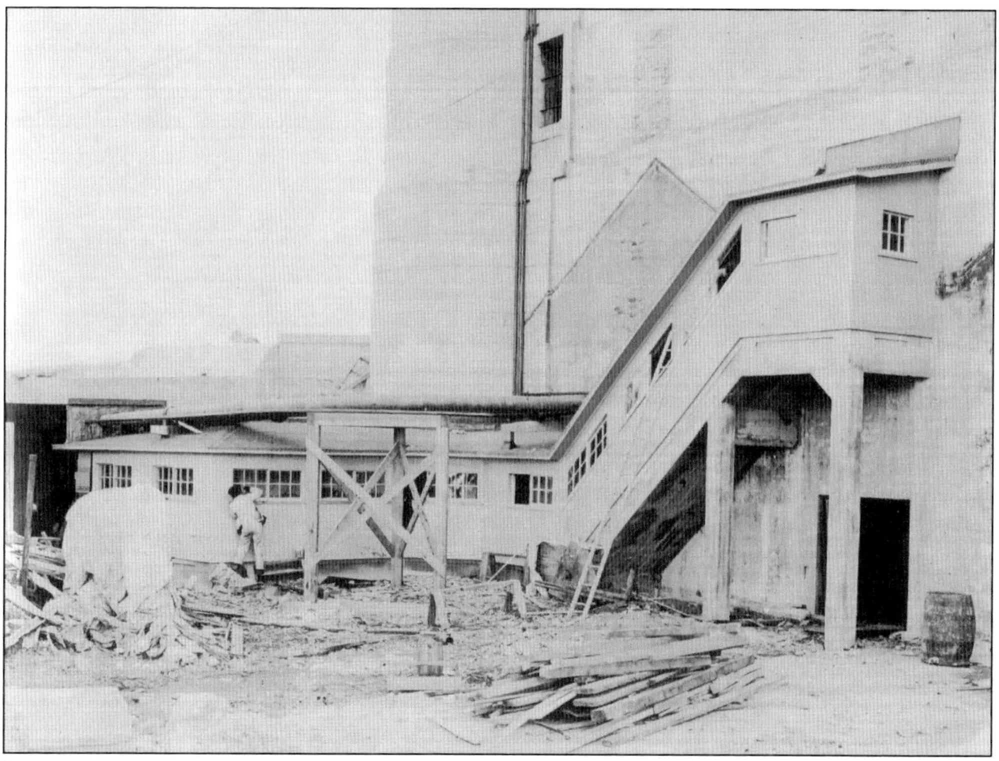

Prison to Tunnel Stairway, 1918. The stairway is now completely gone, no longer attached to the prison, as is Building 121, where the tunnel led. (NARACP.)

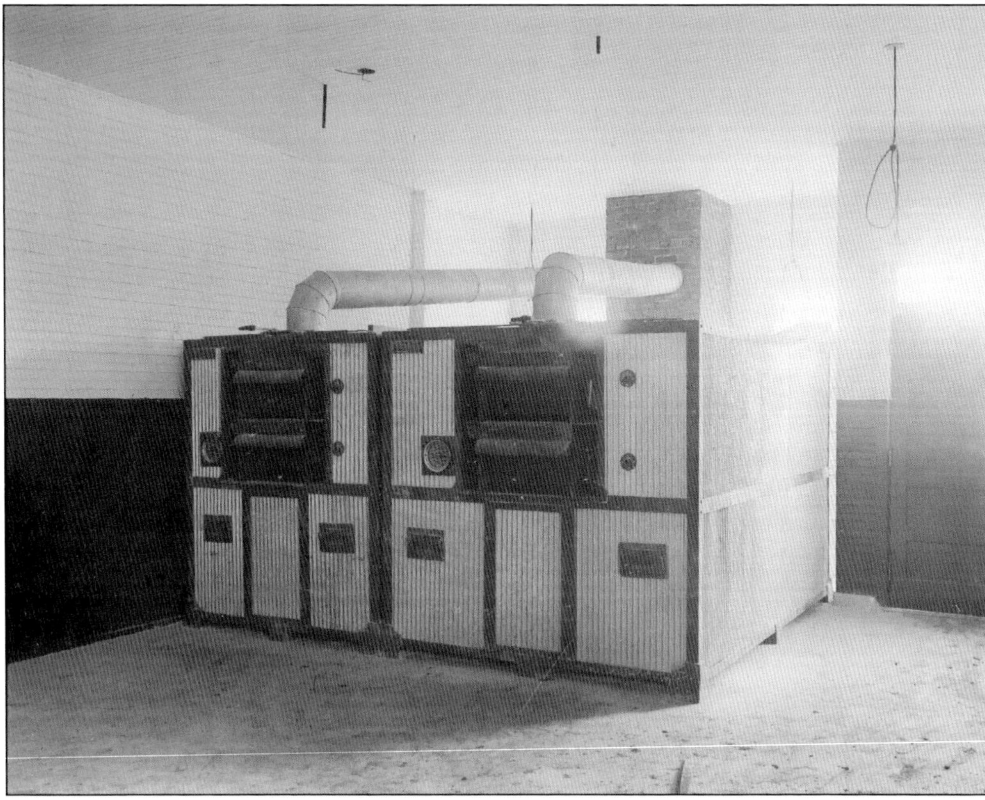

BAKERY IN BUILDING 121. The 1917 annual report indicates that "the bakery operated exclusively by the prison force and turned out excellent work; in addition to the prison demand, it has supplied 2,000 loaves per day for use of the apprentice seamen training in the yard." The apprentice seamen were part of a training program at the shipyard during the war. (NARACP.)

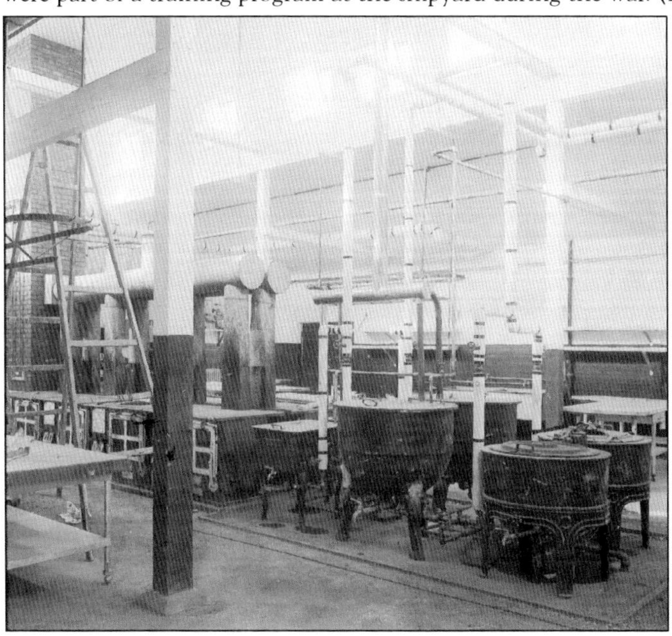

KITCHEN IN BUILDING 121, IN 1918. In June 1917, before Osborne's arrival, Comdr. Henry Lee noted in his annual report that "a huge truck garden in the front of the prison is operated entirely by prison labor. The products obtained from the garden greatly improved the bill-of-fare through the summer and fall, extending into December. Work is now in progress clearing and grading the stockade for planting a late crop of cabbage, potatoes, turnips and parsnips for use in the winter months." (NARACP.)

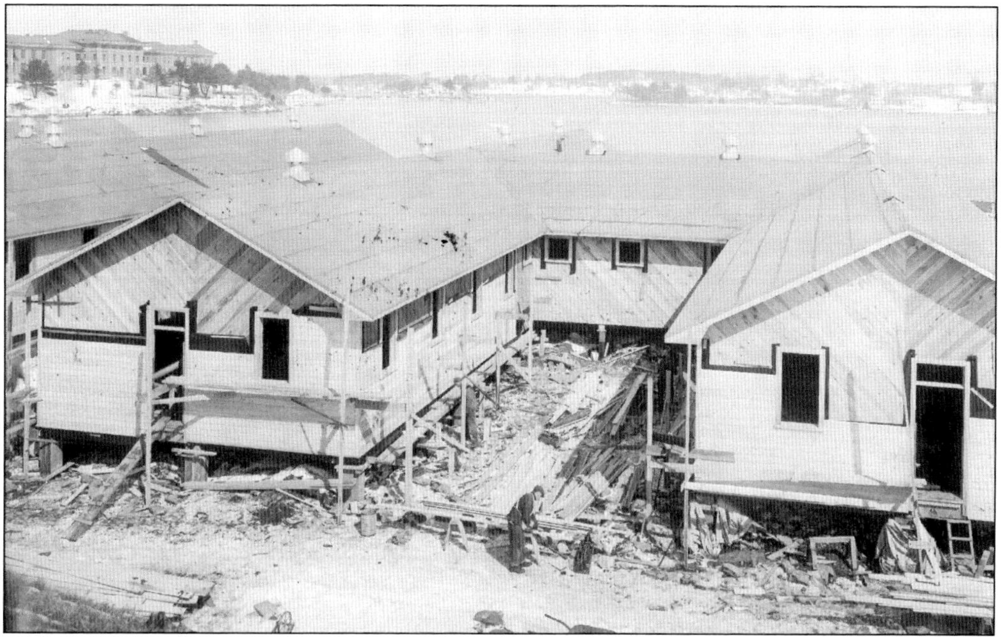

Barracks under Construction, 1918. The new H-shaped barracks, the first of which opened March 25, 1918, were organized into a "fleet," with each one given the name of a ship and men assigned to bunk there. (NARACP.)

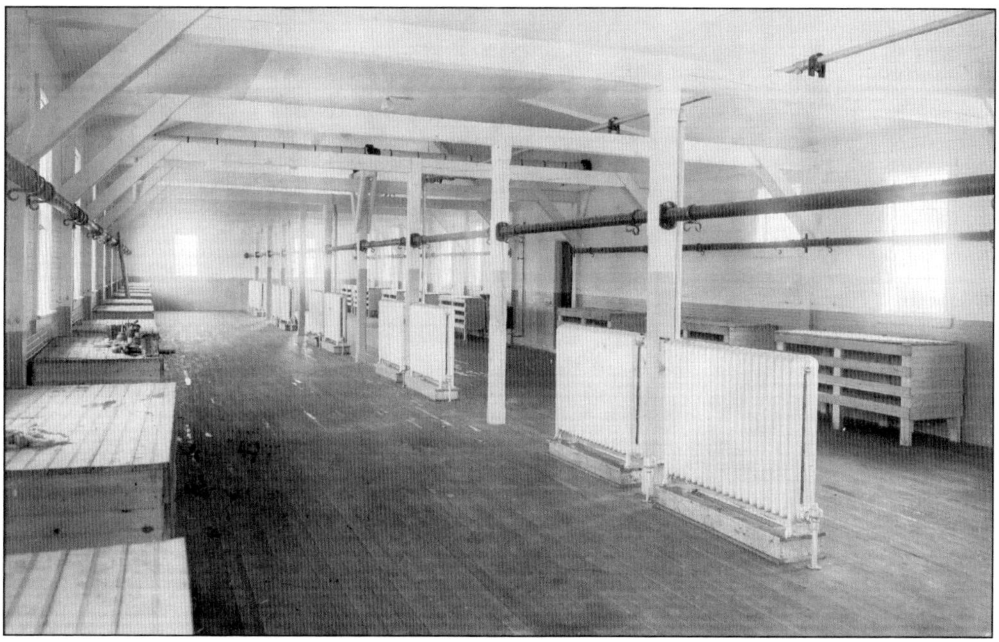

Typical Barracks Interior, April 1918. The Delaware was the flagship, housing many of the prominent league members. The Pennsylvania was for men under 21 years old. The New Jersey quartered men working in the mess halls and on general working details. The Connecticut also quartered men working general details and members of the band. The Virginia was for men who worked in the clothing factory and reading room as well as general working details. (NARACP.)

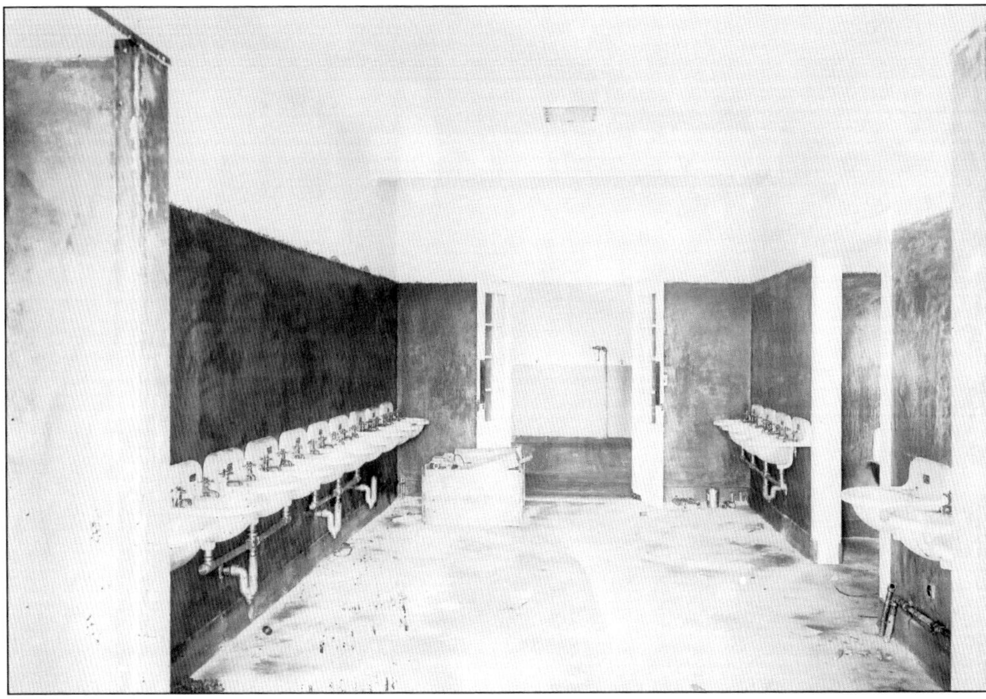

Washroom in the Barracks. The Massachusetts also housed the men who "policed" the other prisoners according to the rules of the Naval Welfare League. As well, the Massachusetts held those infected with venereal disease in a mid-ship compartment and aft contained the prison library. (NARACP.)

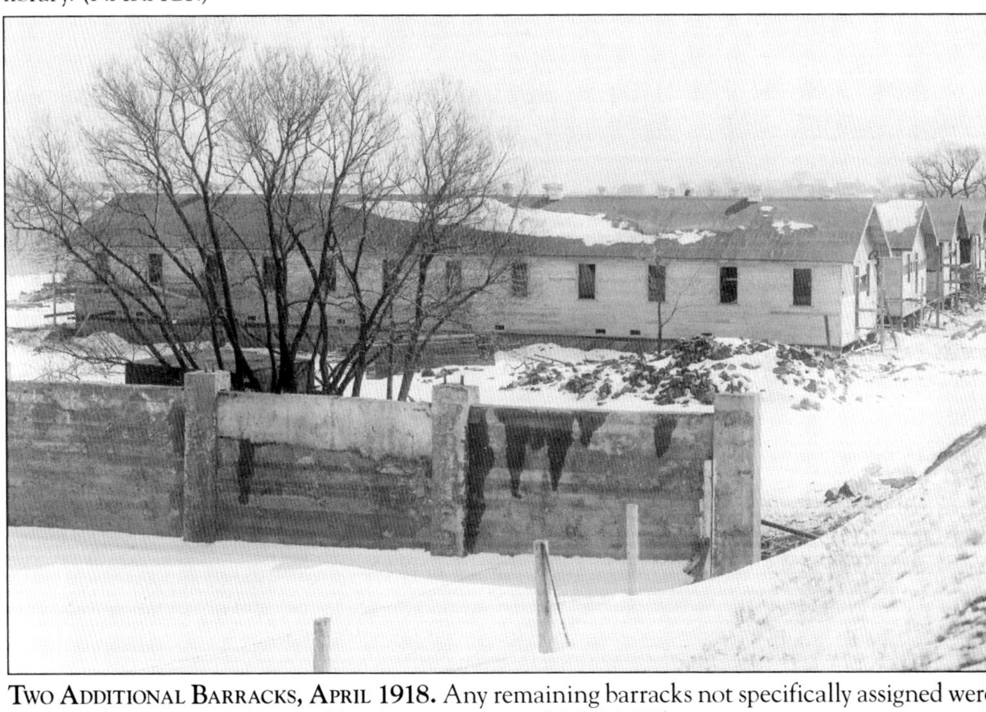

Two Additional Barracks, April 1918. Any remaining barracks not specifically assigned were used for the Marines, as general housing or storage. (NARACP.)

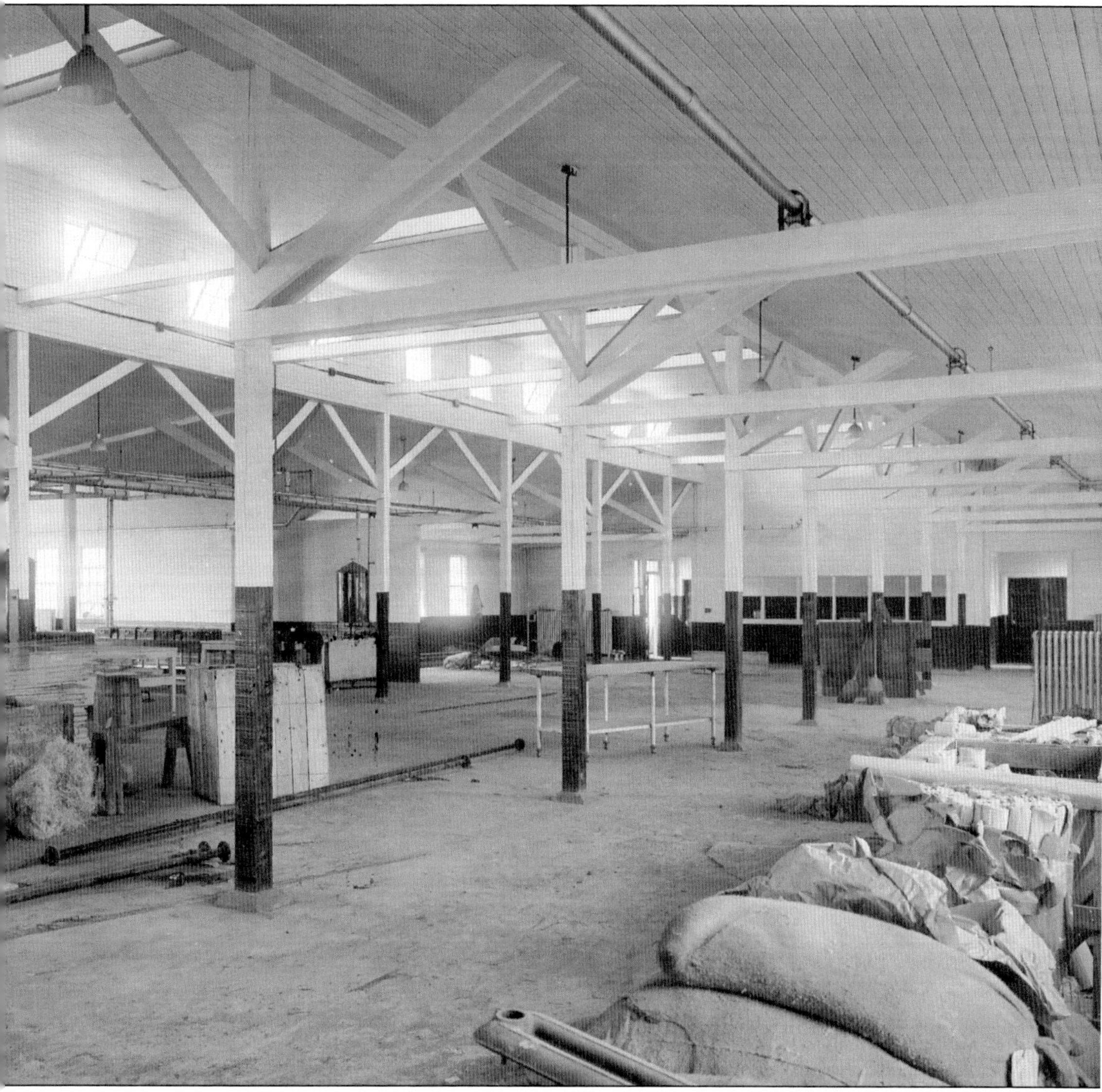

BUILDING THE MESS HALL, MARCH 1918. In 1918, there were 2,295 men at the prison, both in the cell block and the lower reservation. Noteworthy is the logbook, a detailing of the day's events, for that January day records a 3:00 p.m. shipment from Unity Confectionery Co. with the following: 192 Peanut Bars, 288 Nut Tootsie Rolls, 120 Filbert Bars, 240 Nut Malabars, 360 Mint Faries, and 240 Walnut Fig Bars. On February 16, the National Biscuit Company out of Boston brought 240 pkgs. Lorna Doones, 120 Frotanas, 180 Malbours, 120 Fig Newtons, 96 Peanut Butter Sandwiches, 120 Lotus, 120 Anolas, and 120 packages of ZuZus. The fare for somebody had indeed changed. (NARACP.)

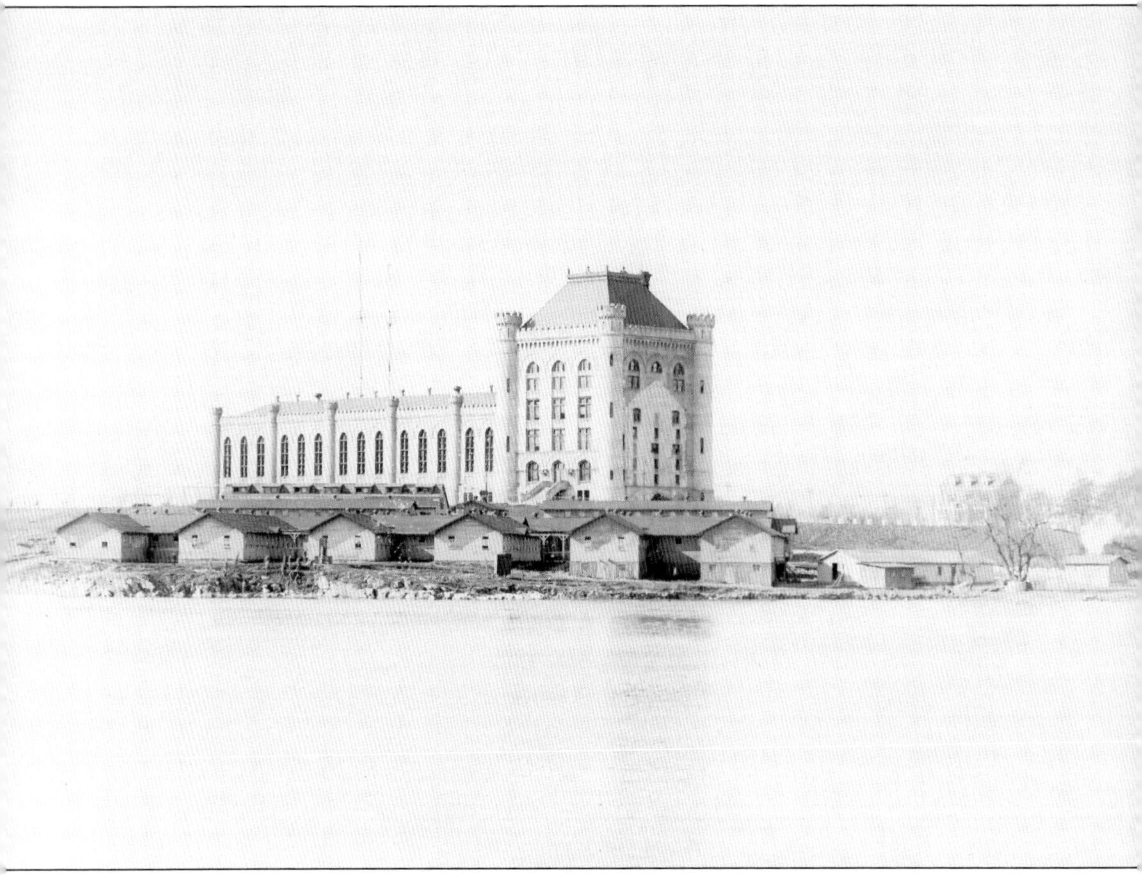

Prison, Lower Reservation, Quarters Q, Undated. In 1917, eighteen prisoners died of the Spanish influenza in the outbreak that had swept the nation. On the day the armistice ending World War I was signed, November 11, 1918, there was an epidemic of escapes. Ten men fled in nine days, and according to a report, all were captured except one. In January 1920, however, old colleague and Assistant Secretary of the Navy Franklin D. Roosevelt spent six hours at the Navy Yard inspecting the prison and investigating charges against Osborne. The *New York Times* then debunked the ongoing myth that no one ever escaped from the prison: "There is no need for the people to fear escapes, as they have not been so numerous as in outside institutions and number only eight to ten in the two and one-half years of Mr. Osborne's administration." (PNSYM.)

Seven

Crackdown and Breakout

On July 5, 1921, Lt. Col. Hamilton D. South became the new commandant. Sixteen days later, he disbanded the Naval Welfare League, took the Prisoners' League insignia, dispersed the 52 prisoner-guards elected by the league and replaced them with 160 Marines, and sent many men back into their cells. The previous commandant, Thomas Mott Osborne, had finally created enough bad publicity, and he had resigned his post in June 1920; however, his reforms and the Naval Welfare League did not leave with him. Comdr. A.V. Wadhams, who followed Osborne, stayed until July 1, 1921, keeping the prison essentially as his predecessor had left it. In the interim, Colonel South, reportedly a popular Marine, had conducted an internal investigation of the prison under the direction of Secretary of the Navy Edwin Denby—who three years later would resign amid the Teapot Dome scandal. South's marching orders were clear: crack down. In his annual report, South discusses the fallout. "There was a noticeable and marked resentment on the part of a number of prisoners who had long enjoyed the privileges afforded them under the league, with the result that there were numerous cases of infractions of prison rules. In the month of August, the maximum month, the Commanding Officer awarded 169 punishments; in May, the minimum, he awarded 12." The average was 58 a month. Punishments, not enumerated in the report, usually consisted of few to no privileges such as visitors, movies, and mail; less recreation; diminished rations, usually bread and water; and harder work. Solitary confinement cells were not built until the World War II era, but in one annual report leg-irons had been purchased. Three years almost to the day of Colonel South's arrival, one of the more spectacular escapes in the life of the prison took place. It was noteworthy in the planning, the length of time the prisoners were on the run, and the expense and manpower it took to apprehend them. Although the escapees would all eventually be caught in Connecticut, this was, for one man, just a dry run. Four years later, he would escape again for good.

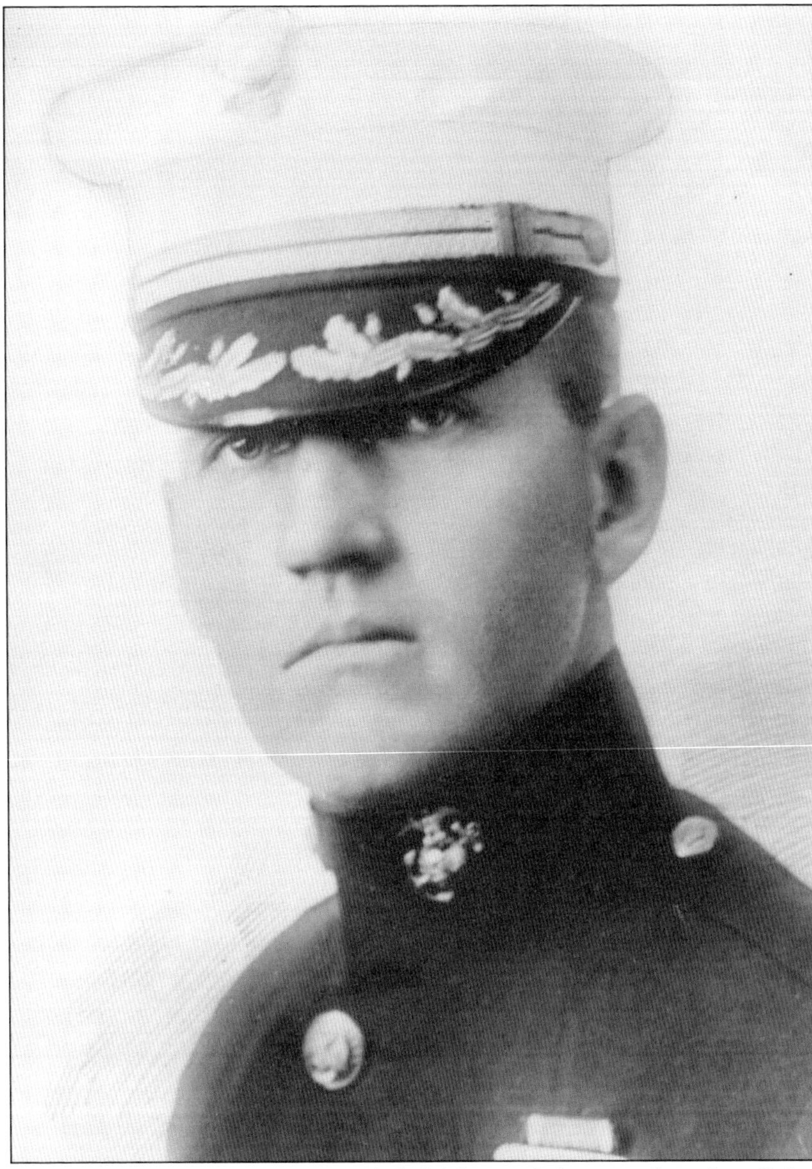

Lt. Col. Hamilton D. South. Born in Philadelphia and the son of a judge, Colonel South had served in Guam and Nicaragua before being appointed Marine Officer of the Atlantic Fleet in 1919. On June 30, 1921, he was ordered to command Portsmouth Prison. There, as well as dismantling the prisoner-run Welfare League, he was forced to belt-tighten when the economy and government funding became precarious. This included keeping prisoners' rations below the 45¢ daily maximum and creating a Clothing-Salvage Program. South wrote in his annual report that "records were kept of each prisoner's clothing surveyed and any case of improper care of garments by individuals was made the subject of investigation and disciplinary action where necessary." Colonel South's initiatives yielded significant savings and he was commended by the First Naval District. Although his thrift was rewarded, the prisoners were probably not as enthusiastic. Commander South further states, "The cold season here is long and rigorous. The coldest day during this winter was twenty degrees below zero." The prisoner breakout in July 1924 should not have come as a surprise. (NHHC.)

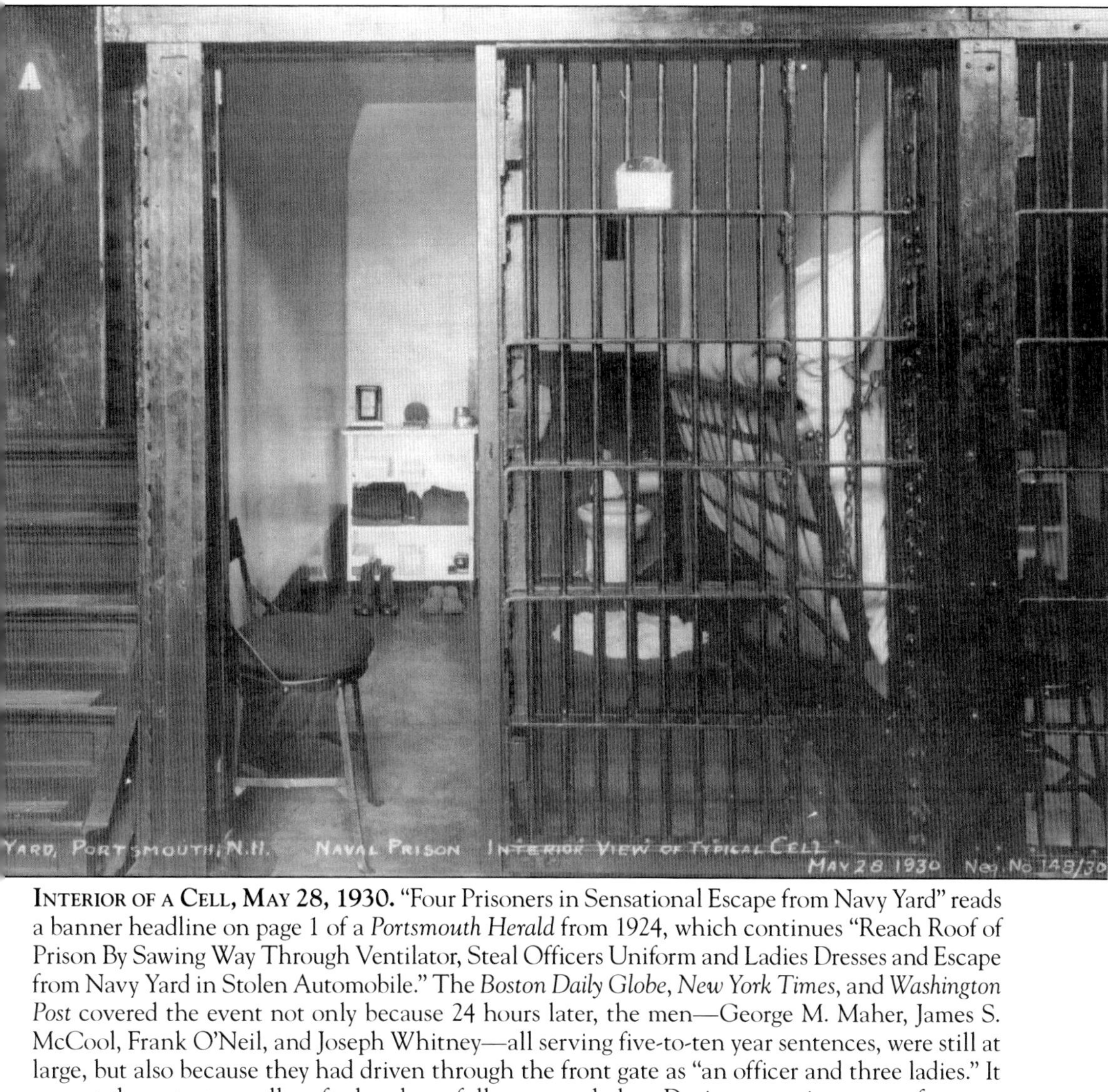

INTERIOR OF A CELL, MAY 28, 1930. "Four Prisoners in Sensational Escape from Navy Yard" reads a banner headline on page 1 of a *Portsmouth Herald* from 1924, which continues "Reach Roof of Prison By Sawing Way Through Ventilator, Steal Officers Uniform and Ladies Dresses and Escape from Navy Yard in Stolen Automobile." The *Boston Daily Globe*, *New York Times*, and *Washington Post* covered the event not only because 24 hours later, the men—George M. Maher, James S. McCool, Frank O'Neil, and Joseph Whitney—all serving five-to-ten year sentences, were still at large, but also because they had driven through the front gate as "an officer and three ladies." It was, at the outset, a well-crafted and carefully executed plan. During a movie—a now frequent and popular earned privilege that continued over the life of the prison—they navigated their way to the roof in the semi-darkness on a Sunday night between 7:30 and 9:30. Having somehow procured a new rope and a tinsmith's scissors to cut through the ventilator shaft, the men lowered themselves 70 feet to the ground. (PAC.)

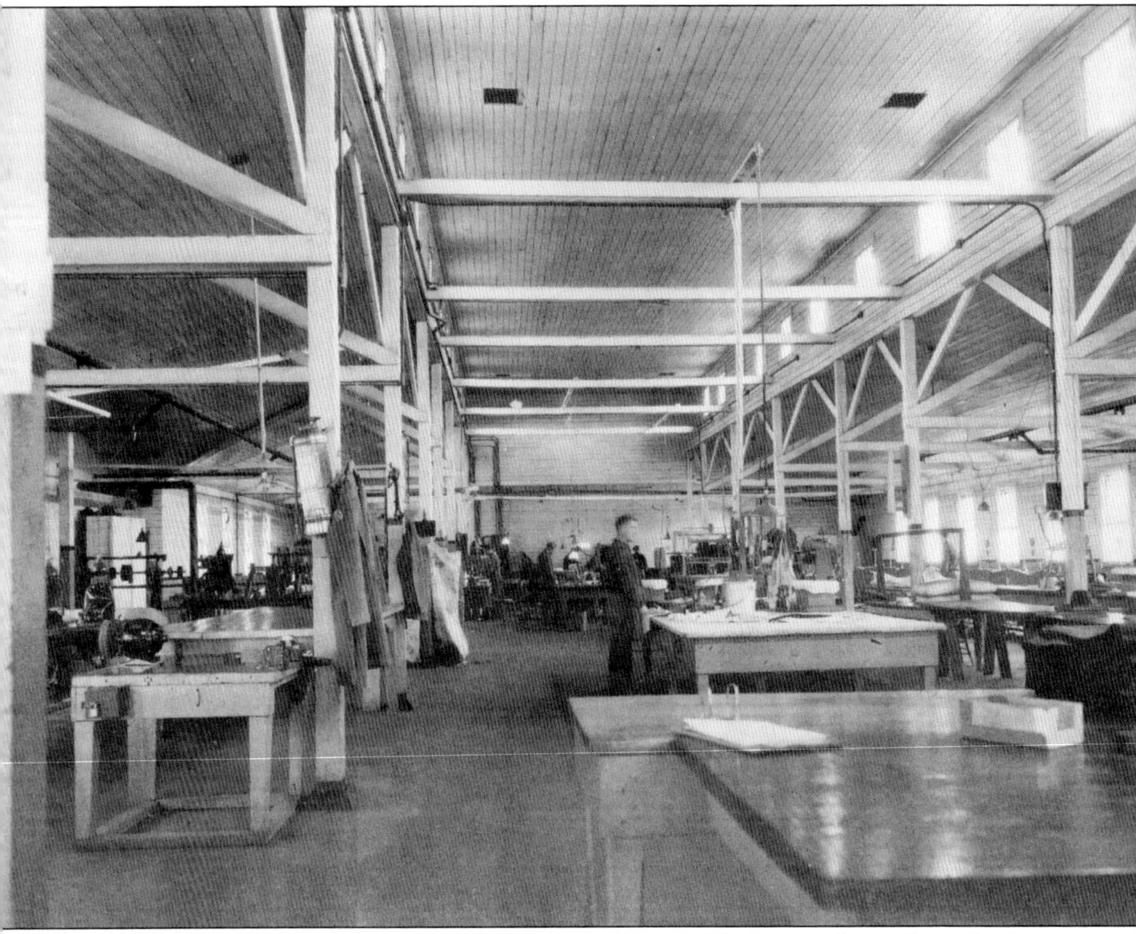

CLOTHING FACTORY, BOOK BINDERY, AND SHOE REPAIR. This was perhaps where the four men obtained their escape tools. Breaking into Gunner Frank Wallace's quarters, they took his uniform and several of his wife's dresses and emerged as an officer and three ladies, piling into Lt. W.D. Baker's blue Nash with Michigan plates parked outside of the officer's quarters. They drove the length of the 27-acre shipyard, out the front gate, and into the night. They had learned perhaps from 19-year-old V. Crosier's 1920 Christmas Day leap into the Piscataqua from the USS *Southery*—and his badly mutilated body washing up some weeks later, identifiable by only his prisoner's suit. A similar event had taken place six months later when the body of Marcus W. Jones, 19, was found floating under the stern of the *Southery*, his body first stuck in the mud and then breaking free. Jones was under a two-year sentence by a general court-martial and had been at the prison only a month. (PAC.)

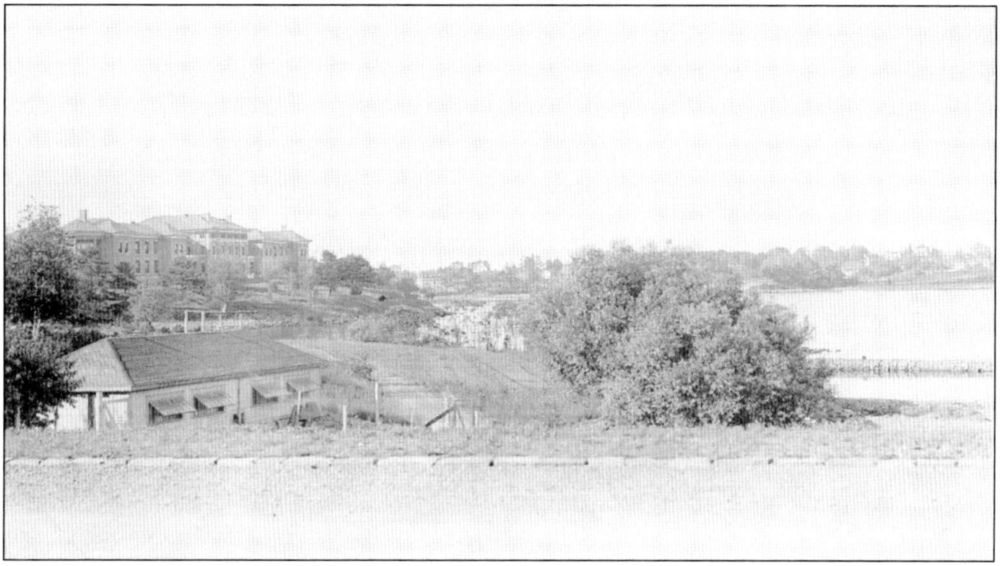

Naval Hospital. Or perhaps the men were heartened by the apparent escape in the fall in 1919 of two general court-martial prisoners from the new Naval Hospital located in the Navy Yard, where prisoners were sent if their illness warranted, prompting a recommendation in the commandant's 1920 annual report to permit "the medical officer to perform major surgery at the Prison, with the addition of necessary equipment and personnel." It may have been warranted. (LMCQ, White Collection.)

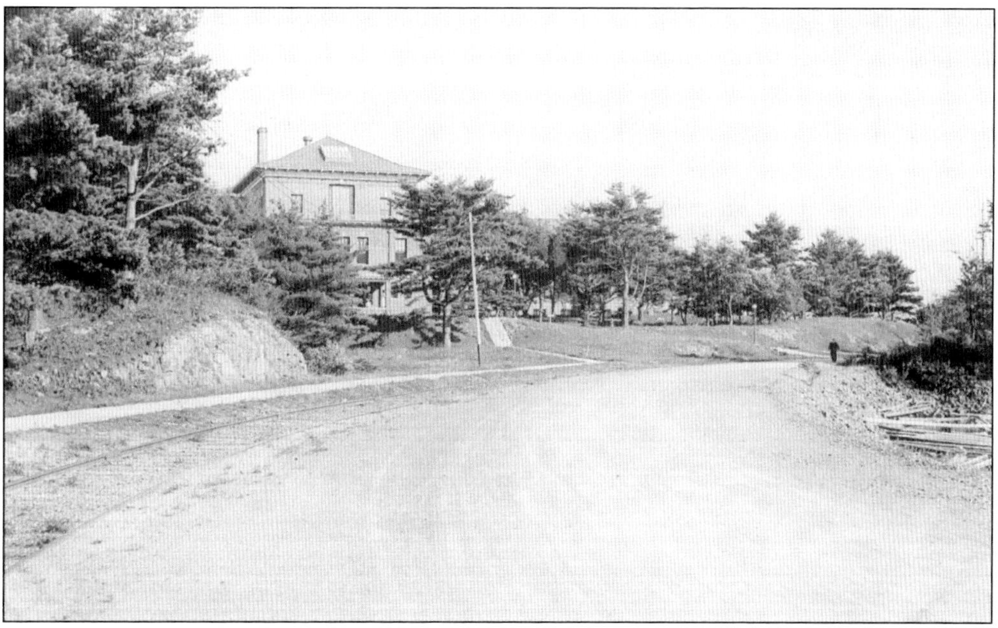

Side View of Escape Route, Naval Hospital. Just a year after this four-man breakout, James R. Hartwell, 33, also escaped from the Naval Hospital, in September 1925, by sawing the bars of the window in his cell and substituting look-alikes, a task the authorities said took some time. Apparently leaving in the night, his absence was not noticed until breakfast. Clearly, escaping from the hospital located in the Navy Yard itself presented fewer obstacles. (LMCQ, White Collection.)

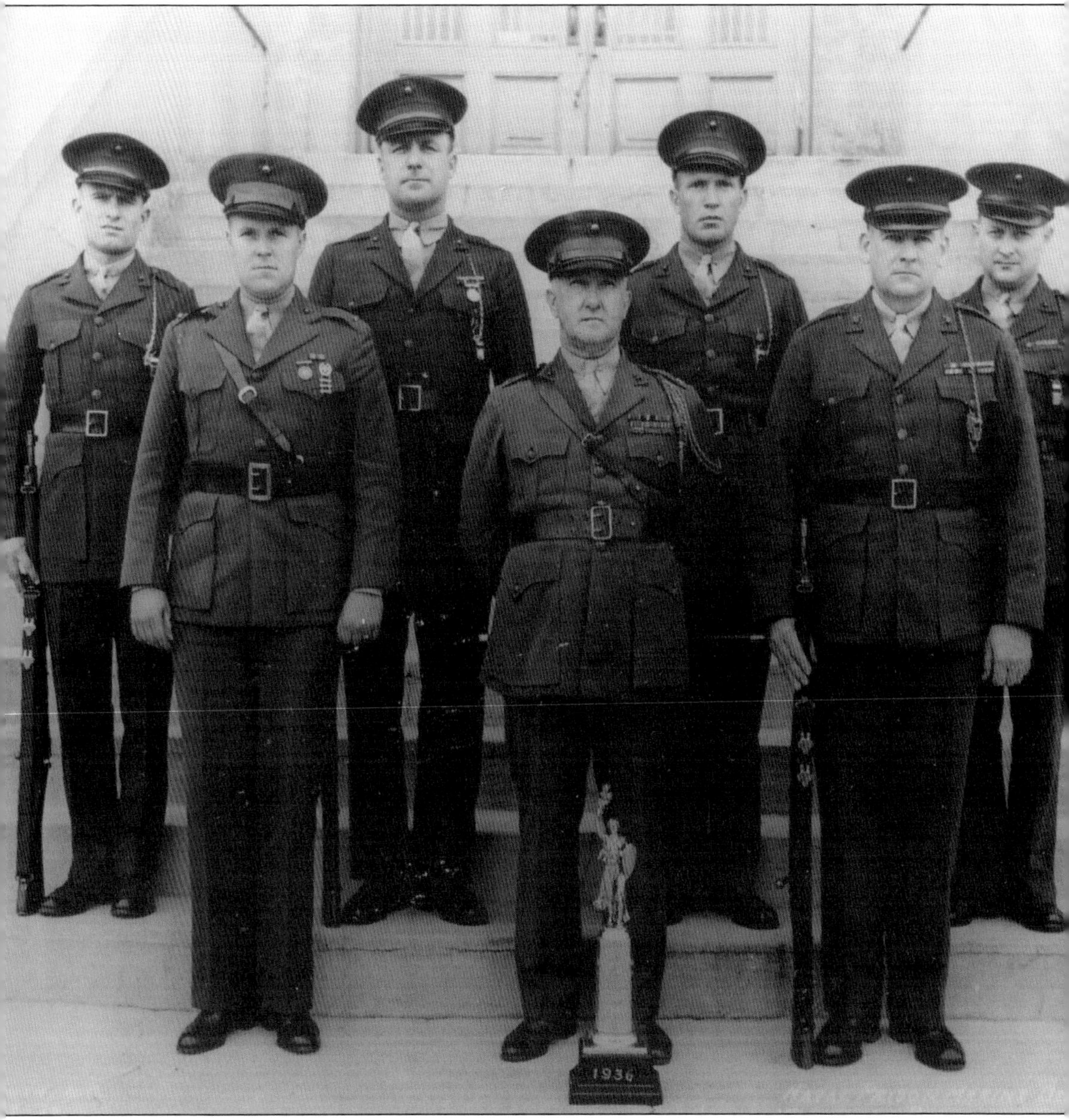

Prison Detachment, 1936 Tournament Winners. When it was finally clear that four prisoners were missing, lockdown would follow, then the long scream of a siren that jolted residents in Portsmouth and Kittery, the arrival of the commandant, the riot squad, and the dogs. The dragnet would fan out as state and local police in six towns were notified, closing the shipyard, blocking roads, and throwing schedules off kilter. Days later in Poquetanuck, Connecticut, the four ran low on gas and eased into Joseph Hastedt's gas station early on July 9. Low on funds, they broke the lock on the pump and filled up. Hastedt, seeing no one paying, went out to inspect. As he did, the three started to drive away, pausing briefly to pick up the fourth. That single act of camaraderie did them in. Hastedt caught up to the Nash and asked the driver to pay. The driver rolled down his window, stuck a .38 caliber gun in Hastedt's face, and asked, "What do you propose to do about the matter?" and gunned it. (NHHC.)

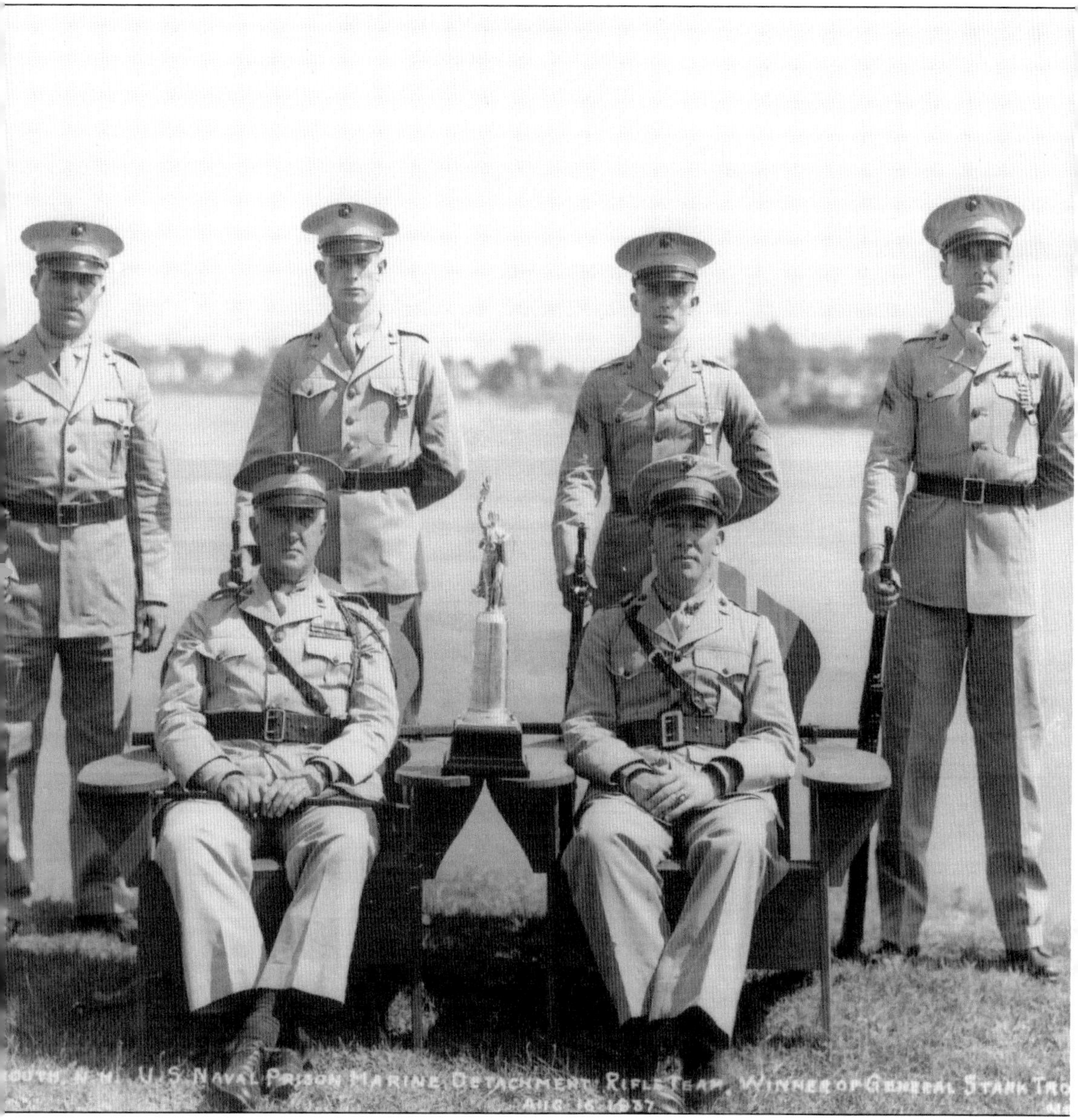

PRISON DETACHMENT, AUGUST 1937. Perhaps similarly dressed in summer service uniform A, Marines fanned out looking for the four escapees. Outside Norwalk, Connecticut, however, rookie patrolman George McCoskey saw a Nash automobile drive by. For reasons he could not articulate, the car looked wrong. He decided to stop it. The chase and shoot-out took the vehicles through the town from the corner of Harris and Winthrop Streets down to Thames Street, ending only when one of the policeman's bullets pierced the Nash's gas tank. For the third time in almost as many days, the four hit the national news in a story that sold newspapers. Upon their return to the prison, they were brought before Commander South to explain themselves, but no one spoke up. Finally, George Mahar, previously charged with manslaughter, summed it up: "It was a chance worth taking." Apparently, it was. Four years later, almost to the day, Frank O'Neil was once again on the lam; this time a little bit older and a whole lot wiser. (NHHC.)

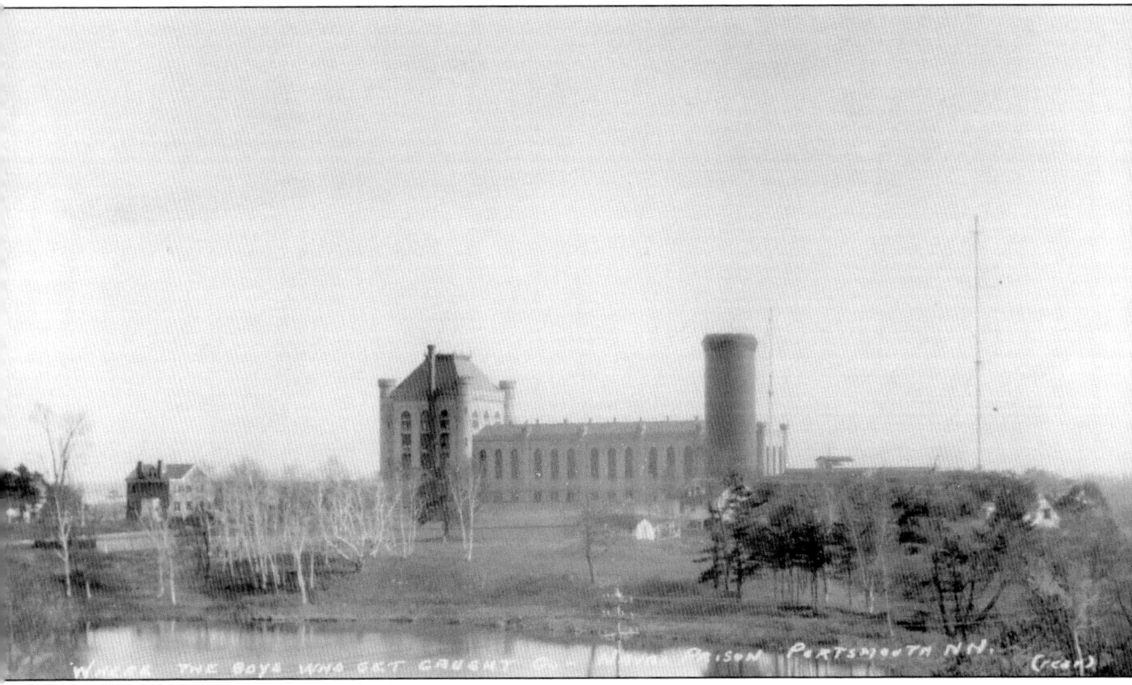

REAR VIEW OF THE PRISON, 1920. In writing about the breakout, carried in East Coast newspapers, reporters repeated a long-standing prison myth: if a prisoner escaped, the guard would have to serve out the remainder of the prisoner's sentence. This was also supposedly the case if a prisoner crossed the outside prison yard boundary, the "dead line," and the guard did not shoot, allowing him to escape. None of it is true; nor is the often repeated phrase "brought back dead or alive." Most men were captured, some were shot and wounded, some were killed, but a handful escaped. Frank O'Neil was still at large. The caption on this photograph reads, "Where the boys who get caught go." (UNHL, Gustave Freret.)

Eight

World War II and Further Expansion

Robert J. Verge in his 1946 *History of the Portsmouth Prison* describes the decade just before the outbreak of World War II, when the prison population was declining and allocated government funds were dwindling, as follows:

> This decade was one of little or no development in prison policies of administration. It bordered on the routine program of peacetime, undermanned Navy with its expenditures limited and its complement at a minimum. In general, this phase of the prison development consisted of minor constrictions and small changes in prison policy but on the whole it stayed in the near vicinity of the already established norm.

The lowest population in the prison's history, 85 men, was recorded in May 1940, just before America entered the war. A mere five years later, in both April and August 1945, count would reach 3,088, the peak in the prison's 66 years of operation. As during World War I, great changes would take place in both the physical plant and the activities of the men. During the war years 1941–1945, Col. Joseph A. Rossell, the prison commandant, would restore many men to service. More importantly, he would stay for four years. During the ebb of the prison population, from August 1934, until Colonel Rossell's arrival in June 1941, six commandants had come and gone. The last commandant to remain for four years was, interestingly, Rossell, when he had assumed the same post from July 1930 to August 1934. Taking this position six months prior to Pearl Harbor, he was—perhaps like Osborne—at the right place at the right time. And like Osborne, as the war ended, Rossell would leave the prison under a cloud, which eclipsed his good works and prior service.

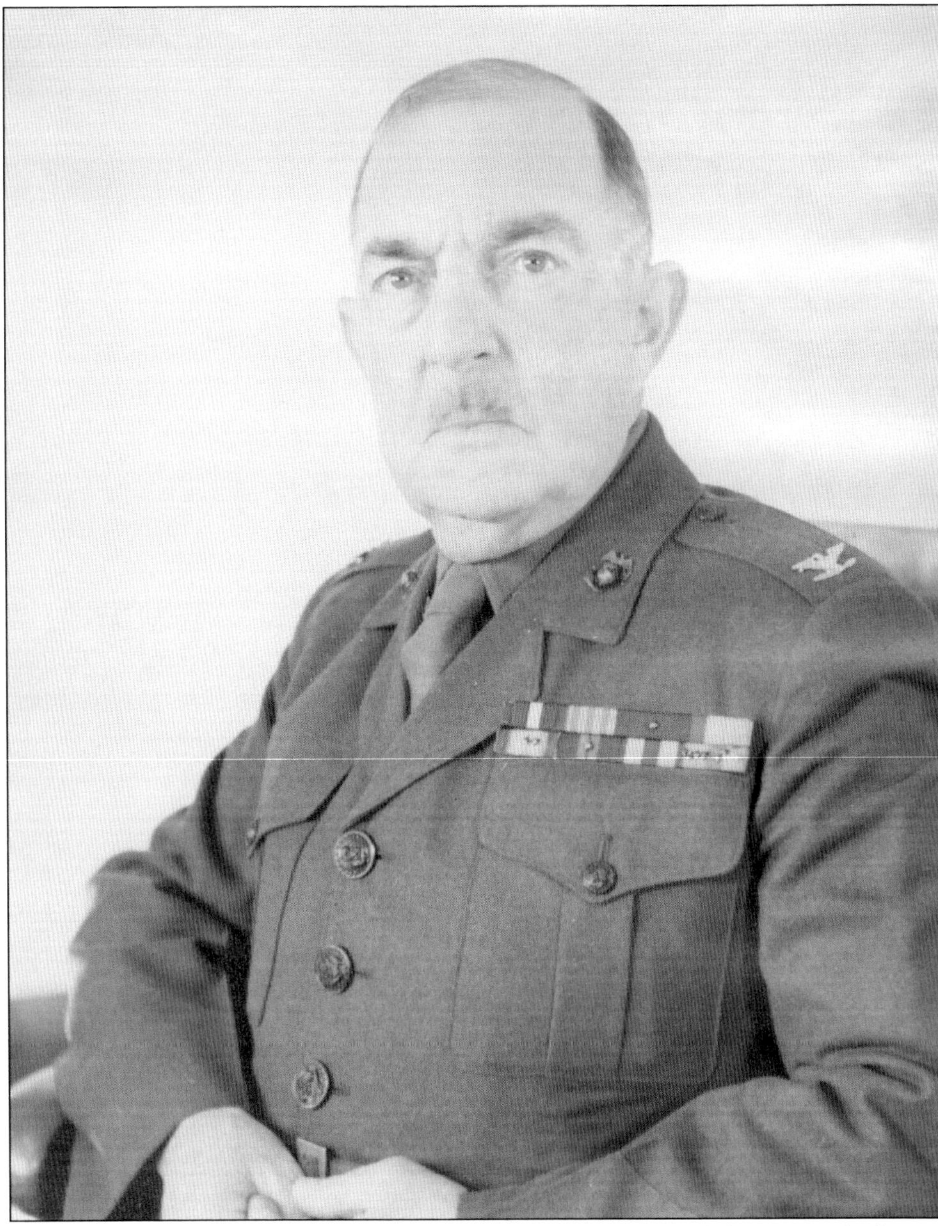

Col. Joseph A. Rossell. Before coming to Portsmouth, Rossell attended seminary for four years in preparation for the priesthood; in 1902, he joined the Marines instead. As several before him, Rossell received the Navy Cross in Nicaragua in 1928. According to Robert Verge, in his 1946 history of the prison, Rossell "was a firm advocate of individual treatment and he would go to great lengths to promote, develop and encourage a prisoner in any wholesome project or enterprise." Rossell did his homework. During his first command at the prison, he made a tour of other penal institutions, bringing back programs and policies he thought might work at Portsmouth. His itinerary included brigs, jails, and prisons in Massachusetts, New Hampshire, New York, Pennsylvania, New Jersey, Ohio, and Connecticut, as well as the Army prison at Governor's Island and New York Police Department jails. World War II broke out during Rossell's second stint at the prison. (NHHC.)

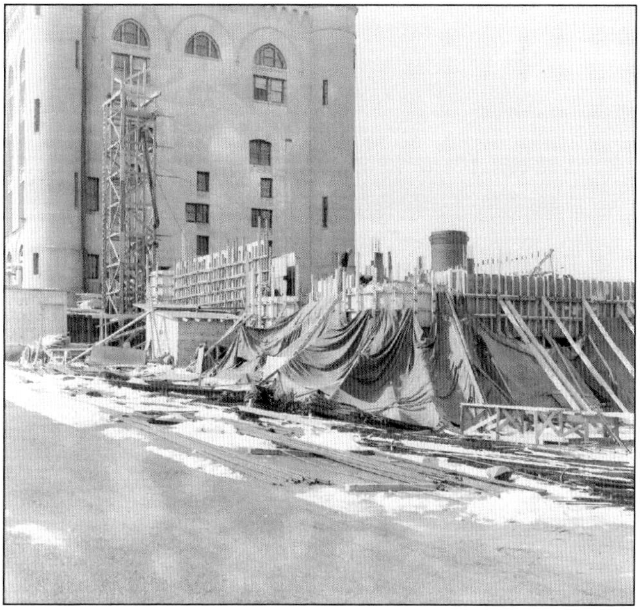

ADDITION TO THE PRISON, FEBRUARY 1942. The war years, 1941–1945, were probably the busiest and most productive in the life of the prison. The highest number of prisoners, an extensive building project, and many men restored to duty characterized Rossell's second four years at the prison. The large and continuous influx of men—an increase of 1,397 in one three-month period—also necessitated both hiring new personnel and constructing additional facilities, most notably the northeast extension, which was completed in November 1942. (NARACP.)

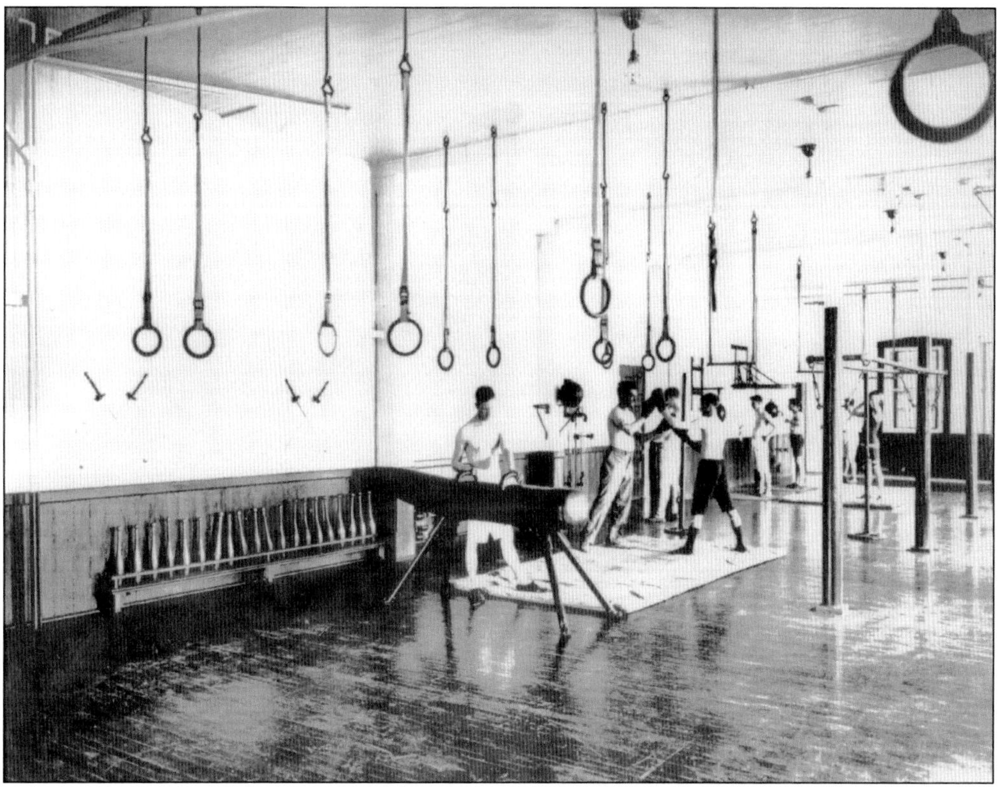

GYMNASIUM, UNDATED. The northeast extension, or north wing, which was part of the original plan, resembled the rest of the prison, with towers on each corner; however, it was a smaller version of what had been originally envisioned. Nevertheless, it allowed the Marines to move off the lower reservation into the third and fourth "decks." A gymnasium was installed on the top deck. (LMCQ.)

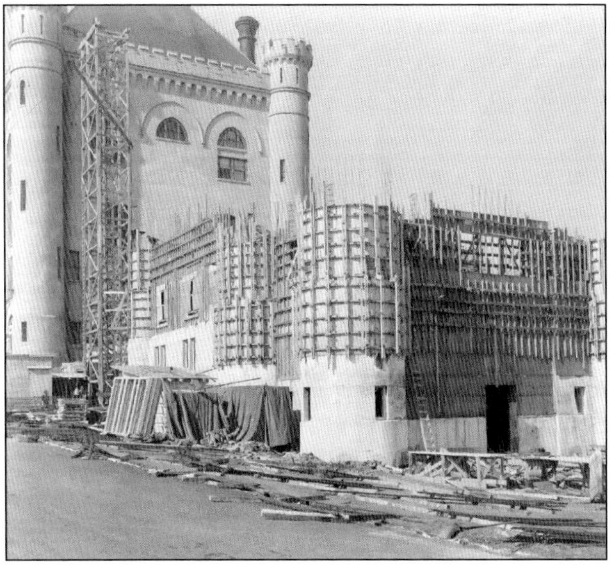

Prison Addition, April 1942. Throughout the war, first the Judge Advocate General (JAG) and later the Bureau of Naval Personnel made restoring prisoners to duty a priority, thus training and work programs that made men fit for service were a priority as well. (NARACP.)

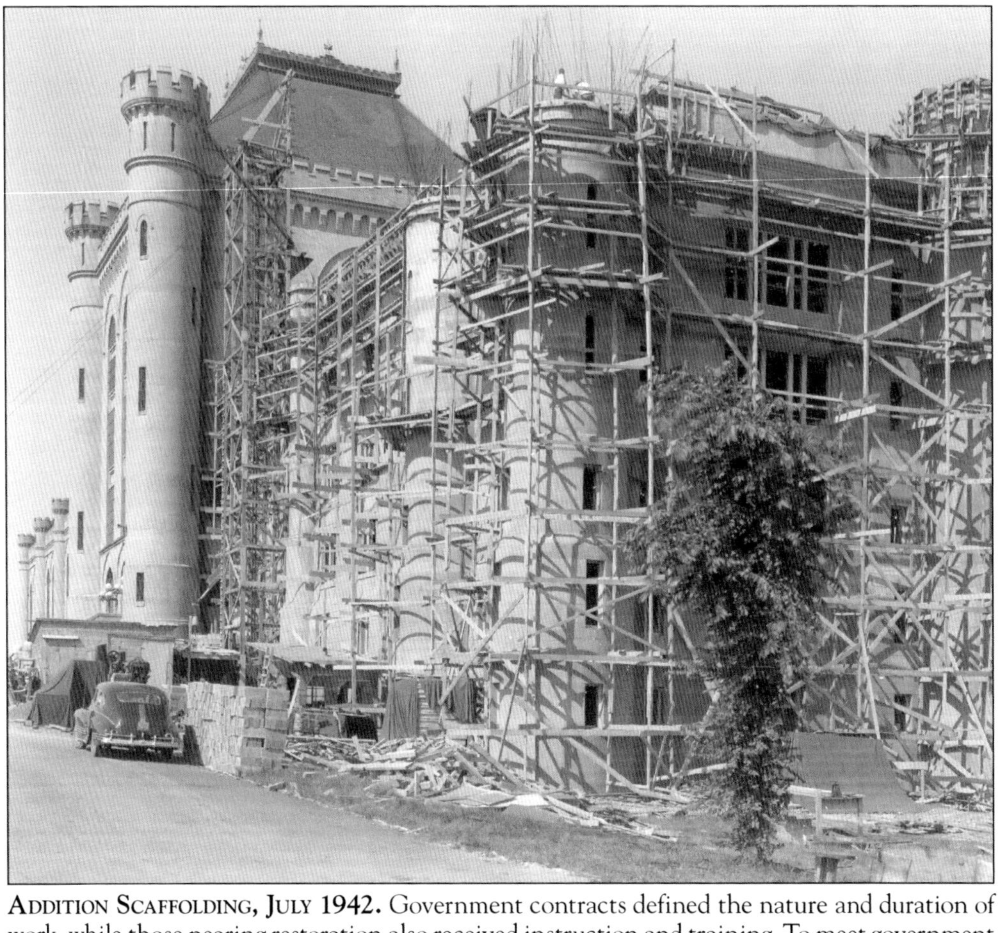

Addition Scaffolding, July 1942. Government contracts defined the nature and duration of work, while those nearing restoration also received instruction and training. To meet government deadlines, the workweek was often extended to evenings and weekends. (NARACP.)

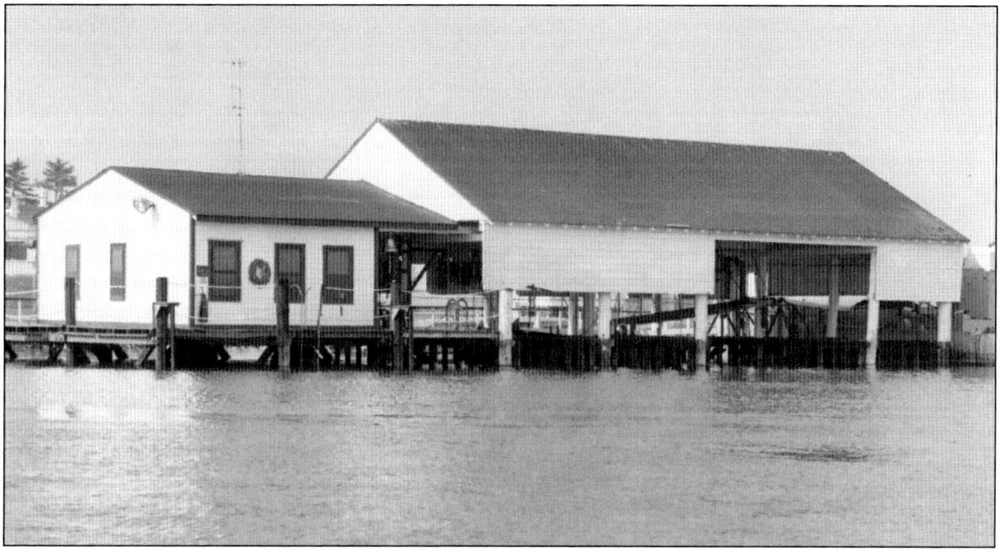

Prisoner-Built Boathouse, 1950s. As during most of the prison's history, inmates (known at this time as GCMPs, general court-martial prisoners) were given increased freedom, responsibility, and privileges based on behavior and in conjunction with an increasingly sophisticated screening when they first arrived as well as periodic reviews. During this time, the population was generally divided into those being restored to duty and those not. (NHHC.)

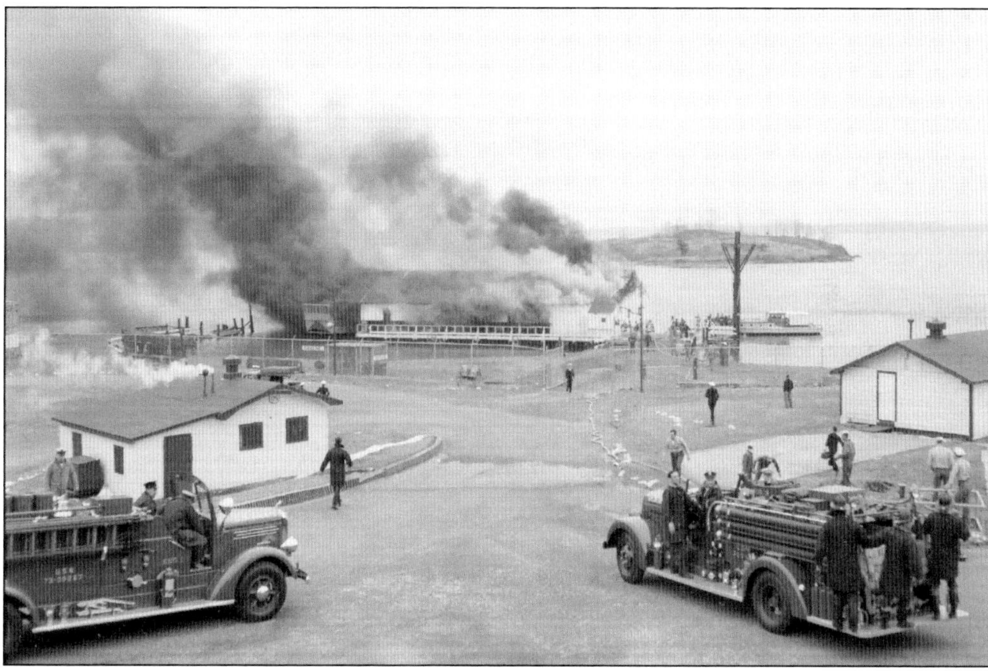

Fire at Boathouse, 1950s. Those not restored because of the severity of their offenses or personality concerns were also fulfilling government contracts that included salvaging radio parts, bookbinding, and manufacturing wooden boxes. As well, they were maintaining the grounds, building a boathouse and a dock, crushing the 70 tons of rock used daily in the shipyard, and repairing and maintaining roads. The boathouse burned in the 1950s, but was repaired and remained Building 193 until being demolished in 2007. (NHHC.)

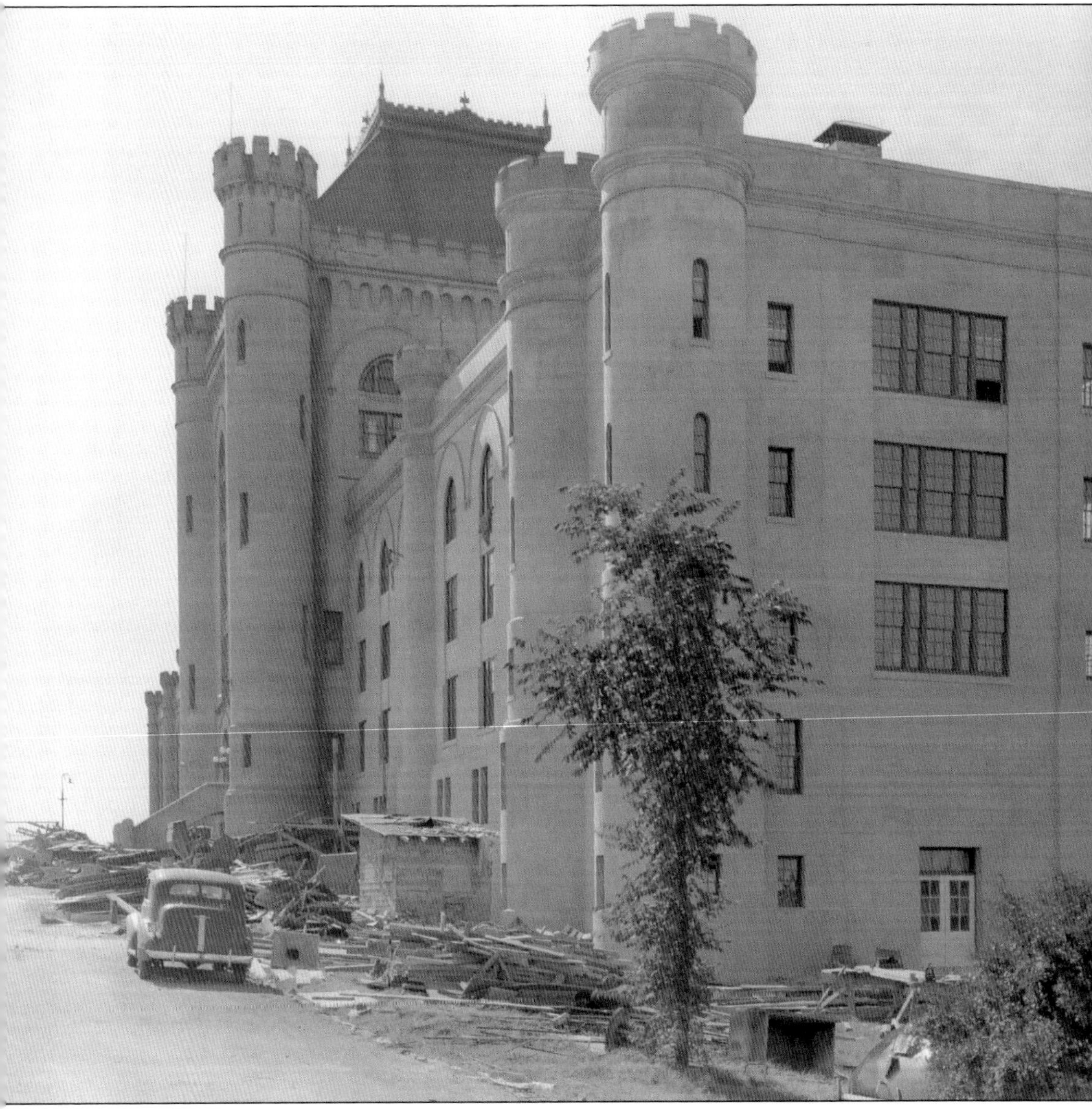

Completed Addition, October 1942. The addition provided much-needed space for the numerous wartime programs. Those recommended for restoration—about 1,000 men—directly helped with the war effort. The print shop ran almost around the clock, printing for much of the Navy Yard. The tailor shop made 70,000 suits for the prison as well as for men in other facilities. The net detail manufactured masses of camouflage and cargo nets, rope, and cable slings. Those slated for restoration were offered training in 16 different areas—such as aviation, ordnance, diesel, photographer, radioman, or ship's cooks and bakers—including the basics of small arms for Marines and fireman and seaman for the Navy. Drilling and exercise with weekly parades and occasional exhibitions were part of training. An Honor Company was established, and these men worked unsupervised in the Navy Yard and lived in restoration barracks on the lower reservation. (NARACP.)

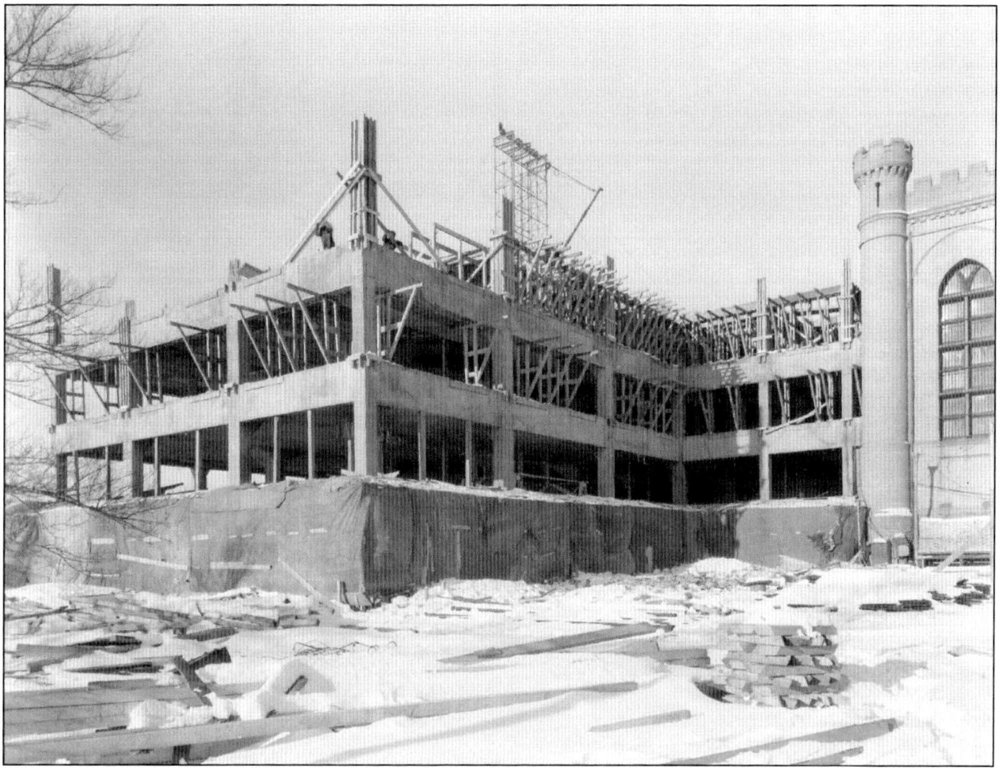

SOUTHWEST ANNEX CONSTRUCTION, APRIL 9, 1943. The seven-story southwest annex was begun several months after the completion of the northeast extension. The annex was a departure from the "castle" architecture, although it incorporated many similar elements of design. The basement contained several shops: tailor, printing, upholstery, book binding, and shoe and automotive repair. The first deck was a galley and mess hall, which could seat 1,000 men. (NARACP.)

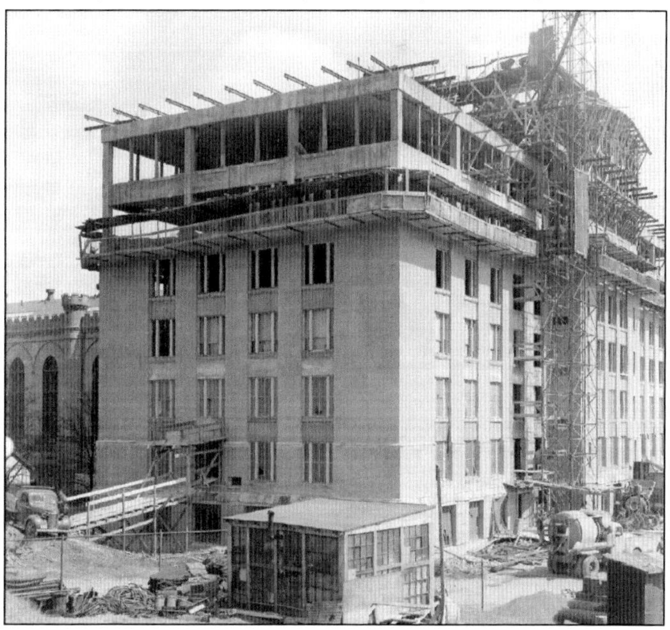

ANNEX CONSTRUCTION, JUNE 6, 1943. An auditorium occupied the top deck, which was used both for evening movies and Sunday services. The second, third, fourth, and half of the fifth could hold 1,600 prisoners in one of eight large, open squad rooms or squad bays; only 300 men remained in the cell block. The rest of the fifth deck was the sick bay with an operating room for minor surgery and dental offices. (NARACP.)

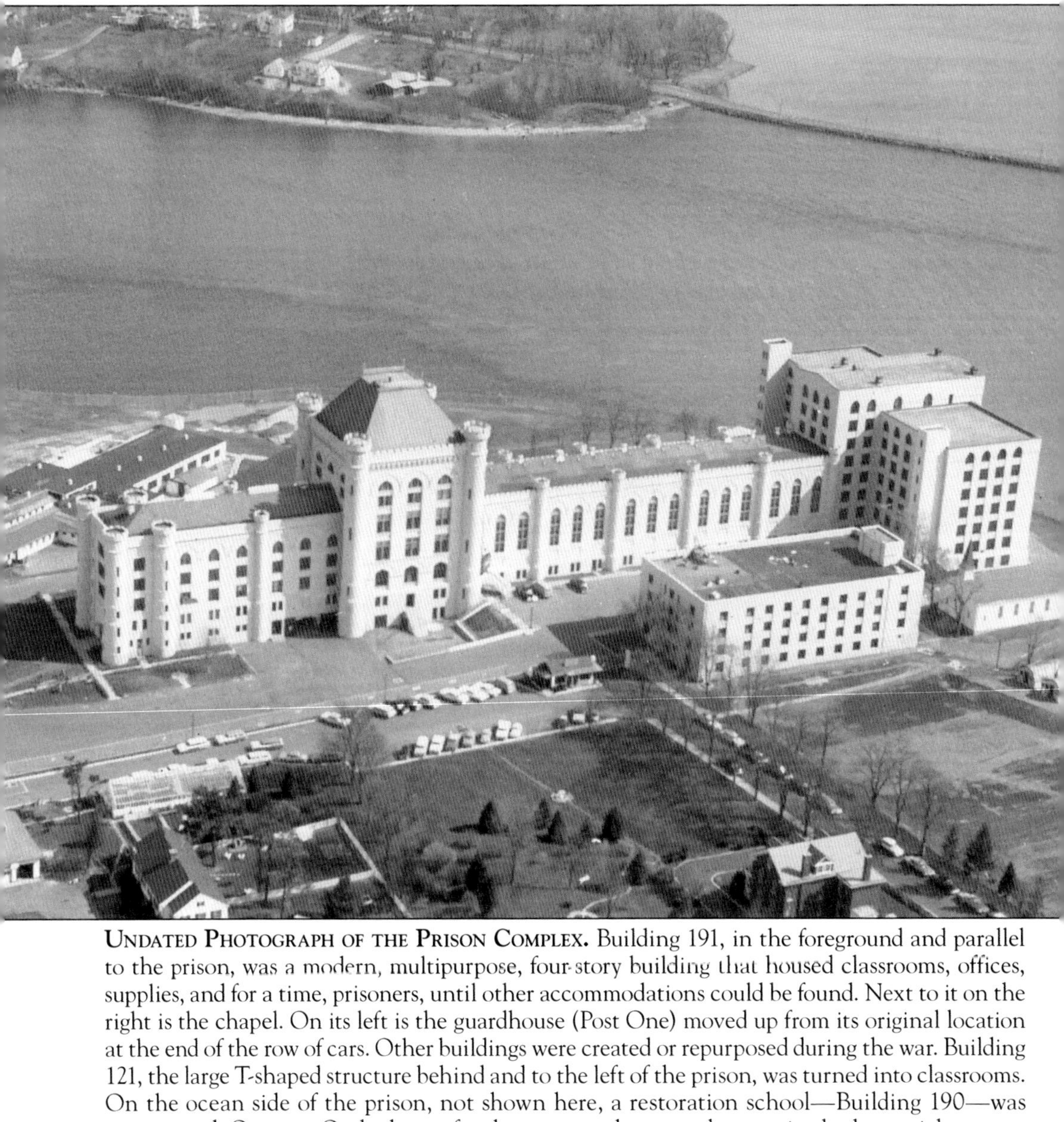

UNDATED PHOTOGRAPH OF THE PRISON COMPLEX. Building 191, in the foreground and parallel to the prison, was a modern, multipurpose, four-story building that housed classrooms, offices, supplies, and for a time, prisoners, until other accommodations could be found. Next to it on the right is the chapel. On its left is the guardhouse (Post One) moved up from its original location at the end of the row of cars. Other buildings were created or repurposed during the war. Building 121, the large T-shaped structure behind and to the left of the prison, was turned into classrooms. On the ocean side of the prison, not shown here, a restoration school—Building 190—was constructed. Quarters Q, the house for the commandant, can be seen in the lower right corner of the photograph. In all, of the 5,894 men who entered the prison between December 7, 1941 and November 30, 1945, approximately 1,566 were restored to duty. (UNHL.)

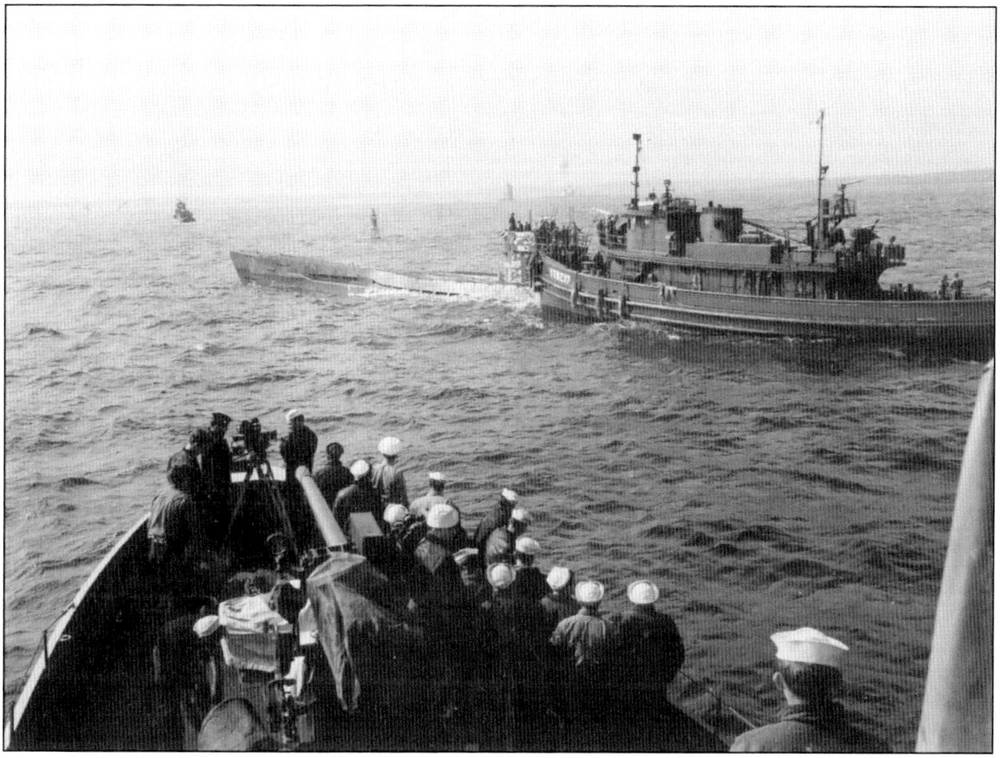

Escort Approaching German Submarine, May 1945. As the war wound down, in the spring of 1945, three months before Hiroshima, a series of events occurred at the prison that became national news, spawned several books, and led to Colonel Rossell's dismissal as commandant. Shortly after Hitler committed suicide and Europe surrendered to the Allies on V-E Day, German navy admiral Karl Dönitz ordered all of the U-boats (*Unterseeboote*, or submarines) to surrender to the nearest port. For those U-boats in the Atlantic, that meant Newfoundland or Portsmouth. The Allies indicated that they would sink on sight any renegade U-boat that did not comply. (NARACP.)

Shipyard with U-805 Crew, May 1945. Shortly after a freak May snowstorm that decimated the Maine apple crop, German submarines were spotted off the coast of Newfoundland and escorted into Portsmouth Harbor. Their arrivals, one after another for a week, were well publicized. Newspapermen and the local citizenry clambered for good vantage points, and because of the enormous crowds and commotion, security was compromised. (NARACP.)

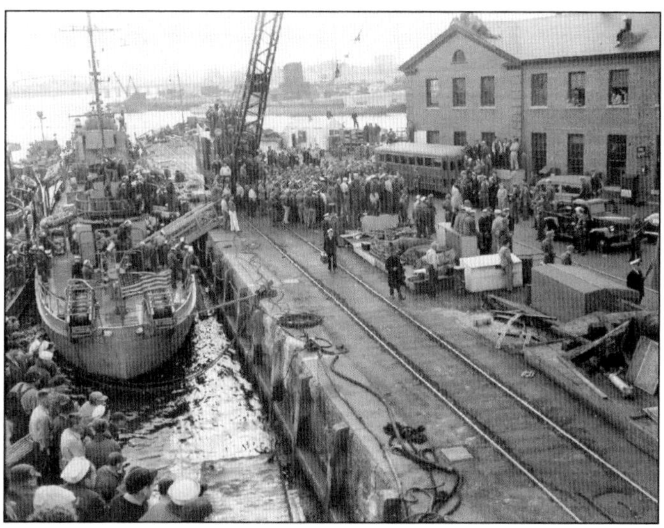

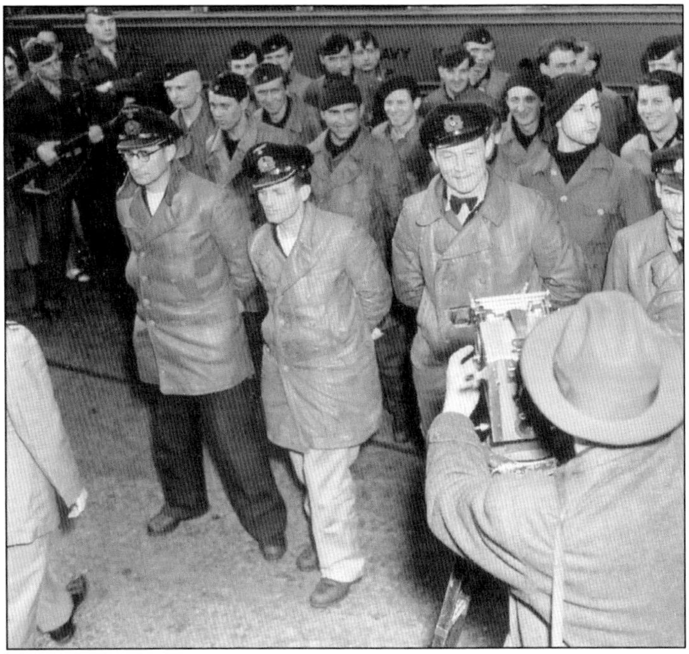

The Crew of U-803, May 1945. The Germans were initially grateful to be in America since surrender to the Russians or French was unthinkable. But because of the lax security, it was hard to keep order. What happened next was perhaps inevitable, despite assurances of the Geneva Convention. (NARACP.)

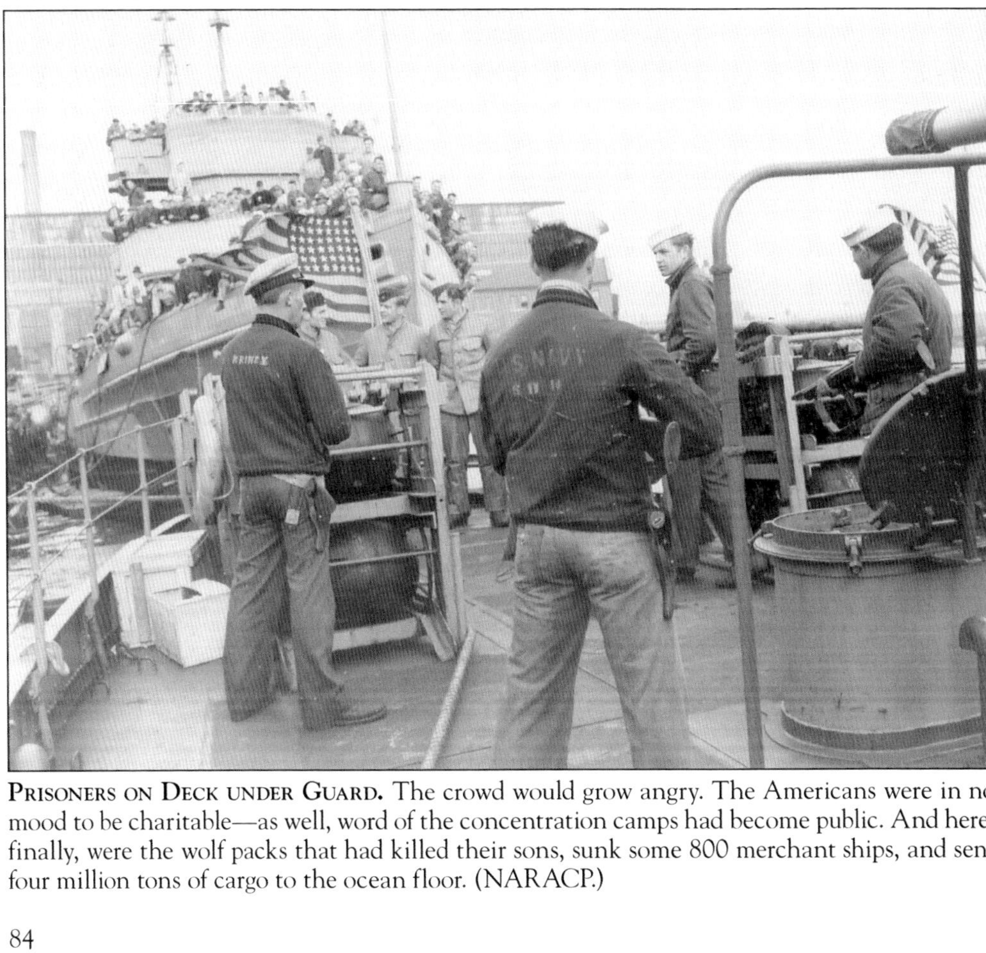

Prisoners on Deck under Guard. The crowd would grow angry. The Americans were in no mood to be charitable—as well, word of the concentration camps had become public. And here, finally, were the wolf packs that had killed their sons, sunk some 800 merchant ships, and sent four million tons of cargo to the ocean floor. (NARACP.)

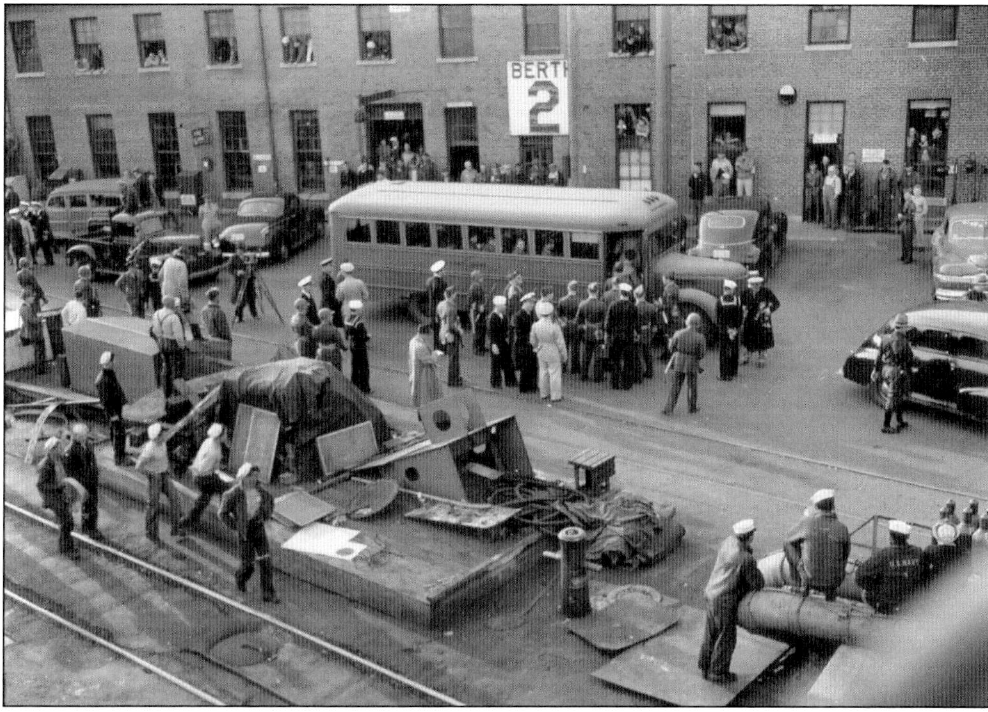

German Crew Loaded into Buses, May 1945. As the Germans, escorted by Marines with automatic rifles and tommy guns, filed into buses that would take them to the prison, the crowd spat on them, swore at them, hurled insults, and grabbed at their clothing. Inside the prison, the Germans' possessions were confiscated and sold, kept as souvenirs, or distributed to the locals; the guards beat and humiliated them. (NARACP.)

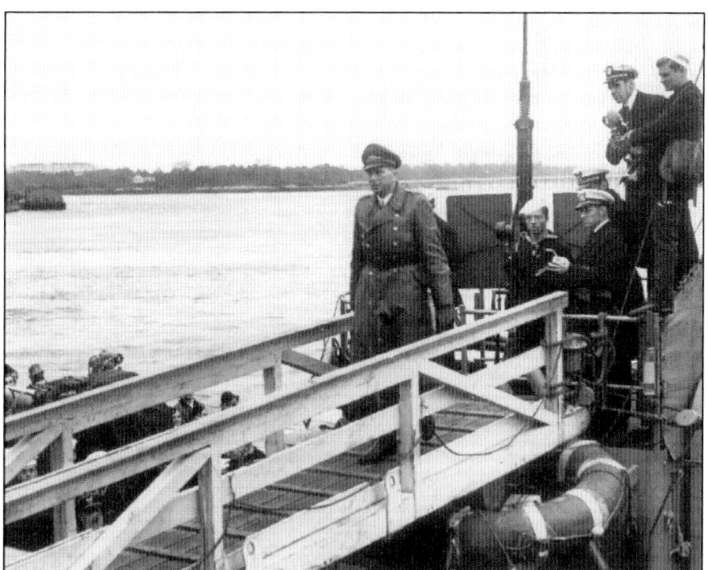

German Officer Disembarking, May 1945. Kapitänleutnant (Lt. Cmdr.) Fritz Steinhoff of U-803 was later transported to the Boston prison, where he committed suicide with his broken glasses. (NARACP.)

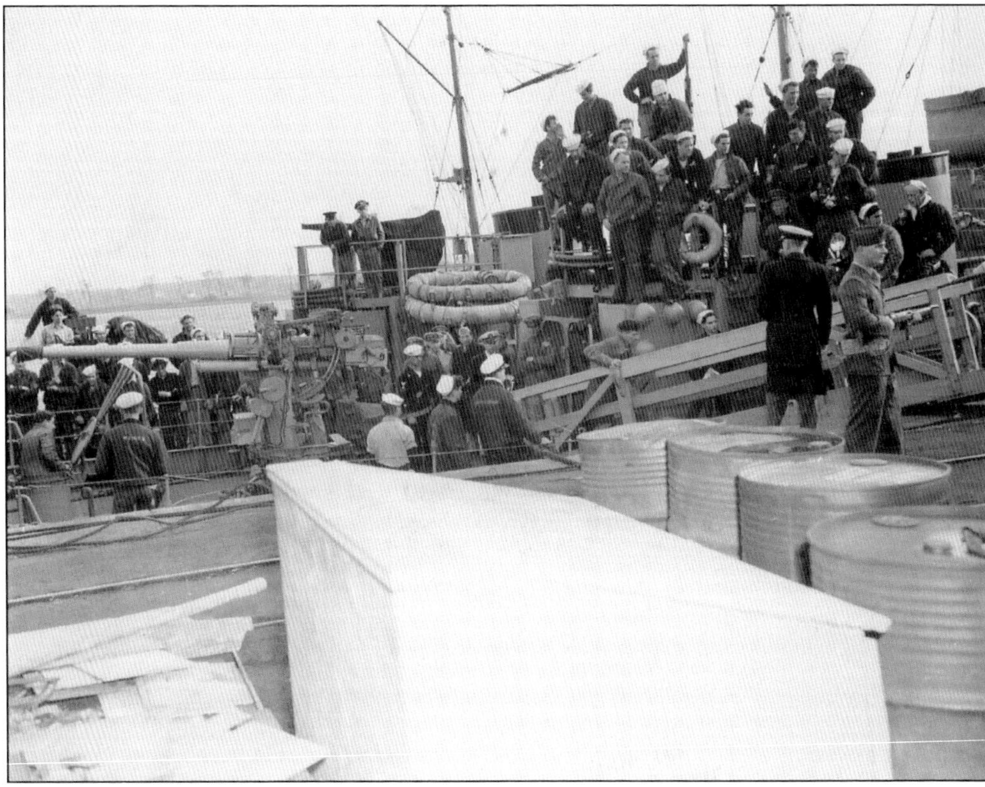

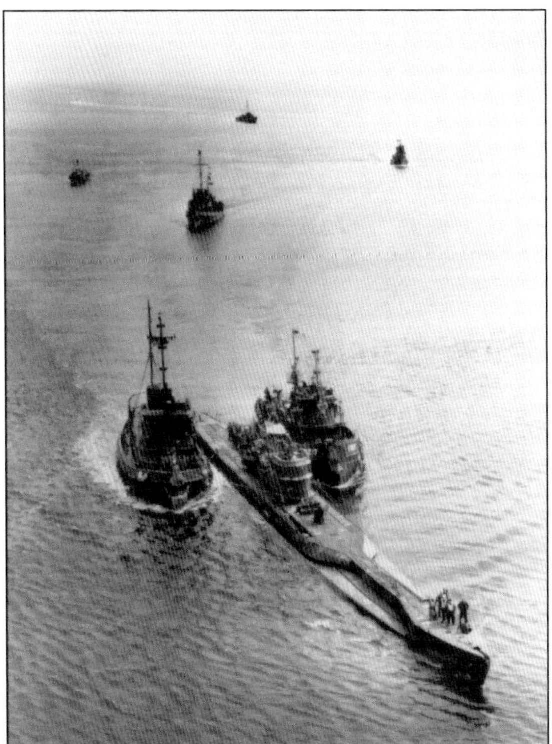

AWAITING GERMANS DISEMBARKING. Others, like Comdr. Johann Heinrich Fehler, were sent to the overcrowded Portsmouth Prison and later south to a prison camp. The rest of his life, he would regret surrendering in America instead of Newfoundland as a result of his treatment at Portsmouth. (NARACP.)

U-234 ESCORTED INTO SHIPYARD, MAY 13, 1945. One of the last U-boats to arrive was U-234, an enormous 1,763-ton, 300-foot mine-layer refitted as a transport ship. In it was 300,000 pounds of Germany's finest weaponry destined for Japan, along with a dozen specialists and scientists who could put the payload into production. (PNSYM.)

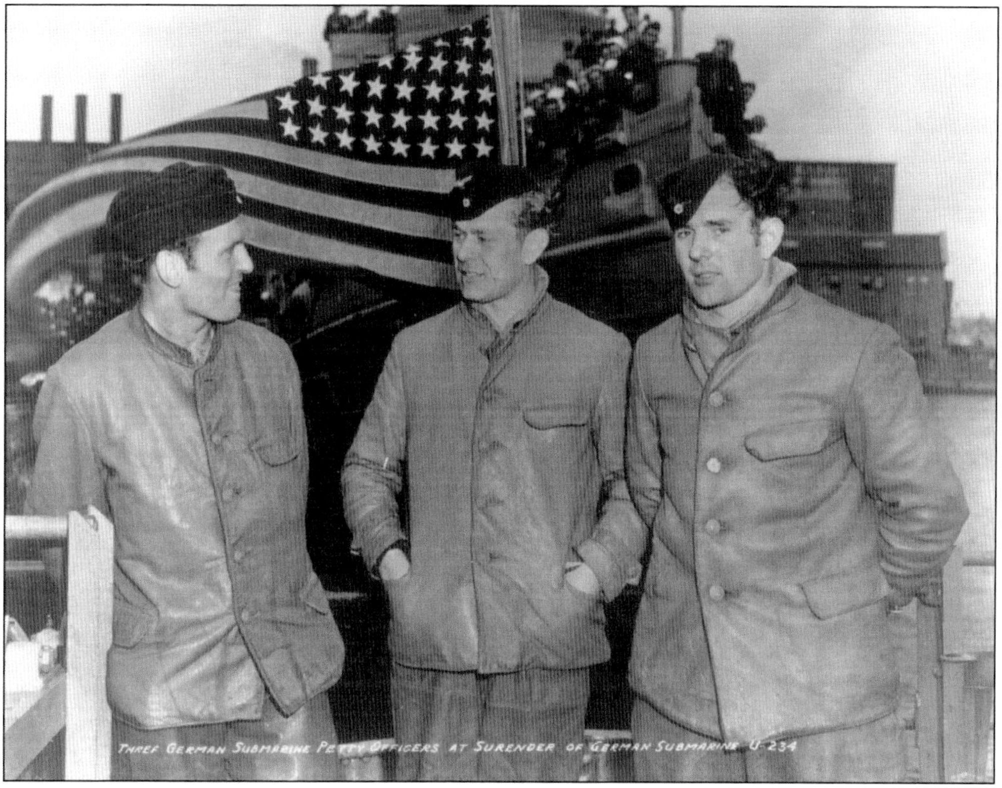

Three Petty Officers at Surrender of U-234. The media had signaled its importance, and rumor was rife: perhaps Adolf Hitler's inner circle was aboard, including Eva Braun or Heinrich Himmler. Mysteriously, two dead Japanese were reportedly on board as well. In fact, only the crew, plus German scientists and engineers disembarked. Hitler's henchmen, if they had escaped, were not found on U-234. The two Japanese were indeed dead but had been buried at sea. Washington had been tracking U-234 and, not long afterward, clamped down on the media and the crowds. Many of U-234's personnel were scooped up by the military for their expertise, and the cargo was impounded. (PNSYM.)

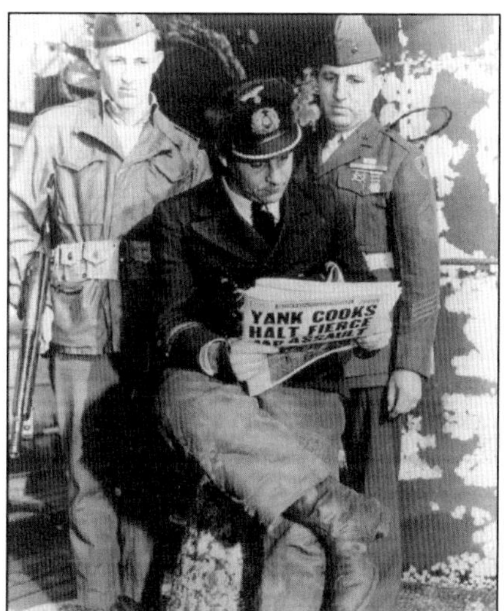

A German Officer from U-234. Several men aboard U-234 would later return to the United States after the war to live and work, despite reported mistreatment at the prison. (PNSYM.)

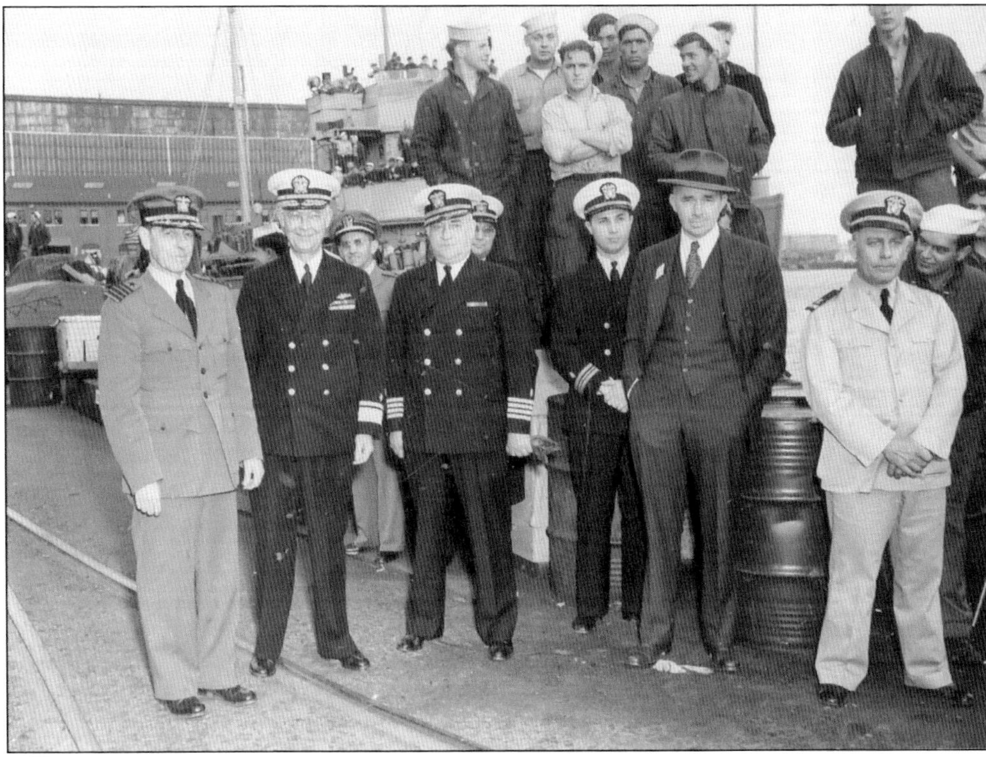

UNIDENTIFIED SHIPYARD OFFICERS, MAY 1945. After the war, an investigation was launched into the treatment of the German prisoners held at Portsmouth. In all, five submarines surrendered at the Navy Yard and most of the crews spent some time in the prison. Those with valuable information were removed more quickly. (NARACP.)

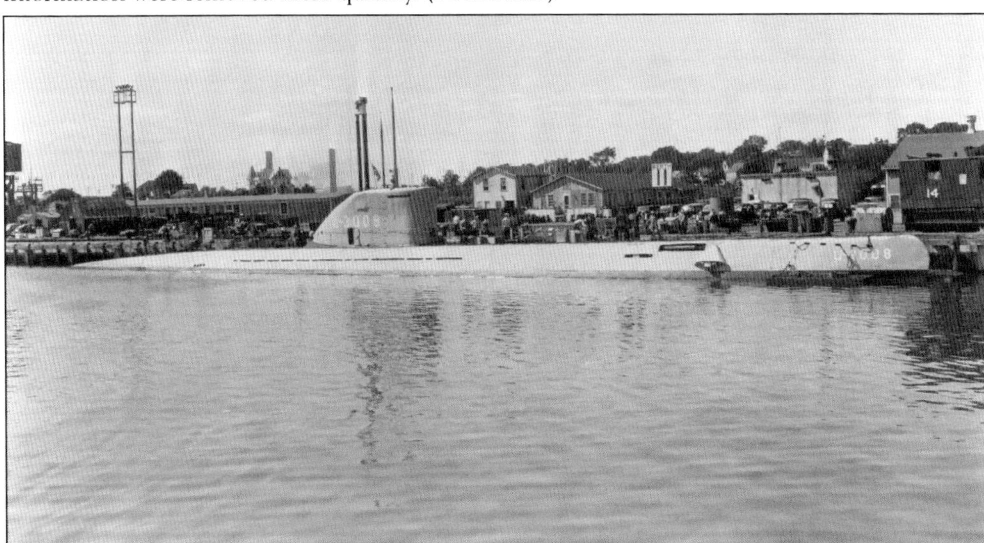

BERTH 11 PNSY, AUGUST 30, 1946. In the resulting investigation, Rossell and several high-ranking officers at the shipyard would be found culpable for the lapse in security and guard behavior. All would be disciplined and Rossell would be forced to leave. Despite his eight years of noteworthy service at the prison, his career would be irreparably tarnished by the incident. (UNHL.)

Nine

Postwar Transformations

The Navy Department would dictate what happened to the prison in the period after World War II until its closing, which included three name changes. The new names reflected the designated function of the prison. From its opening in April 11, 1908, until March 31, 1946, it had been known as the US Naval Prison. From April 1, 1946, to May 30, 1951, it was the US Naval Disciplinary Barracks; from May 31, 1951 to September 29, 1960, it was called the US Naval Retraining Command; and from September 30, 1960, to its closing on June 3, 1974, the US Naval Disciplinary Command. Right after the war, the Navy Department revamped the restoration and discharge requirements, sending men who were slated to rejoin the military to other retraining commands. The prison's restoration and retraining equipment was sent to the new centers with them. Those prisoners who would not be reentering the service but would be returning to civilian life—much of the remaining population at Portsmouth—stayed at the prison and the prison's new mission became one of education and vocational training. In 1945, the command established a new elementary school and a vocational training school. The classifying and sorting, always a part of the entry process, were taken over by the Assignment Board, which screened men during a quarantine period for communicable diseases and determined their educational levels, vocational aptitudes, and levels of guarding required. Because of an influx of new recruits after the Korean War, the Bureau of Naval Personnel, under the direction of the Navy Department, started a training program for all enlisted men and officers working in the prison.

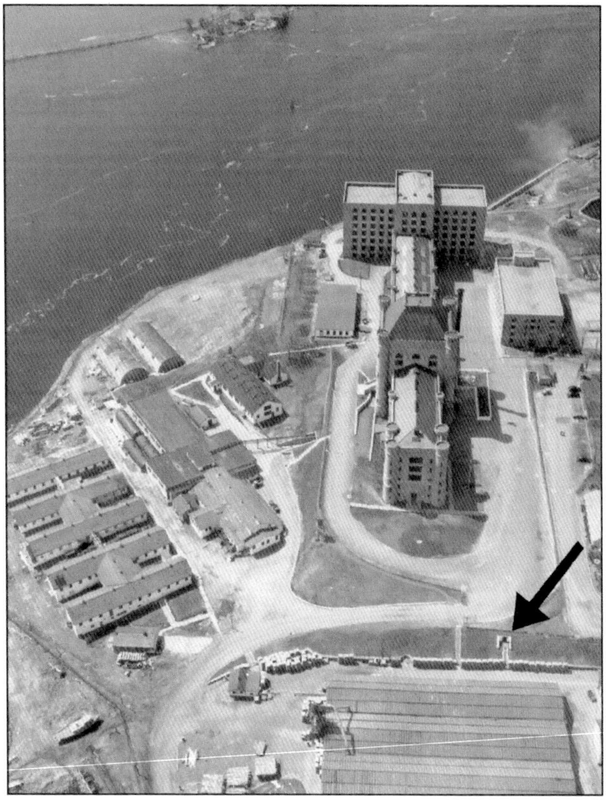

US Naval Disciplinary Barracks Aerial Views, 1948. This is one of the few photographs that shows the special detention center or "Little Siberia," as indicated by the arrow, which contained four cells and no windows. To warrant a stay here, a prisoner's actions or behavior had to be completely unmanageable or disruptive. Or, as one former guard put it, "He had to really screw up." (NHHC.)

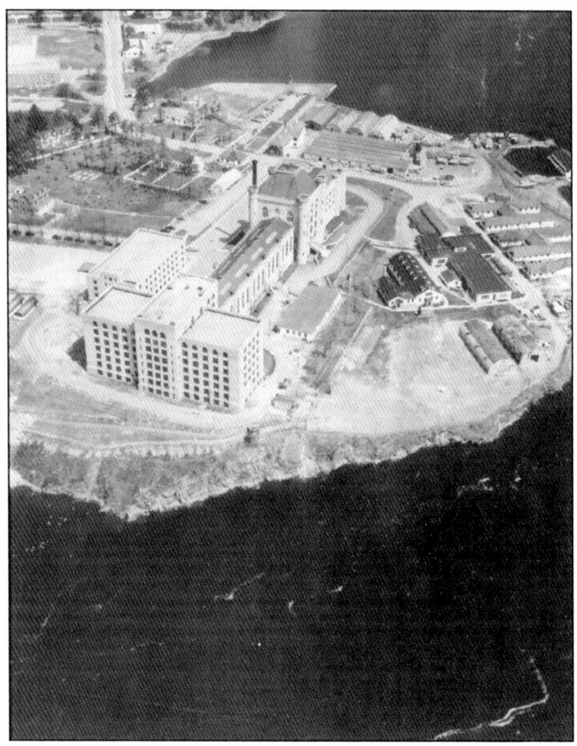

A Prison Aerial View Looking South. With the authorization of the Uniform Code of Military Justice, which went into effect on May 31, 1951, the mission of the prison changed again. Now called the US Navy Retraining Command, its task was both to return men to service and to train those who would not be returning. (NHHC.)

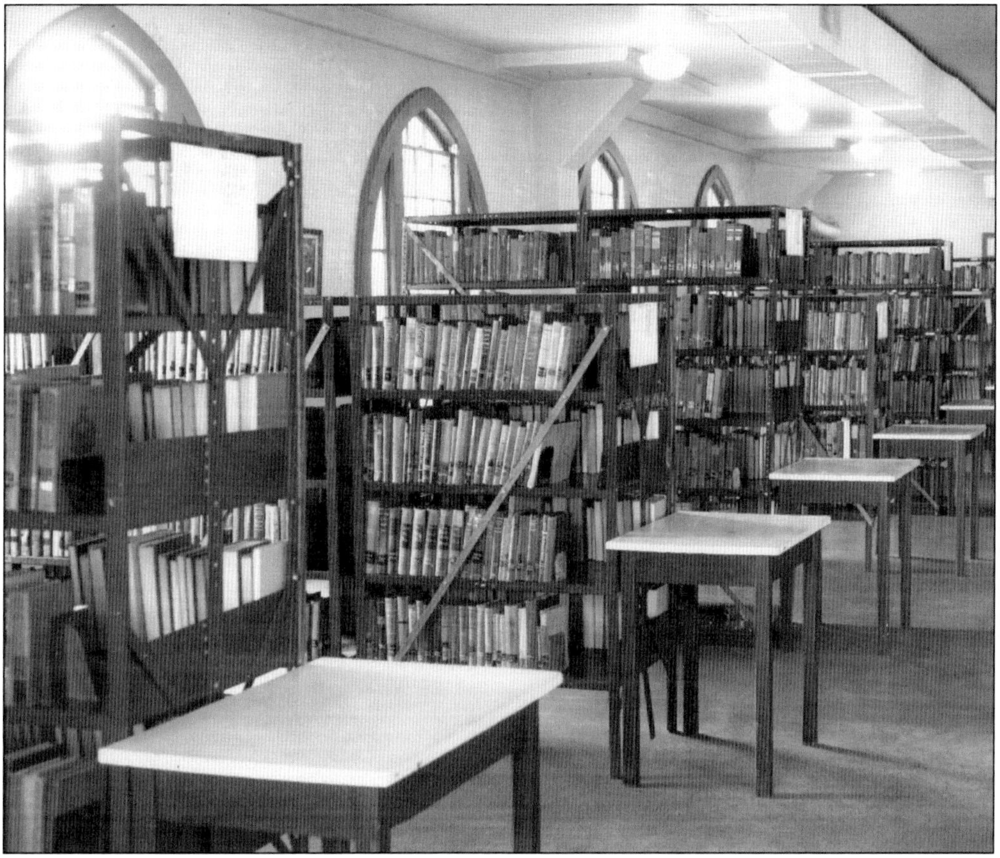

Library Relocated to Annex. As part of its new education mission, the library, now containing over 10,000 volumes, many donated by the New York Public Library, was moved from the lower reservation to the sixth floor of the annex, allowing men to access books themselves rather than have them delivered. The widely read and award-winning prison newspaper *The Castle Courier* was established, which was published biweekly and printed in the prison print shop until the prison's closing. (NHHC.)

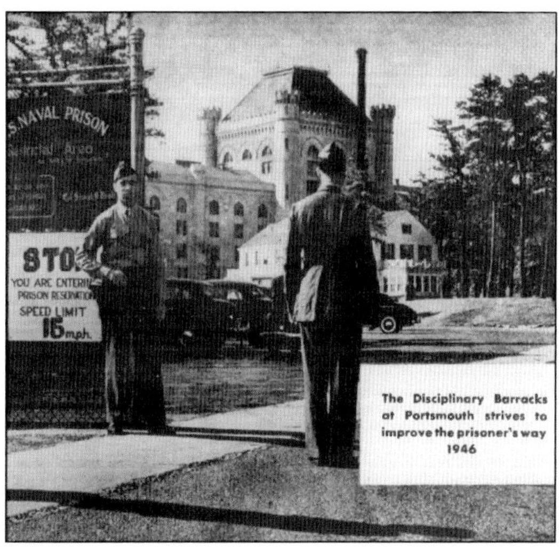

Old Prison Entrance, 1946. In light of the new mission, new policies, and changing prison population, security was increased. The guards at the prison were mostly Marines, but the Navy footed the bill and supplied administration, instructors, and training. In 1946, there were 14 officers and 252 enlisted Marine Corps personnel. (NHHC.)

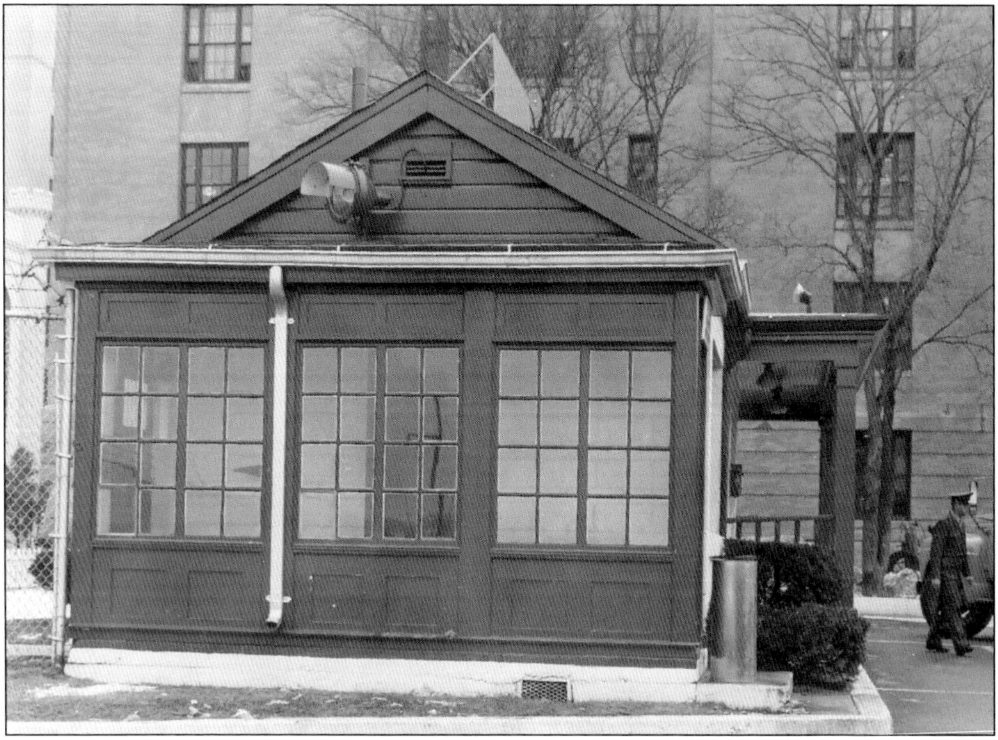

Building 228, Gatehouse, c. 1960s. A gatehouse was erected to monitor those who entered and exited the prison grounds. (NHHC.)

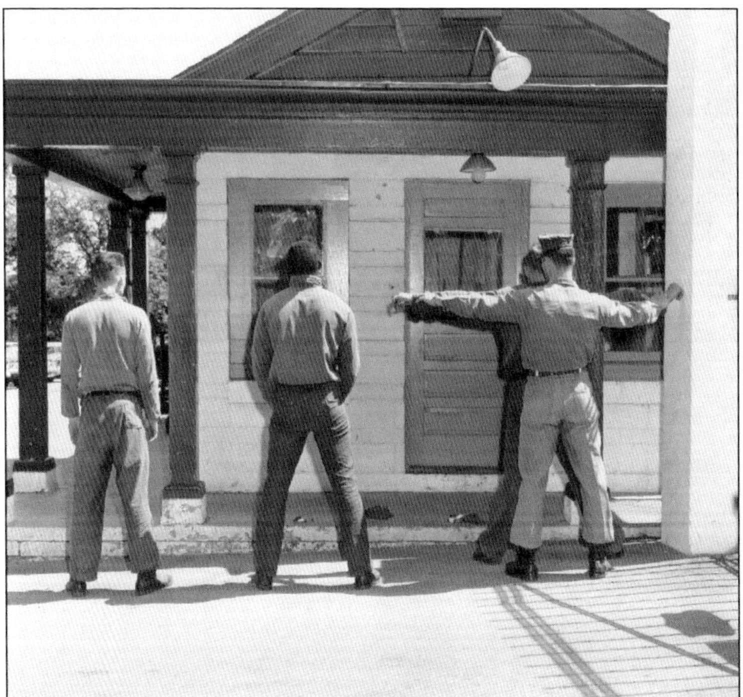

Shaking Down of Prisoners, 1960s. New arrivals at the prison are being searched for weapons at the gatehouse. Although this is a more recent photograph, it shows the heightened security after the war. (NHHC.)

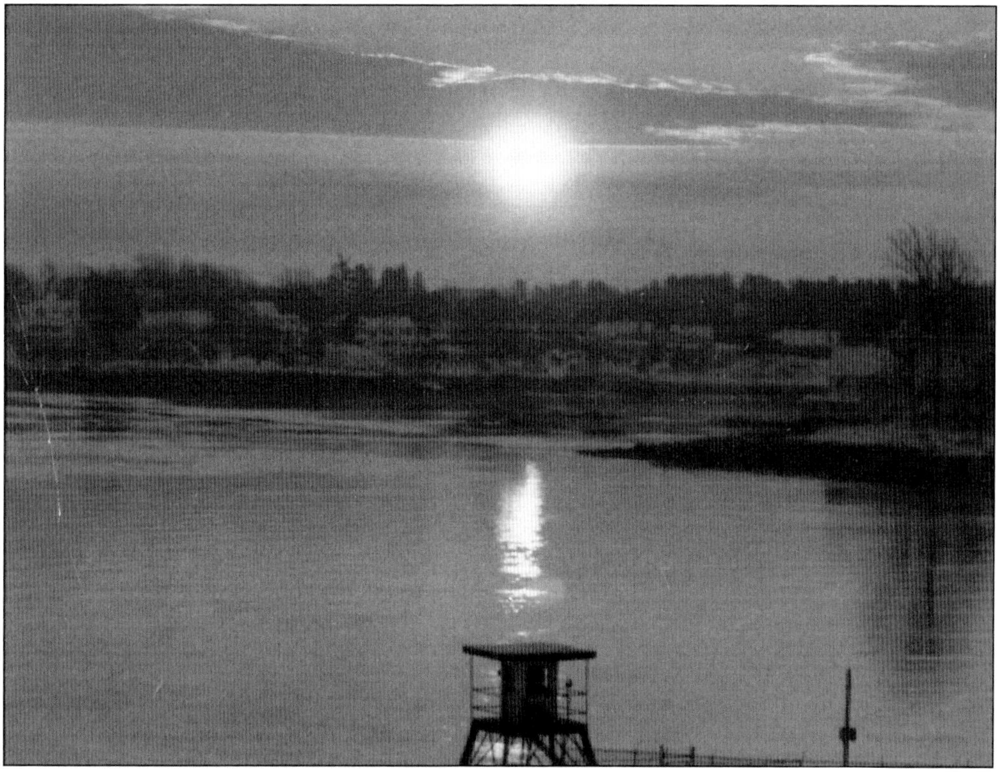

Guard Tower at Night. Guard posts appear in prison maps from its earliest days. Most of the well-armed Marines pulled guard duty at night on all the perimeter guard towers. Duty was usually four hours on and four hours off, with rotating tower assignments and no consecutive nights at the same tower. (NHHC.)

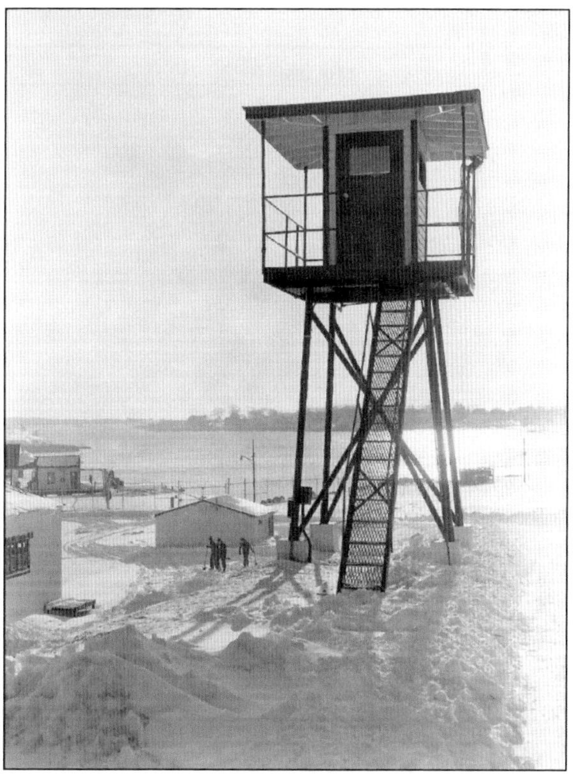

Post Four, "Four on the Shore," February 1964. A station log was a record of daily events and an abbreviated view of life inside and outside the prison. For example, "2325, OOD directed posting of one man fog watch—roving patrol inside compound," means that at 11:25 p.m., the officer of the day assigned a roving guard because of the fog. (NHHC.)

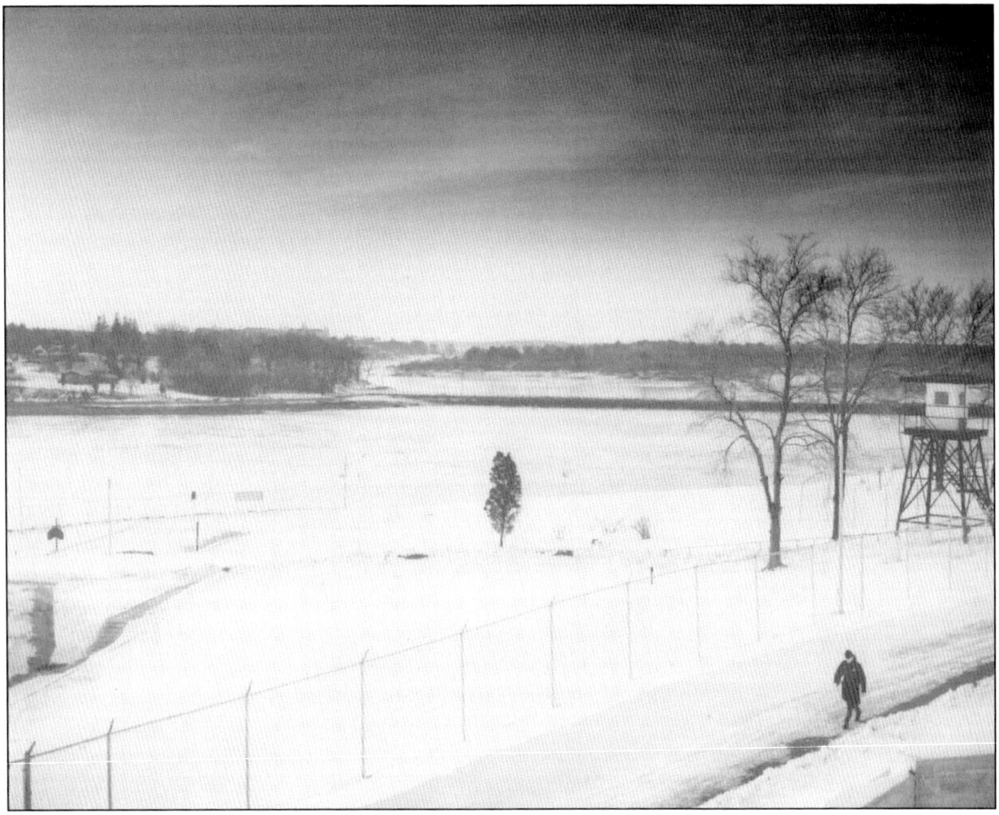

Guard Duty, c. 1973. Some station log entries are easier to interpret: "2350, OOD completed inspection of all posted sentries and barracks, all secure." (NHHC.)

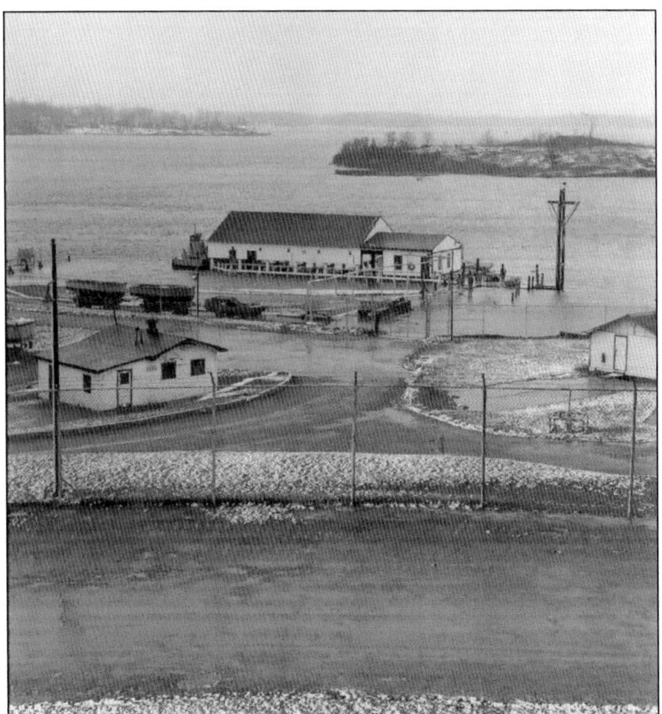

Flood Tide, Boat House, April 1958. This is a view of the boathouse and storage shed on the lower reservation at high (or flood) tide, which made walking the perimeter, a guard duty, challenging at times. In the background are the channel of the Piscataqua River and Clark's Island. (NHHC.)

Tower, Fence, and Flower. This photograph, undated but taken after 1960, shows a version of the fence that was constructed in 1946. As well as a focus on education, security also became a priority. A 10-foot wire fence was installed around the prison complex and the recreation field. It separated the prison from the officers' quarters and the commanding officer's residence, both located on the upper reservation. (NHHC.)

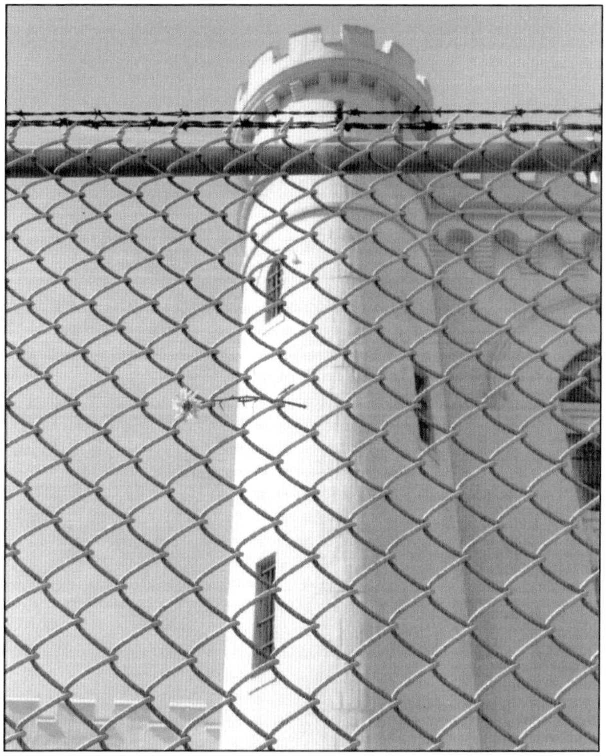

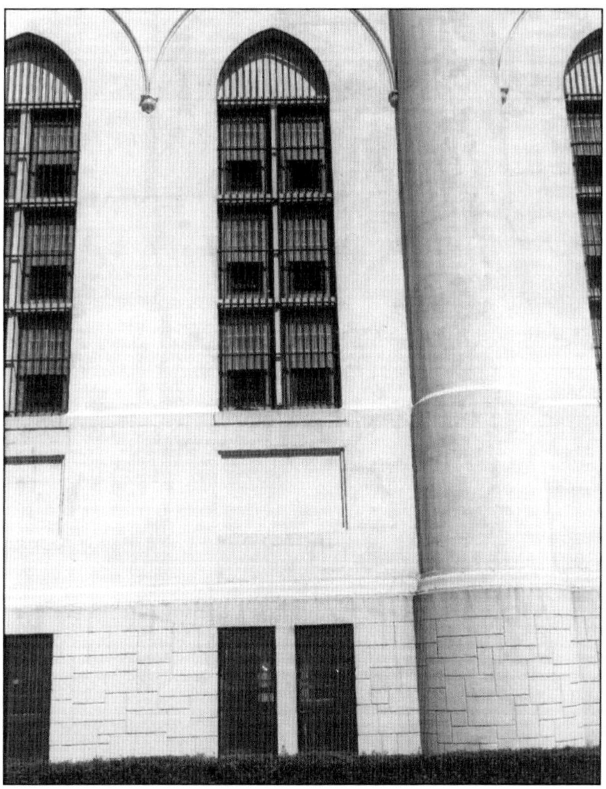

Barred Window Arch, August 1973. The gatehouse and the fence, however, may also have been the result of two prison escape attempts, both reported in the local and national newspapers. The first attempt took place on July 13, 1945, and was covered in the *Boston Daily Globe*, *New York Times*, and the *Washington Post*. The second, March 26, 1946, was reported in the *Christian Science Monitor*. (NHHC.)

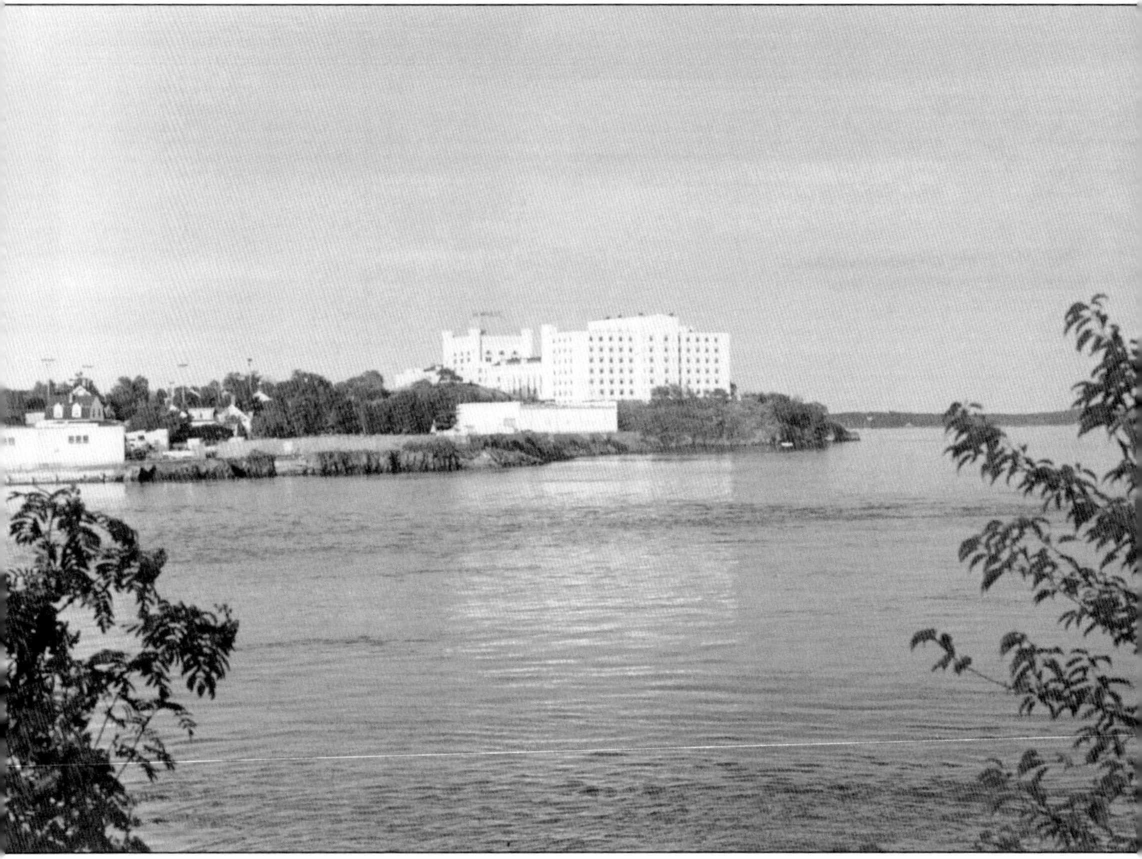

Prison from the Piscataqua. The drama unfolded in the river. Two men, Conrad W. Kirchner and Everett C. Richards, both 20 and both serving lengthy sentences, fled the tailor shops and the net depot, respectively, and jumped into the river. A boatman, not recognizing the two men struggling vainly against the strong Piscataqua current, rowed over and hauled them into his boat. Simultaneously, a Coast Guard boat, alerted to the escape, pulled alongside and ordered the two escapees aboard. They complied but then overpowered the Coast Guardsmen, took their uniforms, commandeered the boat, and ran it aground on Gerrish Island. Unfortunately, the only way off the island was via a now heavily guarded bridge. The 1946 escape involved two Marines and a sailor, who were reported missing after the 12:30 p.m. count. A dragnet was carried out in surrounding towns and on strategic bridges and highways. Charles H. Coleman, the sailor, had made two previous escape attempts. Unlike the other reported attempt, these men were not immediately found. (PAC.)

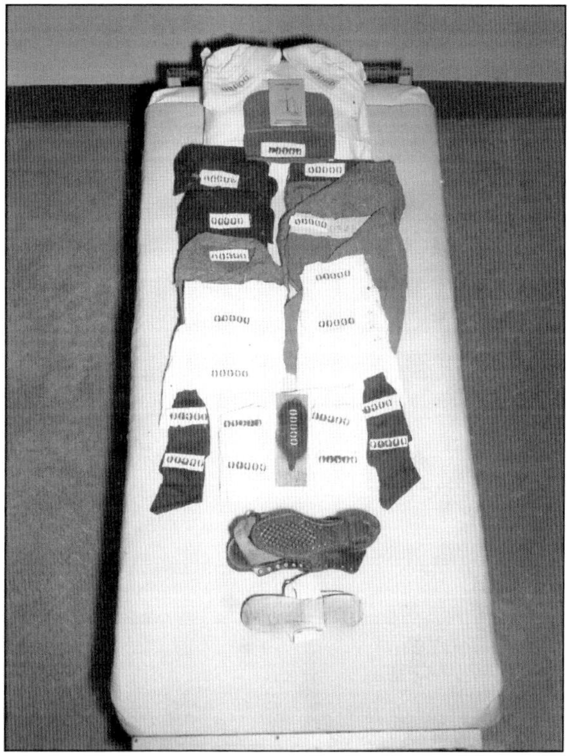

Summer Annex Rack Display, March 1955. The Uniform Code of Military justice provides four methods of dealing with offenses committed by servicemen, depending on the nature of the offense. For the most serious offenses, there is the general courts-martial, followed by the special courts-martial, summary courts-martial, and finally, punishment administered by the commanding officer. Each has different requirements during the hearing and range of punishments. Those in the annex had lesser punishments. (NHHC.)

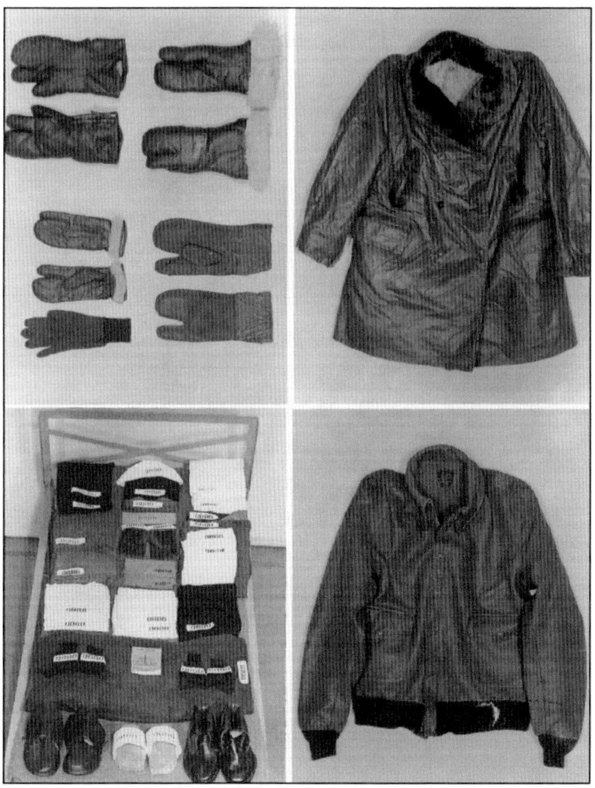

Winter Layout Honor Company, March 1955. General courts-martial have the harshest penalties, including death and life-imprisonment, as well as other lesser penalties. Less serious offenses requiring a special courts-martial have penalties that include confinement at hard labor, loss or forfeiture of pay, and reduction in rank. As a result, the prison had to accommodate both long-term and short-term confinement as well as those men returning to duty and those not. (NHHC.)

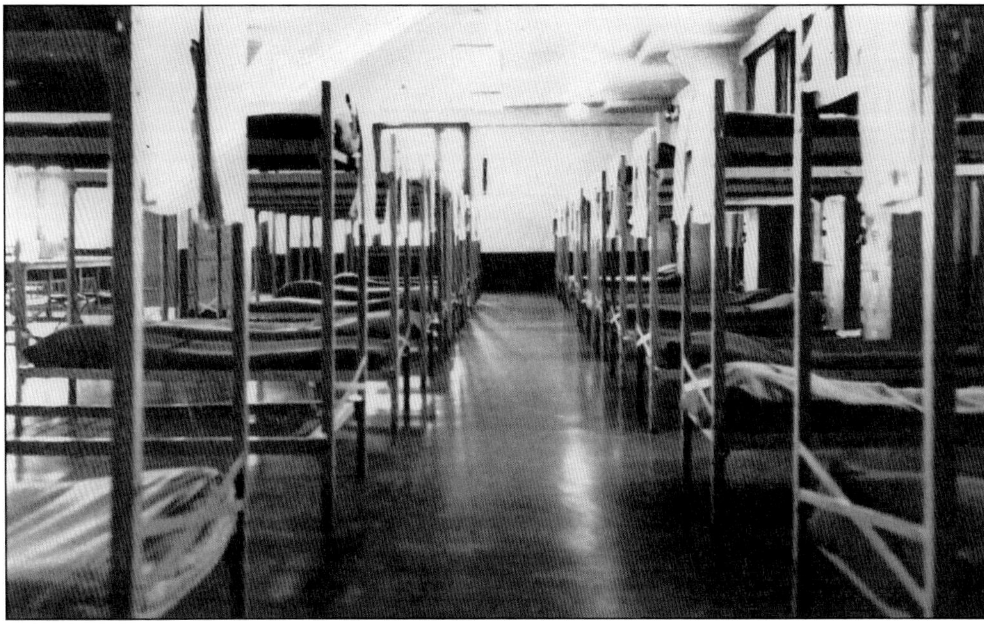

HONOR SQUAD BAY, TWO VIEWS, 1961. The second, third, and fourth floors of the southwest annex were all laid out in the same configuration, as shown above and below. (Both, NHHC.)

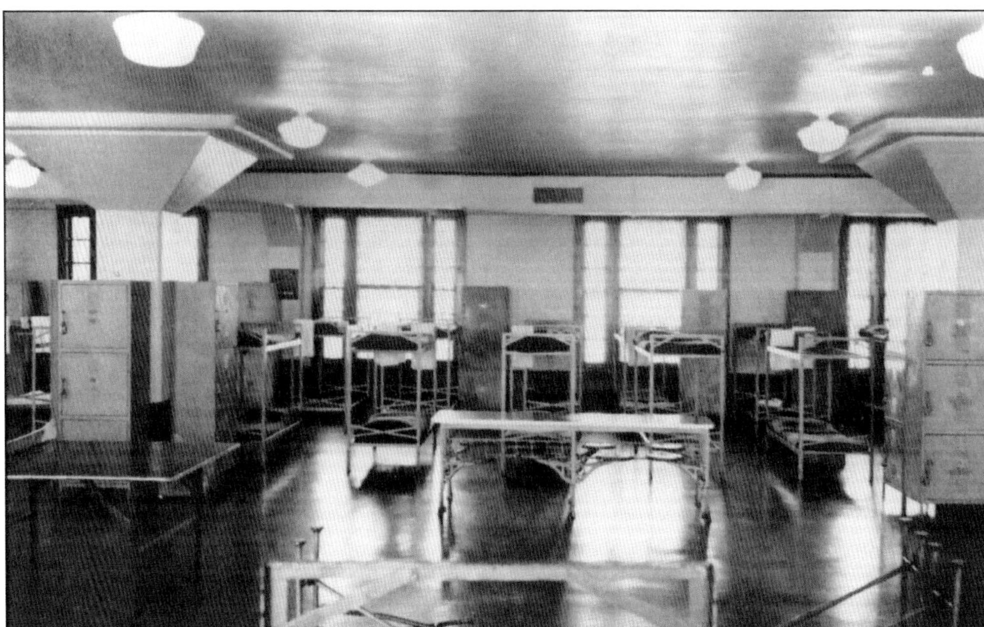

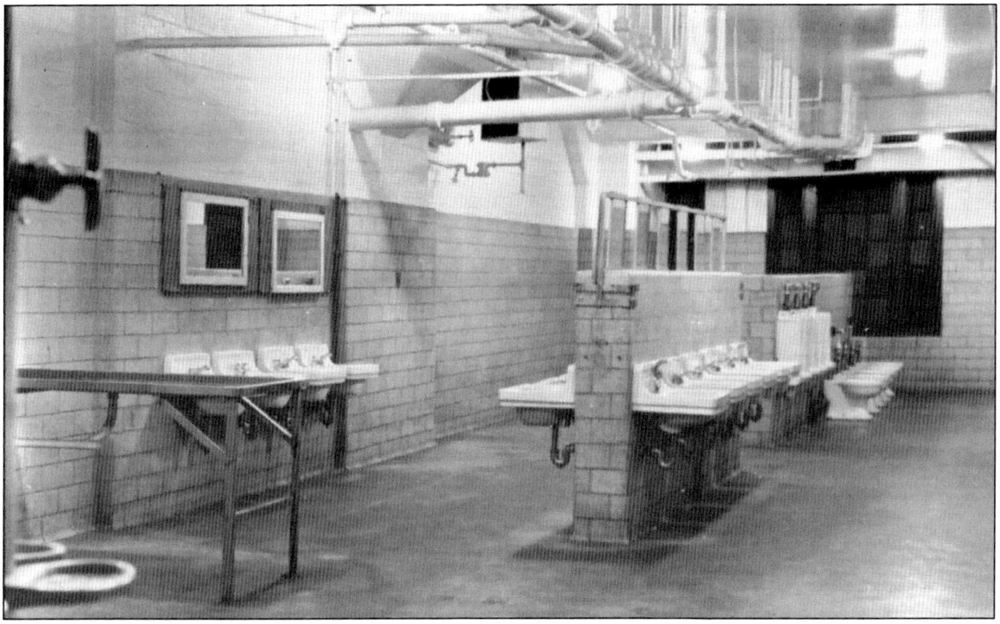

Shower Room, 1959. Shower rooms separated the squad rooms. Each one had a bank of showers and in the center, there were toilets, urinals and sinks. (Both, NHHC.)

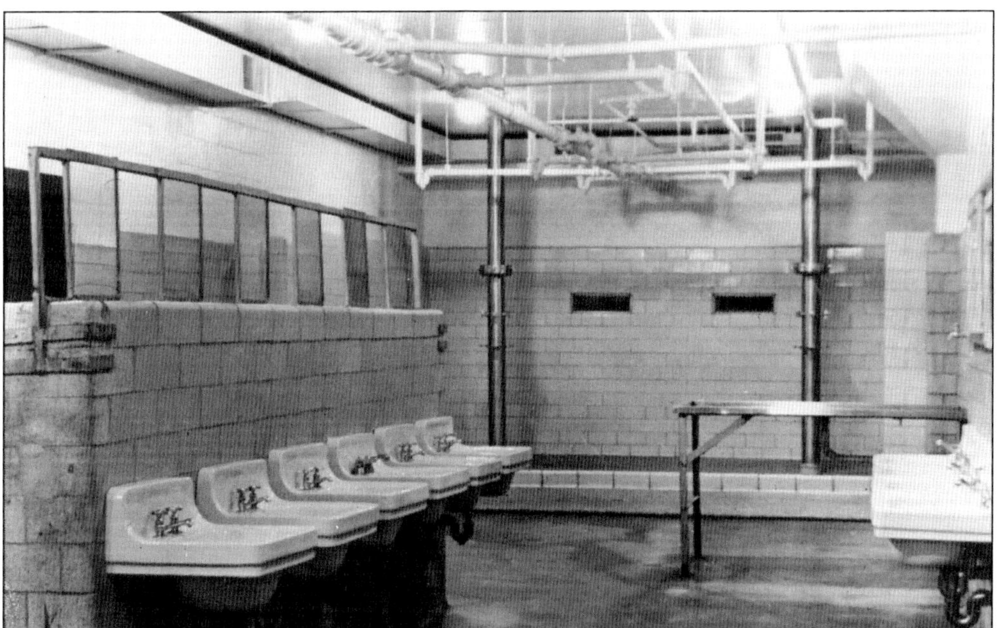

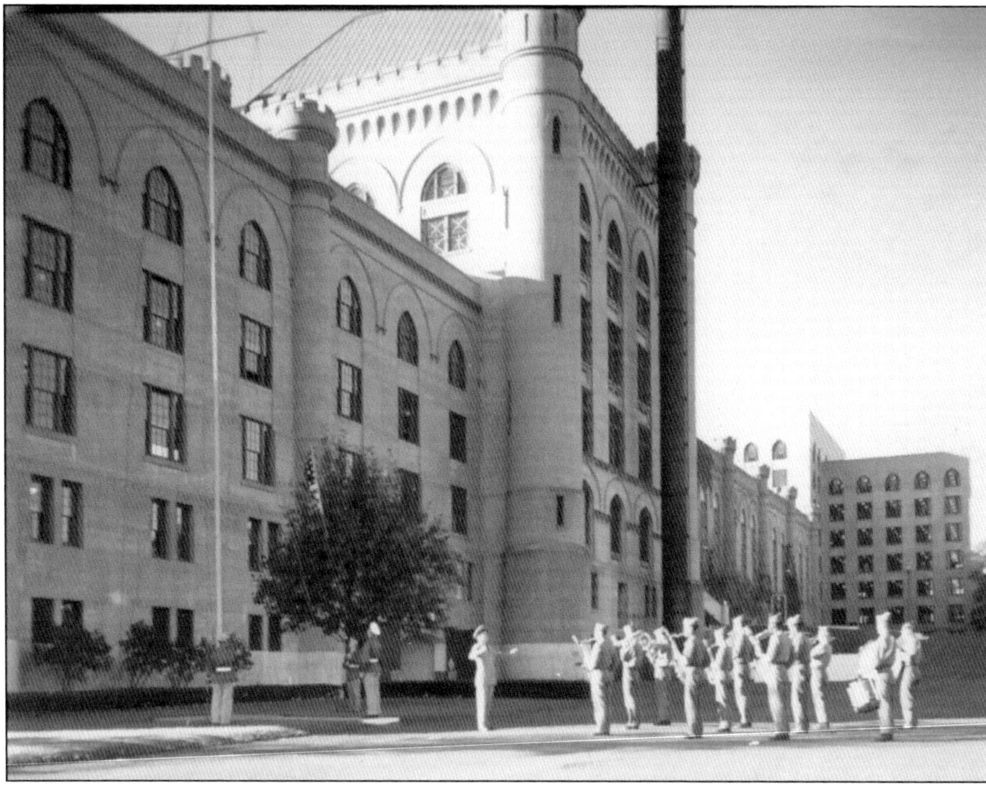

Morning Colors, Retraining Command Band, September 1955. Buglers have long been part of the prison routine. A music program seemed to arrive with Thomas Mott Osborne, himself a concert pianist, who conducted a concert of prisoners at the Portsmouth Music Hall. In 1952, the all-male prison choir performed with the Shipyard Chapel Choir for Sunday services and special events. In 1972, the Portsmouth Naval Shipyard Choir and the DisCom Choirs presented Schubert's Mass in G and Bach's Cantata no. 106 in honor of Navy Day. (NHHC.)

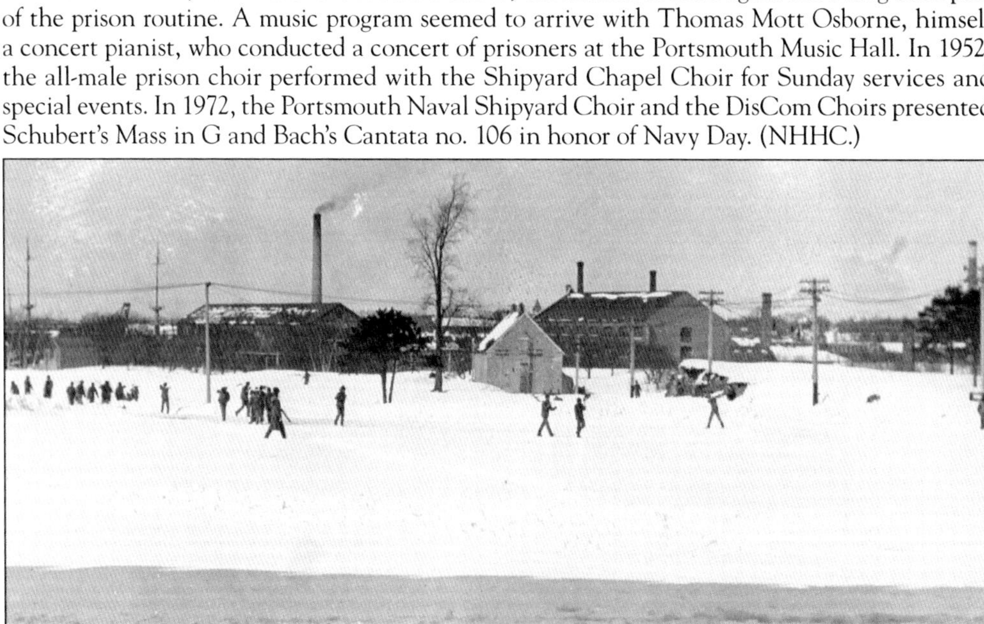

Snow Shoveling Detail, Undated. Most photographs of the prison were taken when the weather was cooperative. However, numerous station log entries discuss snow removal detail, a common task in winter. This is one of the few photographs of that activity. (NHHC.)

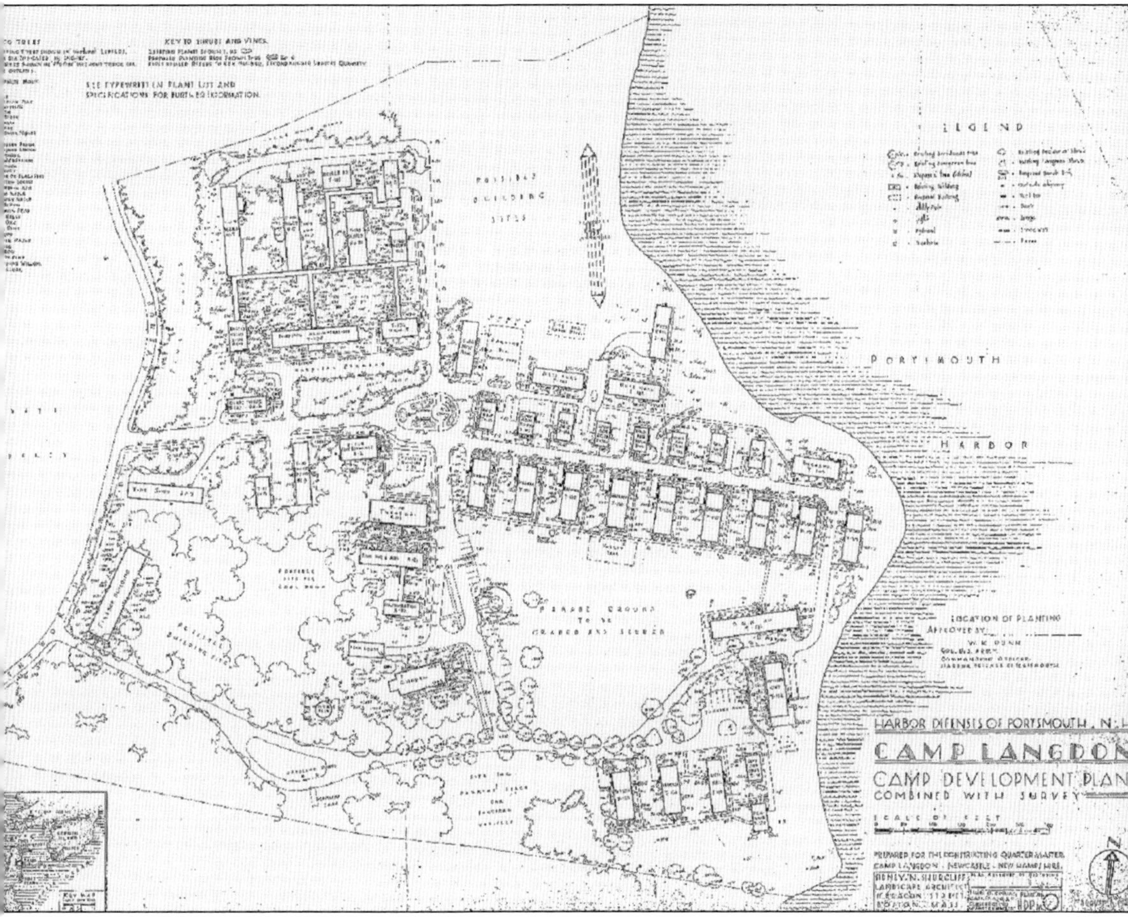

Camp Langdon Map. On July 1, 1952, count at the prison was 625. By December 31, it was 987. A year later, it had risen to 1,303. Since the code provided for the confinement of special courts-martial prisoners as well as general courts-martial prisoners, the prison population grew. Looking to expand, the command acquired a former Army site, Camp Langdon, located in New Castle, New Hampshire, about seven miles distant. Camp Langdon, part of the retraining command, opened on April 2, 1954. Its function was to implement the command's restoration program for men returning to duty. The camp was named in 1940 after Gov. John Langdon, who, in 1916, petitioned Secretary of the Navy Benjamin Crowninshield to keep the shipyard open despite reduced appropriations and cries for its closure—a situation that would reoccur over the course of the shipyard's history. (NCHS.)

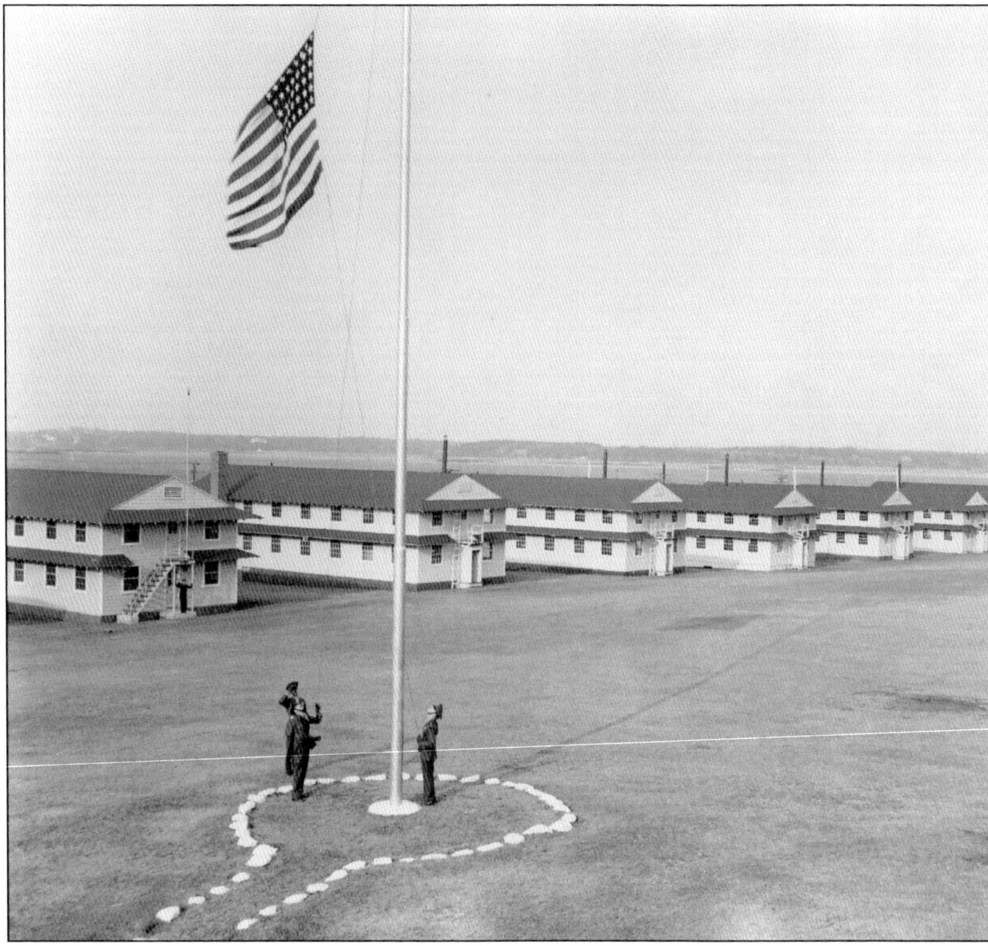

Flag Raising at Camp Langdon. Located between Fort Constitution and Fort Stark in New Castle, Camp Langdon was active during World War II. In some disrepair, it took several months of hard work by the retrainees and duty personnel before it was fully functional. The camp opened on April 2, 1954. Its mission was to implement the restoration program for men returning to duty. (NHHC.)

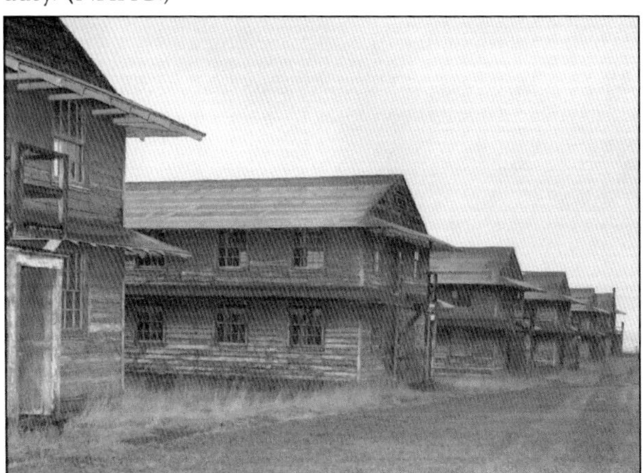

Barracks before Restoration. Inmates convicted of the most minor offenses, in military terms, or near the end of their sentences were assigned to Camp Langdon, also called the Retraining Center annex, across the river from the prison. Unlike at the main prison, there were no cells or bars and the perimeter fence only reached partway around. Anyone looking to walk away easily could. (NHHC.)

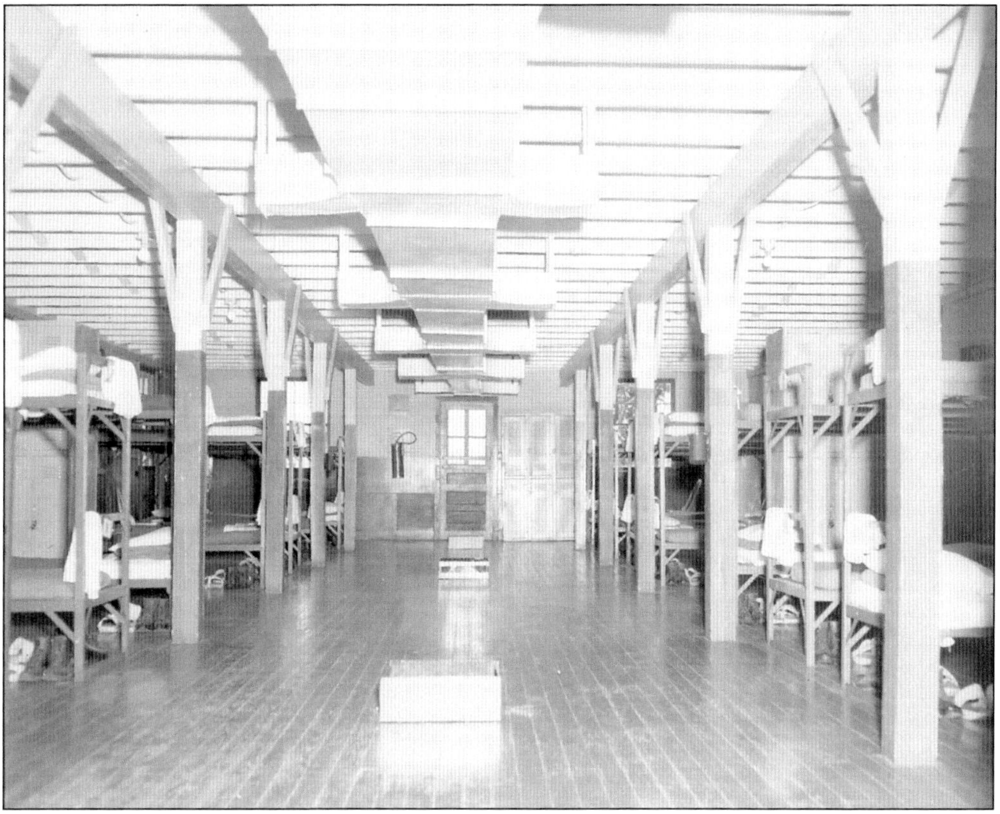

Vagas Barracks, August 1956. This was the winner of five consecutive Awards of Honor Company Competitions at Camp Langdon. Men at the camp enjoyed more privileges. Unlike the main prison where CMPs (court-martialed prisoners) came to a halt without speaking or saluting when an officer approached, those at Camp Langdon did both—preparation for a return to duty. As well, men were given a small amount of spending money and wore parts of their regular military uniforms along with prison garb. (NHHC.)

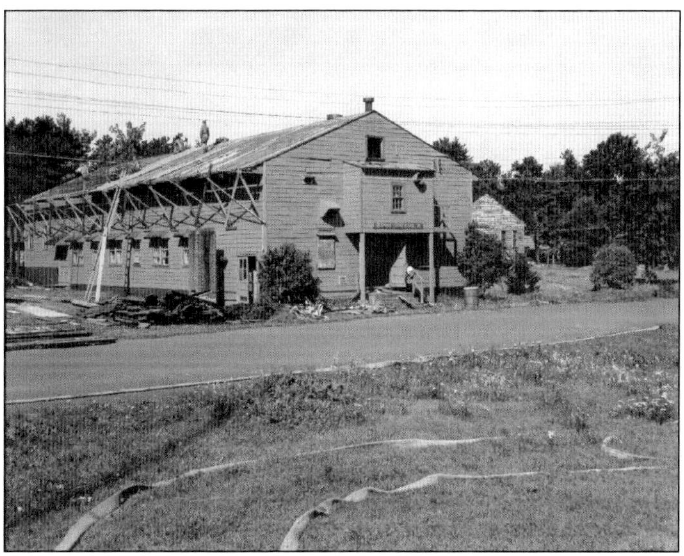

Camp Theater before Restoration. By the time of the first anniversary of Camp Langdon, it was recorded that 86 percent of restorees returned to duty were successes. In January 1958, Camp Langdon completed the construction of its own chapel. Dedication services were held the following month. (NHHC.)

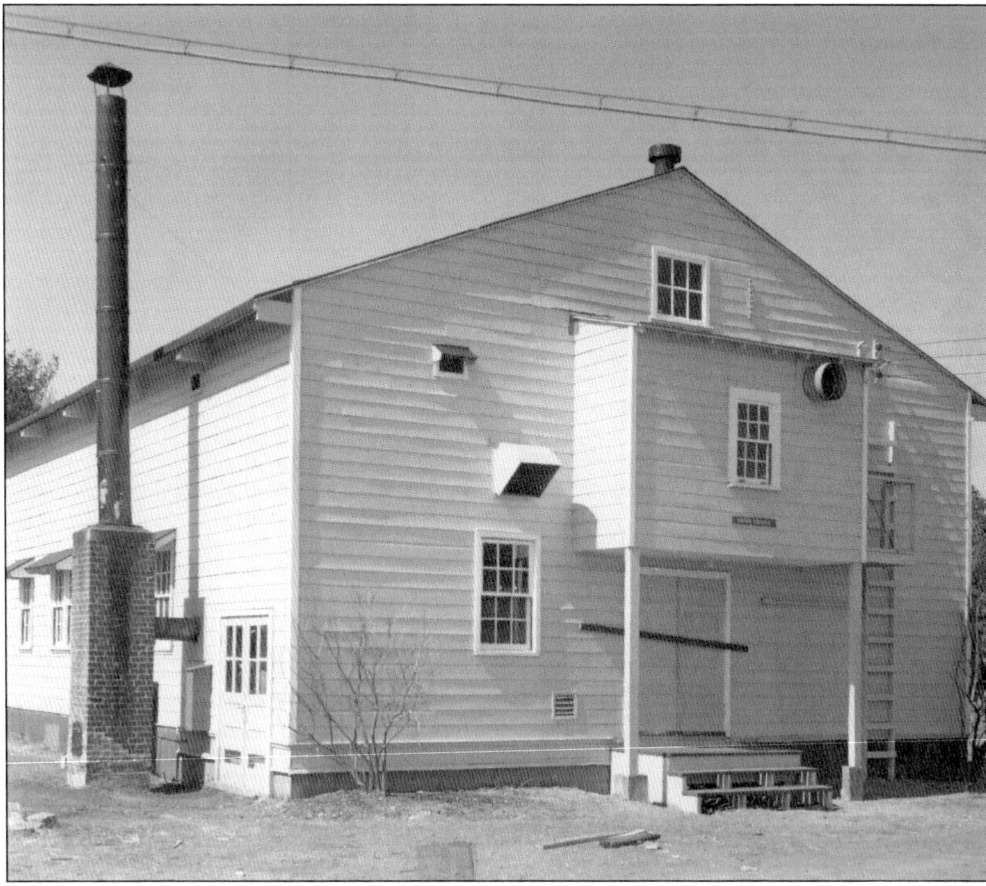

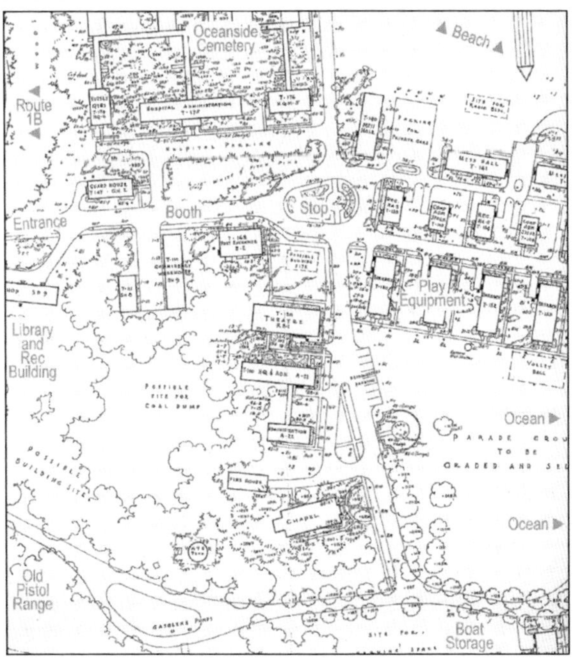

Camp Theater after Restoration. In the 1940s, this structure was known as the Recreation Building, or No. RB-1. First built in March 1941, it had a capacity of 364, with several rooms and facilities. At Camp Langdon, it was the Theater or T-130. (NHHC.)

Camp Langdon Today. Camp Langdon was eventually closed for economic reasons. Much of the former Army and prison camps have been dismantled, moved, or repurposed. Only vestiges remain as indicated on the map above, which labels current New Castle buildings and landmarks. (NCHS.)

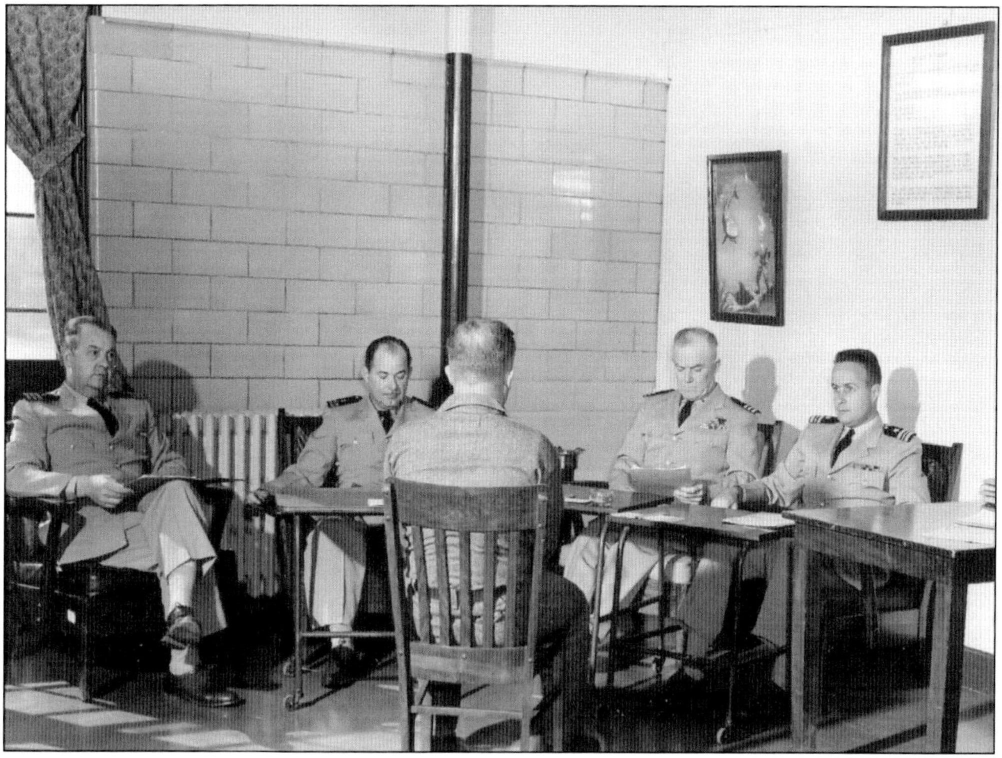

INMATE BEFORE CLEMENCY AND RESTORATION BOARD. Taken May 21, 1959, when the prison was the US Navy Retraining Command, this image of personnel includes, from left to right, Cmdr. Cecil V. Marley, CHC USN; Lt. Clinton DeWitt, MSC USN; Cmdr. John B. Davidson, executive officer, senior member; Lt. Cmdr. William J. Davis, USN, education officer; and John Quinn, recorder. CMPs who came before the board while the prison was the retraining command could be restored to duty. Others would serve their sentences and leave with a dishonorable discharge. (NHHC.)

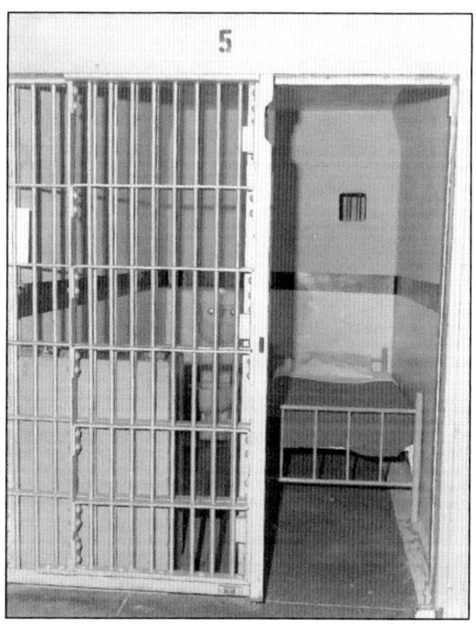

A CELL, UNDATED. A third group, those charged with the most serious crimes, after three or four years of reviews and appeals at Portsmouth, would be transferred to other federal prisons such as Leavenworth. At the time of this photograph, a sailor on the West Coast who had shot his commanding officer was serving time at Portsmouth. (NHHC.)

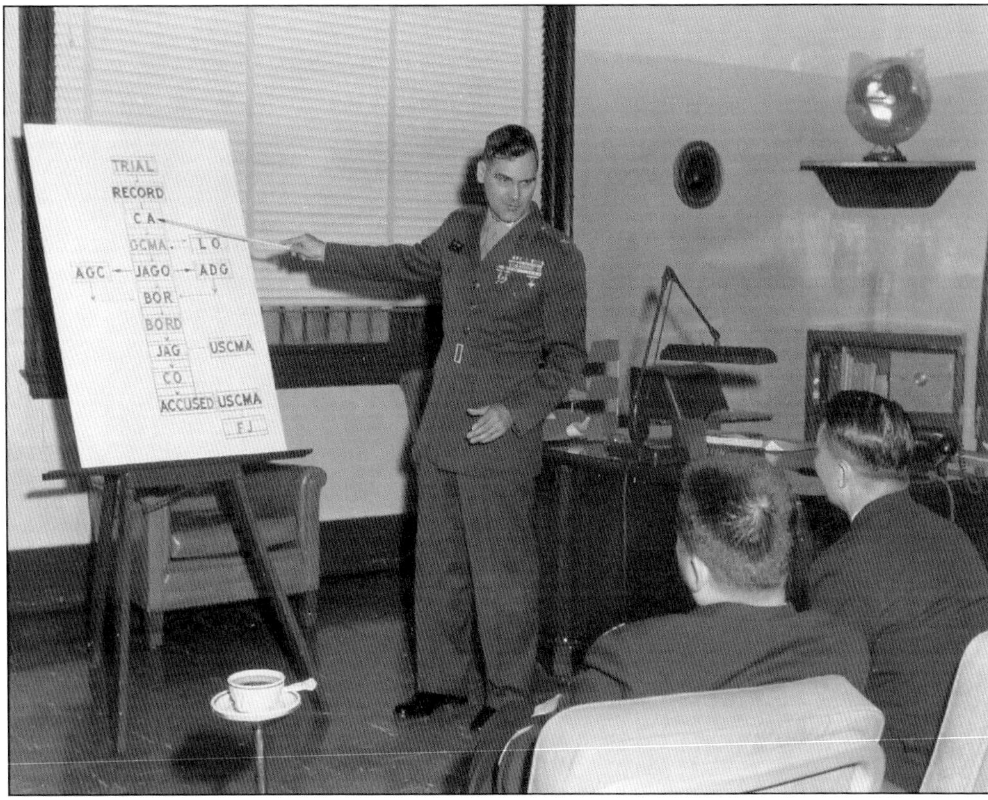

COL. R.E. CAREY, COMMANDING OFFICER. Colonel Carey, commanding officer, is explaining the court-martial review process to two visitors from the Chinese (Taiwanese) Navy in January 1964. There were a number of visitors in the 1960s. (NHHC.)

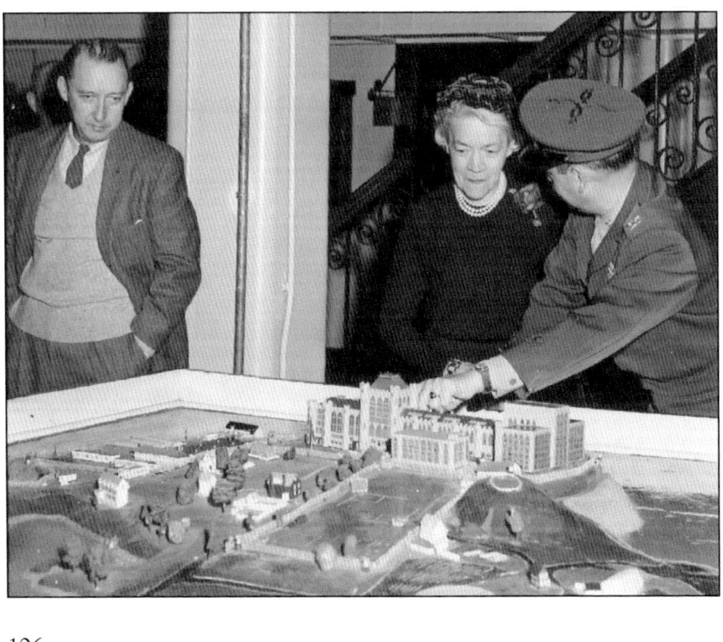

SEN. MARGARET CHASE SMITH, DECEMBER 1960. The senator from Maine is looking at a model of "the Castle" presented by Col. C.A. Rigaud, commanding officer. (NHHC.)

The South Annex, 1943. After World War II, the annex, shown here in 1943, was reconfigured to coincide with the changing mission of the prison. Shops and work areas formerly located in the basement were moved to the lower reservation. (NHHC.)

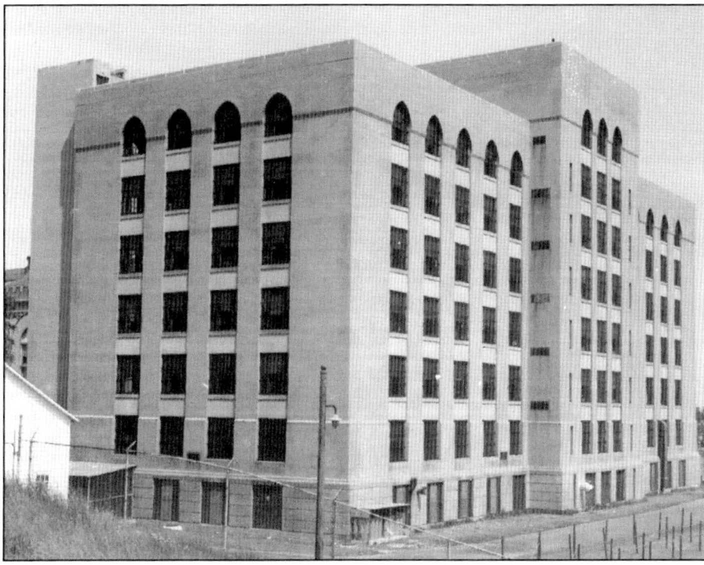

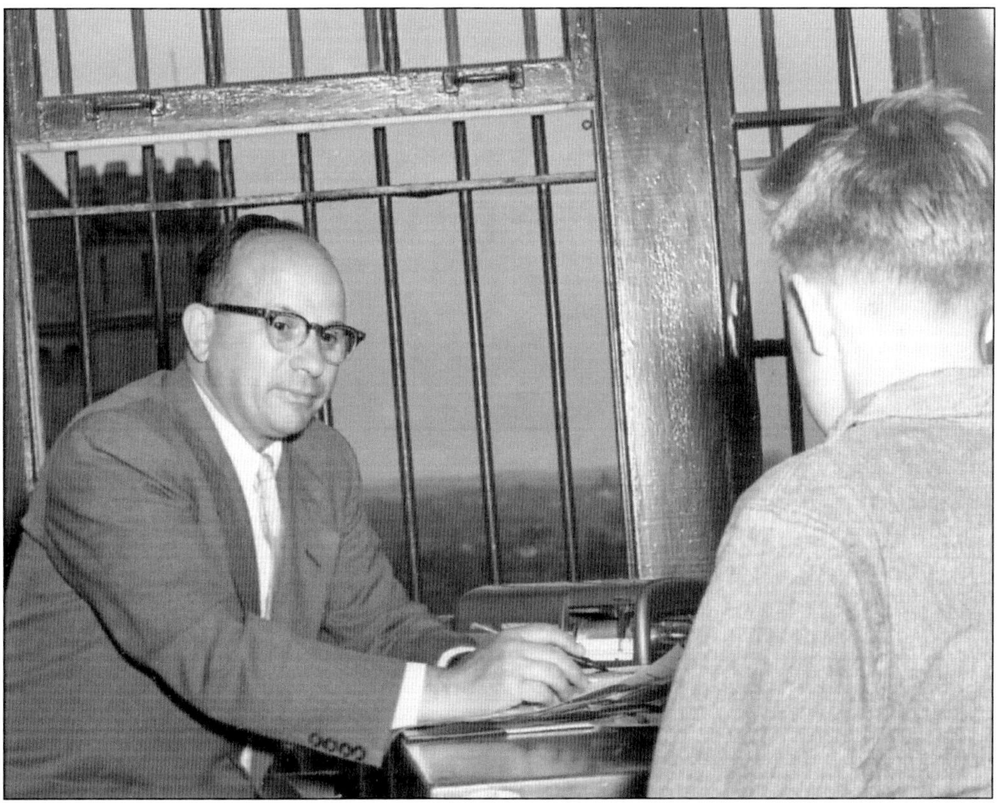

Samuel Gerstein and CMP. The Uniform Code of Military Justice required changes, and the population was rising again. Under the direction and guidance of Col. Charles Rigaud, an extensive program of treatment and counseling was implemented. Here, Gerstein, a clinical psychologist, is interviewing a court-martialed prisoner in medical department spaces in May 1958. (NHHC.)

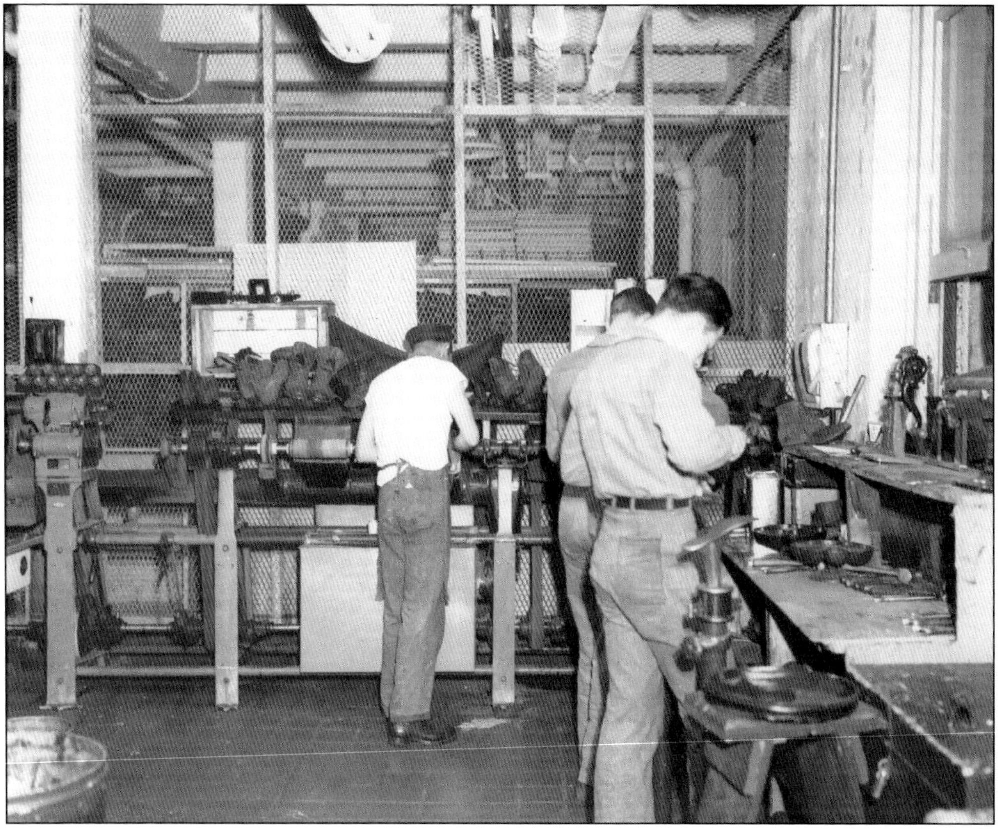

COBBLER SHOP, 1959. The Division of Correction Services mandated schooling for those scoring below a fifth-grade literacy level. Vocational courses were offered part- and full-time days and evenings in most of the trades, including tailoring, electricity, welding, and carpentry among a wide variety. (NHHC.)

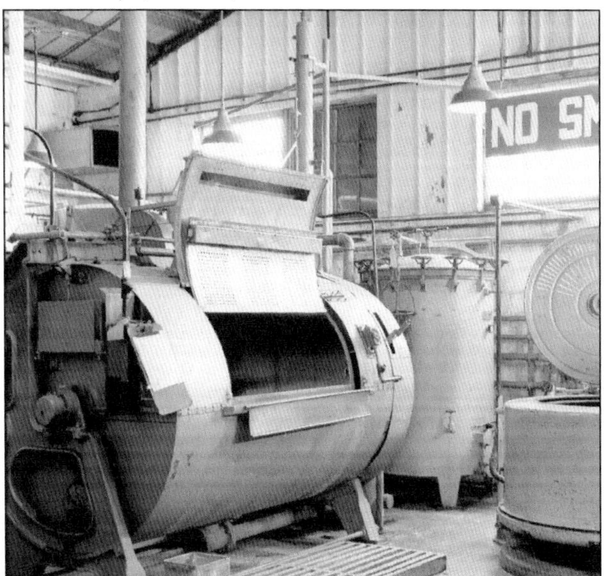

CLOTHING RENOVATION AND DRY CLEANING, 1959. As the annex was reconfigured and repurposed, many of the shops were moved to the lower reservation. The two largest were the tailor shop and the pallet factory, but the prison offered 22 on-the-job training opportunities, of which clothing and dry cleaning was one. (NHHC.)

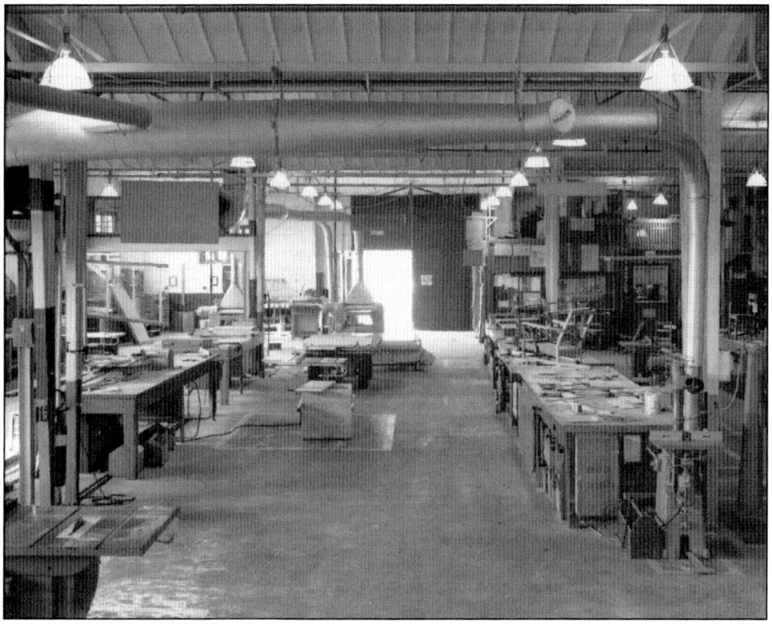

The Upholstery Shop. In addition to the ones pictured here, baking, typewriter and motor repair, painting, and sign painting were also offered along with training for glaziers and printers. (NHHC.)

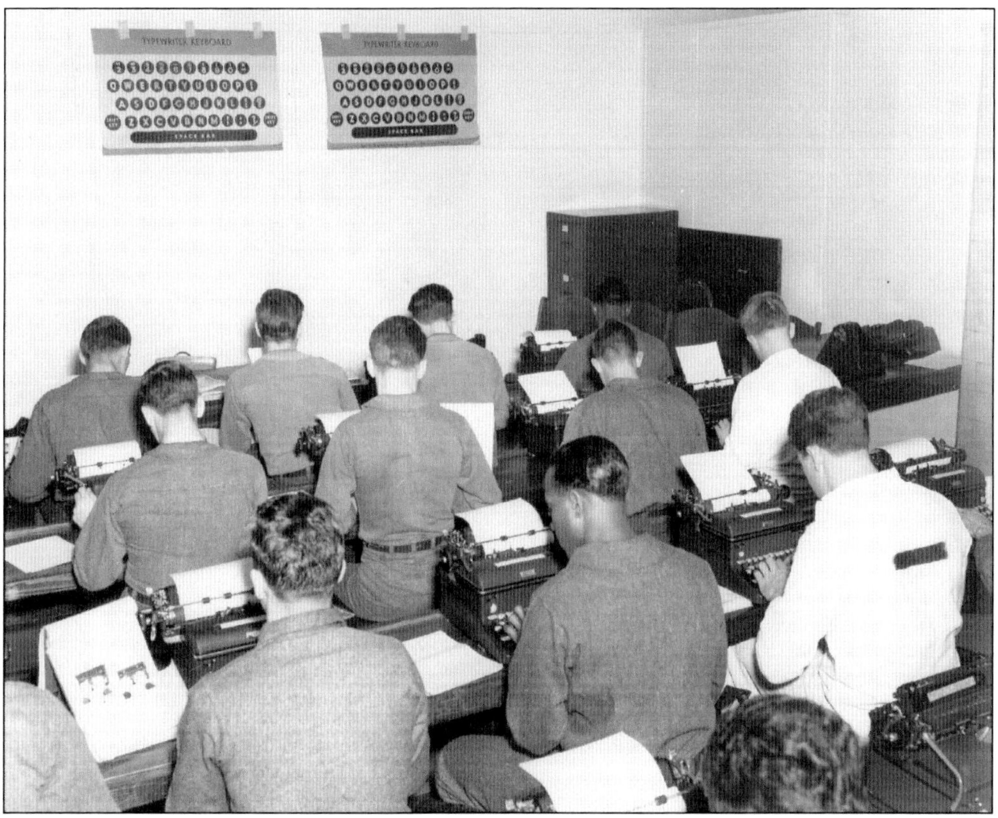

Adult Education Typing Class. Prisoners learning typing and shorthand are pictured here. (NHHC.)

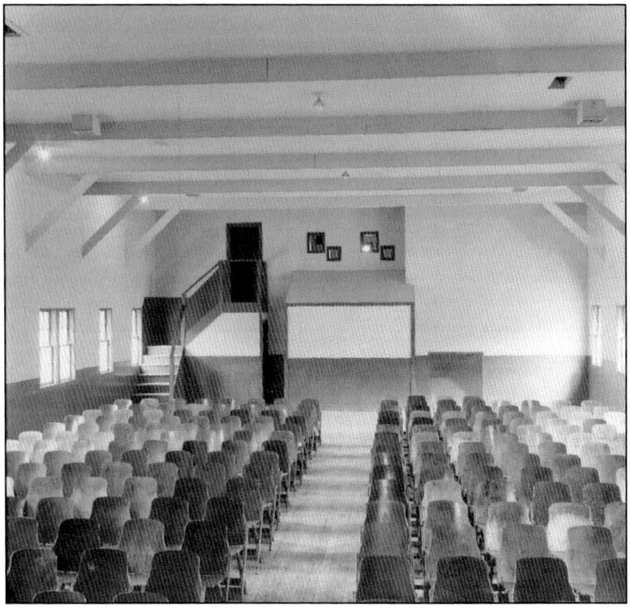

AUDITORIUM PROJECTION ROOM, NOVEMBER 7, 1957. A large, well-equipped auditorium was located on the seventh floor of the annex. In 1946 and 1974, movies were shown most days, with a double feature on the weekends. Pre-releases and the latest movies were often available. Those whose behavior warranted it got more privileges, including more movies. (NHHC.)

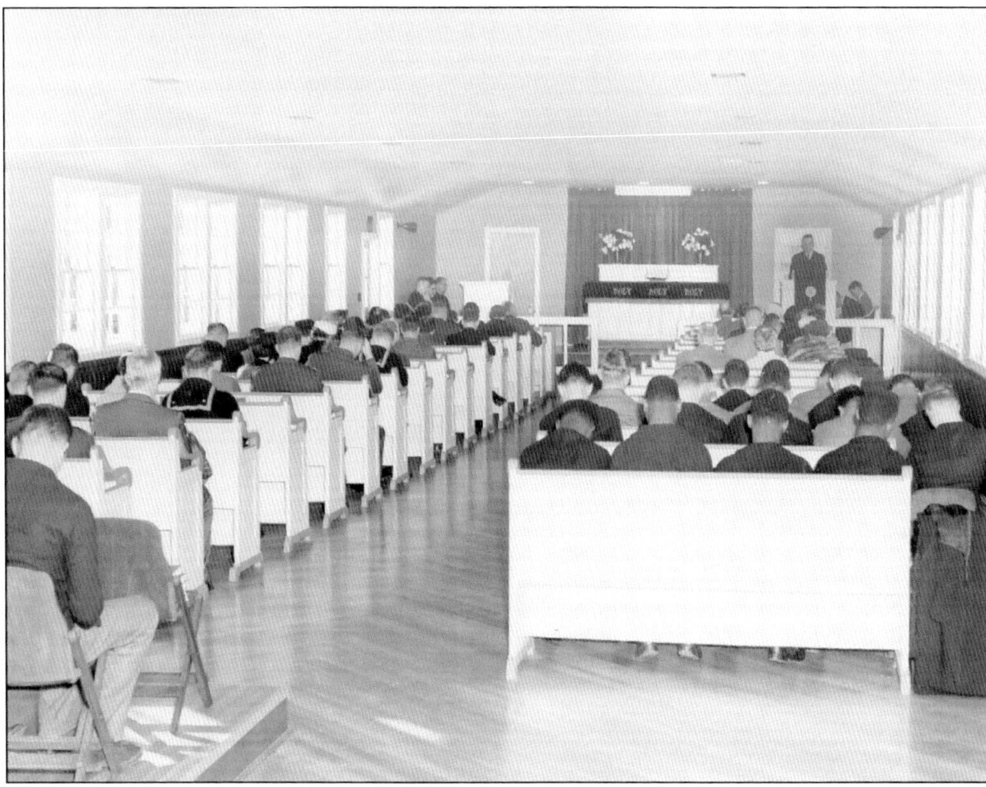

CHAPEL SERVICES, FEBRUARY 1958. In 1949, construction began on a chapel that would be housed on prison grounds. Using materials from the old Army post Camp Langdon in New Castle, the new chapel was built and dedicated in February 1951. From its inception, "divine services"—initially compulsory and Christian—were conducted on Sunday. By 1918, Protestant, Catholic, and Jewish services were all offered. (NHHC.)

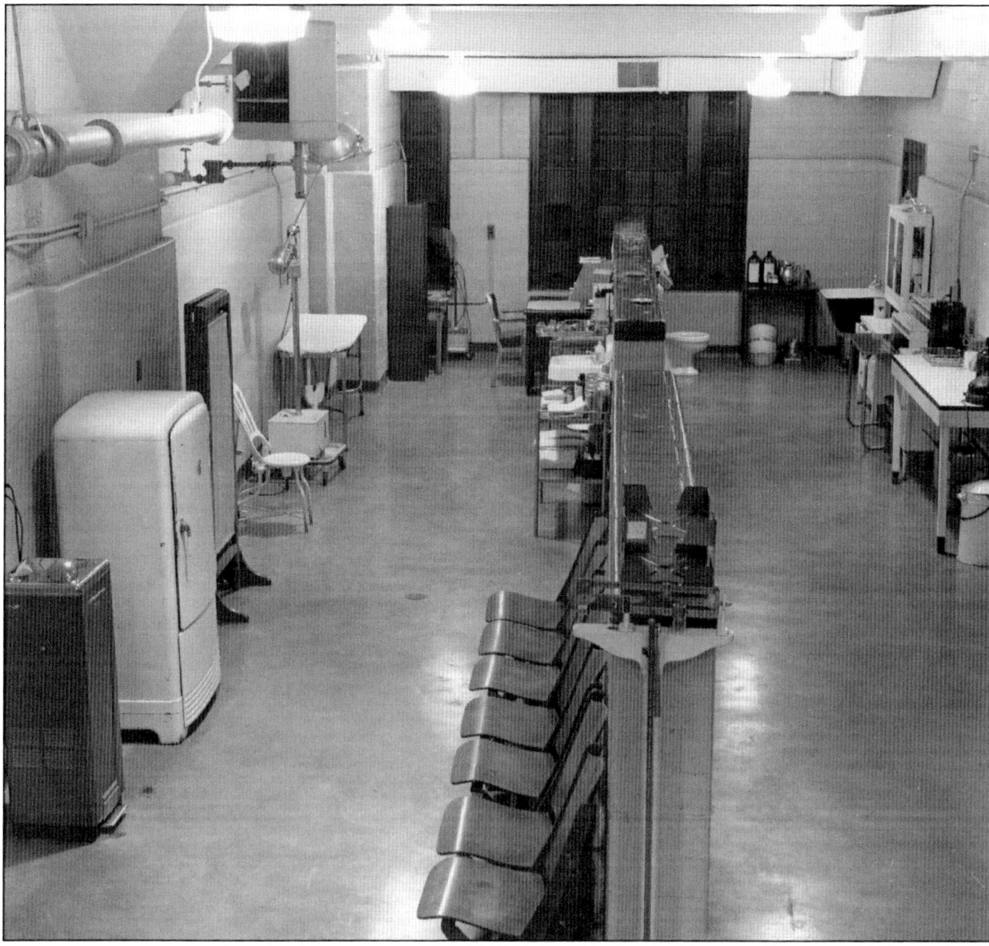

Sick Bay, Sixth Deck, 1959. This floor, or deck, contained a dispensary, laboratory, and a pharmacy. It also had rooms for operating and x-ray as well as a waiting room. (NHHC.)

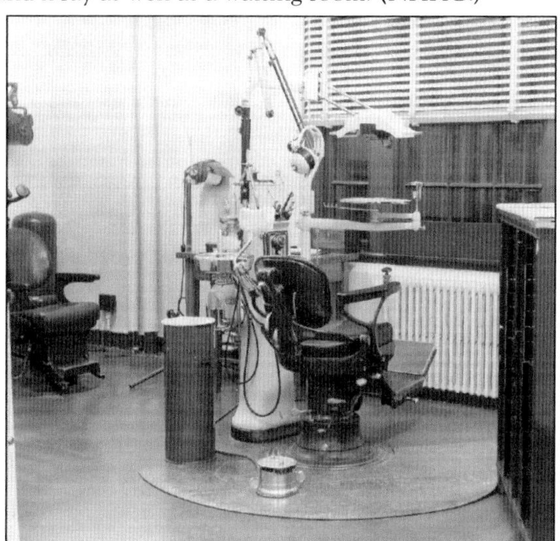

Dentist's Chair. Dentists' offices were also located on the sixth floor. From the time the prison opened, dental services were available. (NHHC.)

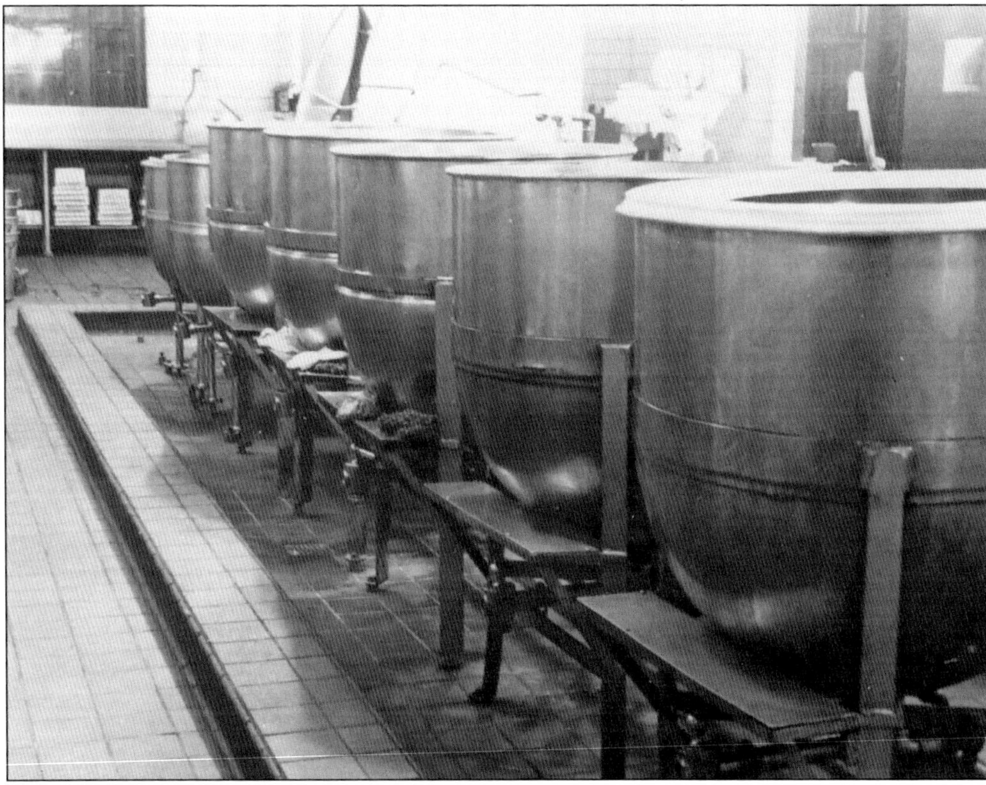

ANNEX FIRST DECK GALLEY AND MESS HALL. The first and second floors of the annex were reconfigured as needs changed. This is how it looked in the late 1950s and early 1960s. Pictured above are cooking pots in January 1960. Below is the CMP mess hall in 1961. (Both, NHHC.)

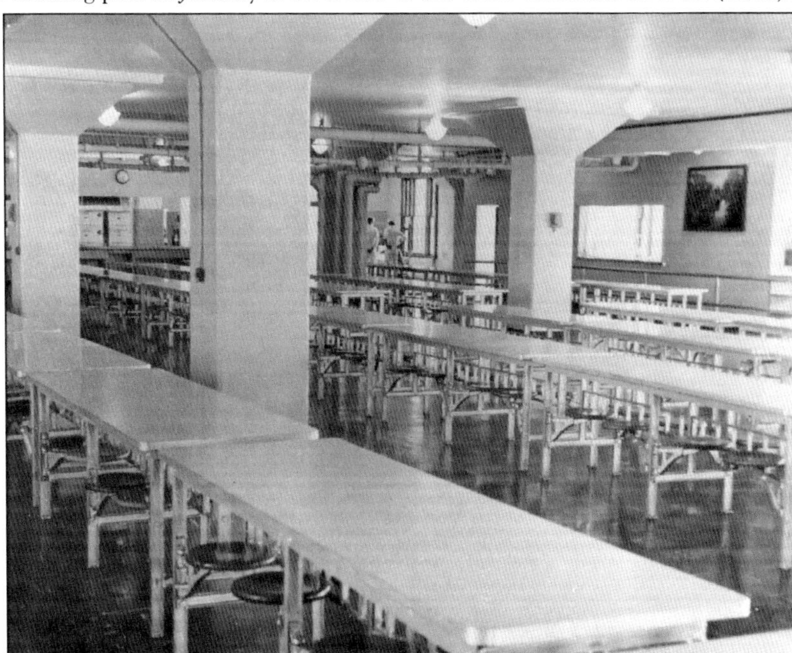

Ten

US Naval Disciplinary Command Closes

On September 30, 1960, the prison was again re-designated as the US Naval Disciplinary Command, or DisCom, and maintained this name until the facility closed in 1974. The prison population continued to decrease until the mid-1960s and the Vietnam War, when the population exceeded 1,300. The turmoil the nation experienced during this era was duplicated in most incarceration facilities around the country—Attica being a prime example—as well as military facilities. There was also unrest, racial tension, and a significant drug problem at the prison. In response to the new type of prisoner and the nationwide changes, the Trusty, Work Release, and Home Leave programs provided more freedom for many CMPs. There were a prisoner rock band, liaisons with local businesses and the Universities of New Hampshire and Maine, a GED program, and 27 trades. The Classification and Treatment Department was significantly expanded, and during the two-week observation period, newly arriving CMPs met with a variety of professionals: psychiatrists, physicians, chaplains, and vocational and marriage counselors. Legal, personnel, and special services were also available. Visitation restrictions were relaxed and a seven-day temporary home-leave program begun. In 1969, a drug dormitory was opened to deal with addictions. Despite these initiatives—many innovative—problems remained, both inherent in the military prison system itself and in the Portsmouth prison in particular. Issues included friction between Marines and the Navy, who solely foot the bill for the prison, the cross-purposes of punishment and rehabilitation, the "problem" of homosexuality, and alleged beatings. Concurrently, the physical plant was also changing, gradually returning to its pre–World War II appearance. Many of the buildings of the war era were demolished in an effort at cost-cutting, which would eventually include the chapel, the boathouse, blacksmith, paint, manufacturing and repairs shops, laundry, gatehouse, and vocational school. The lower reservation gradually returned to its pre-prison state of a grassy slope leading to the water's edge.

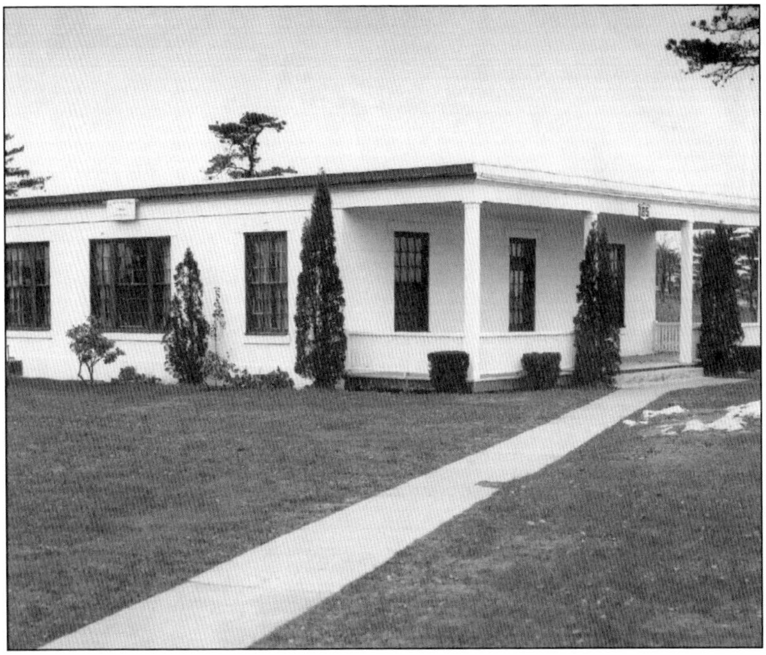

The Visitor's Center, 1961. Court-martialed prisoners as well as the prison staff came from military facilities around the country—Quantico, Virginia; Camp Pendleton, California; Corpus Christi, Texas; and the naval stations at Pensacola, Florida, and Charleston, South Carolina, among many. (NHHC.)

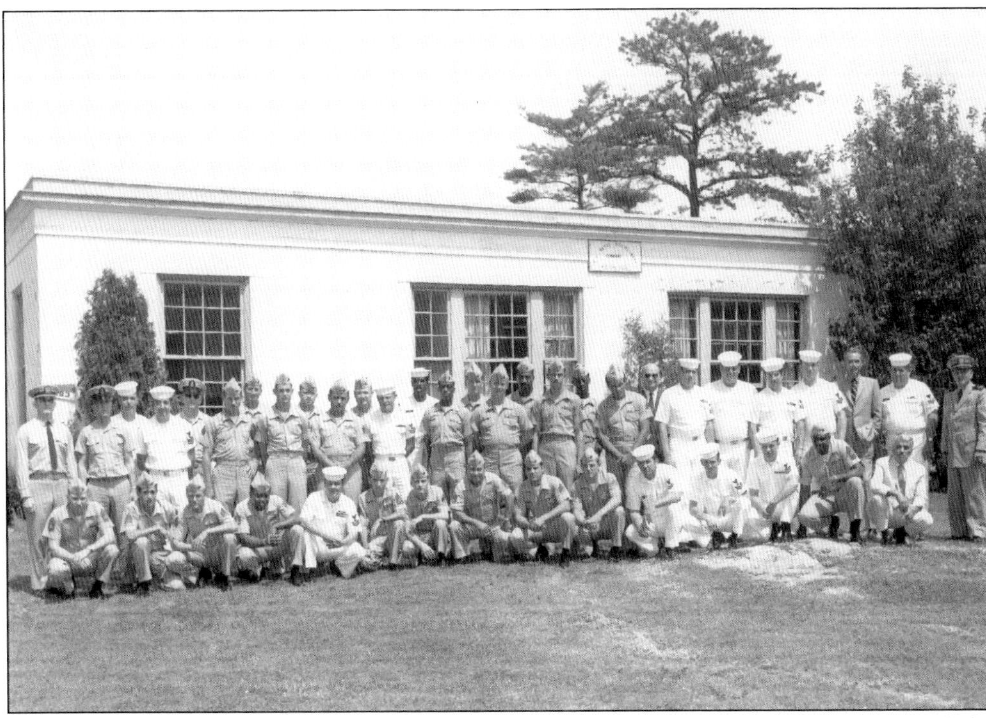

Guard Training Class. The station logs kept careful track of who came and departed the facility: parents arriving unannounced, men reporting for duty, as well as telephone calls about the shenanigans of the Marines in Portsmouth. (NHHC.)

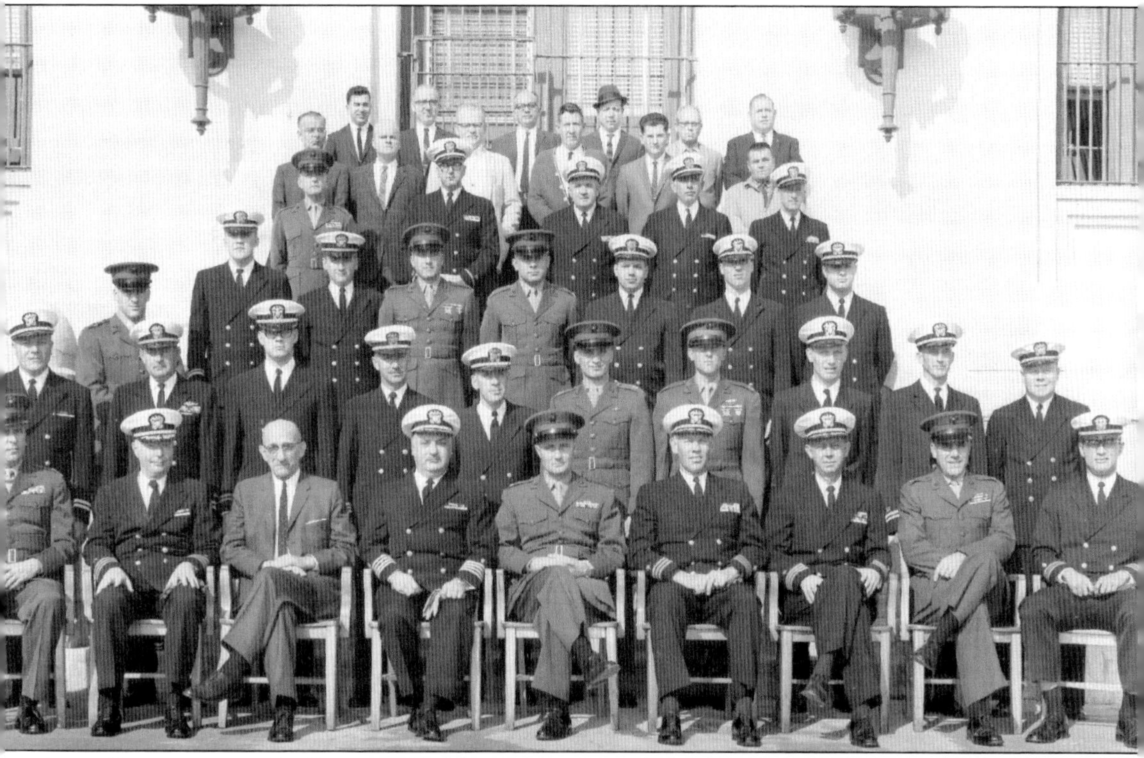

STAFF PHOTOGRAPH, DISCOM, 1965. There is no identifying information about this picture. However, Col. R.D. Kennedy, who arrived five months earlier to command the prison, is seated in the center of the first row. (NHHC.)

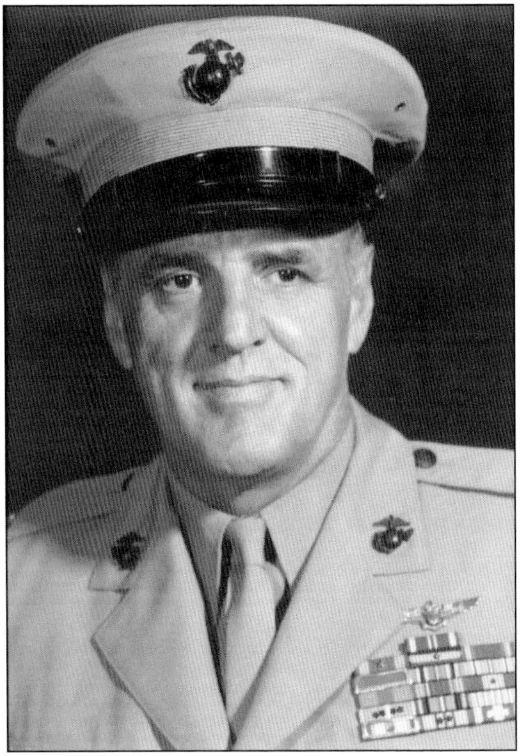

COL. WALTER E. DOMINA, USMC. Colonel Domina served as commanding officer from July 1970 to September 1973. After the Vietnam War, the prison population continued to decline, making it less cost-effective, and the Pentagon—in a sweeping base closure that affected Massachusetts, New Hampshire, and Rhode Island—put the Disciplinary Command and the Naval Hospital on that closure list. (NHHC.)

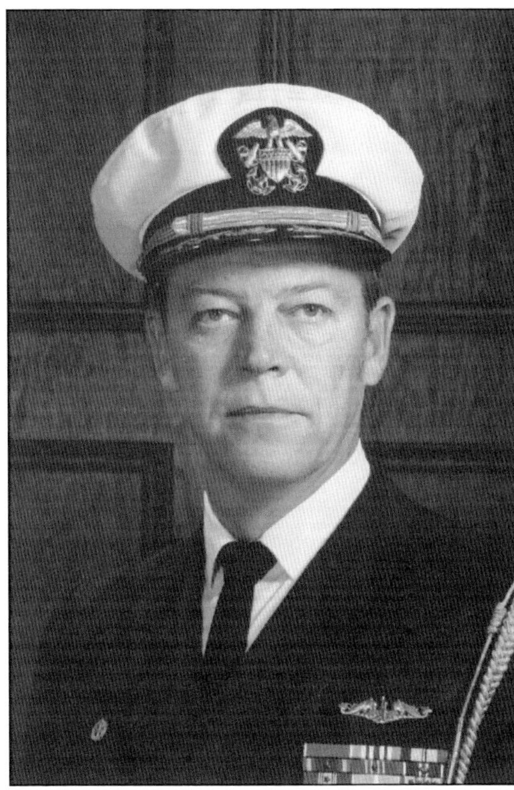

COMM. RAYMOND A. HELGEMOE, USN. After Colonel Domina left the command, Colonel Helgemoe, the executive officer, remained to administer and then close the facility. He was present at the Decommissioning Ceremony in June 1974. (NHHC.)

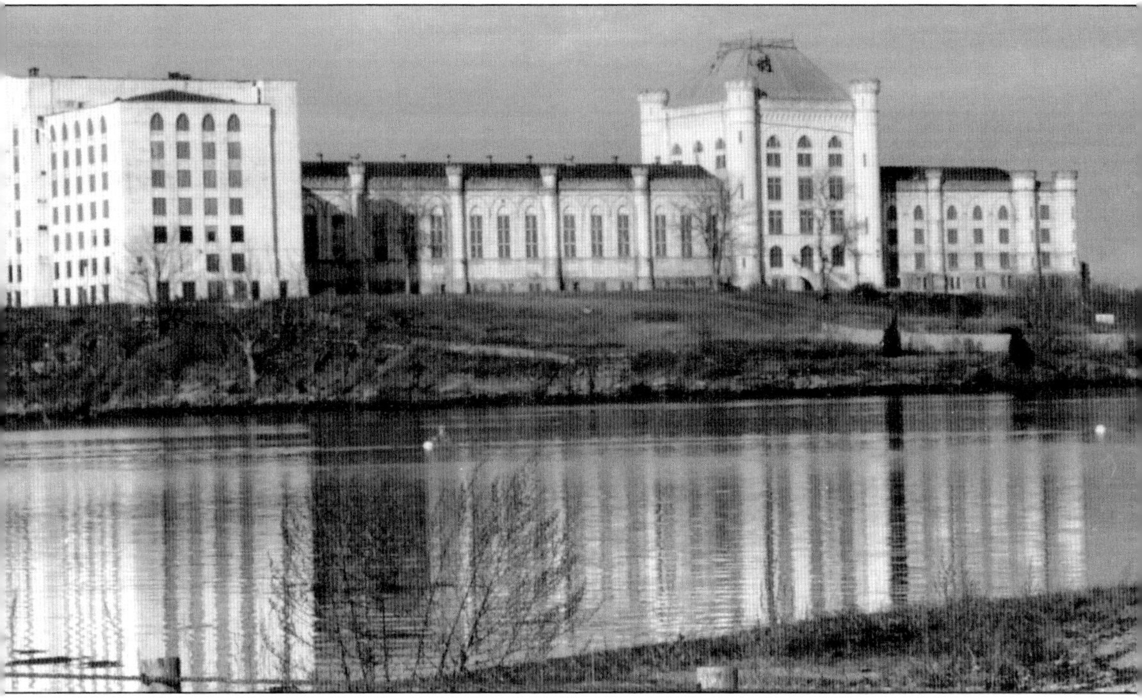

LOOKING ACROSS THE PISCATAQUA, 1999. This is the vacant and mothballed prison when plans were afoot to reopen it. (PAC.)

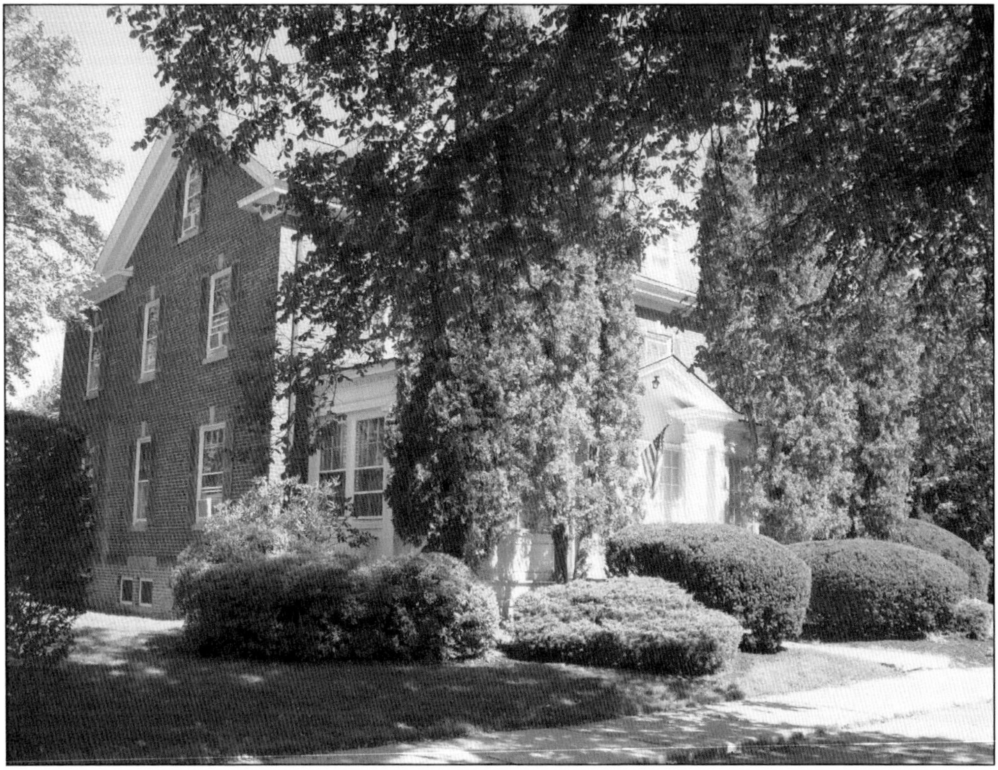

Quarters Q, 2015. Today, the prison commandant's residence is one of the three original buildings, besides the prison and its additions, still remaining on the grounds and in use. (Photograph by the author.)

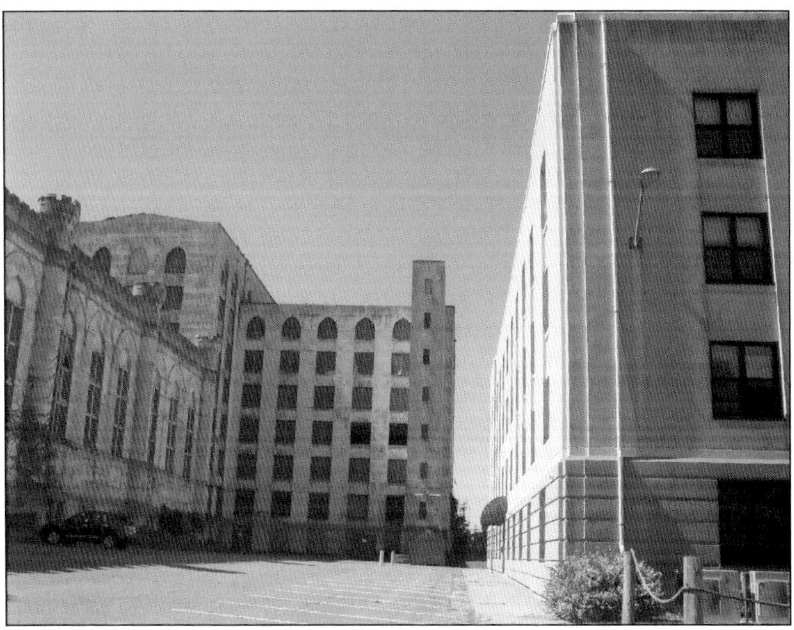

Buildings 93 and 191 in 2015. The prison, Building 93, on the left is boarded up. Building 191, once used as Marine barracks, on the right, is still used by the shipyard. (Photograph by the author.)

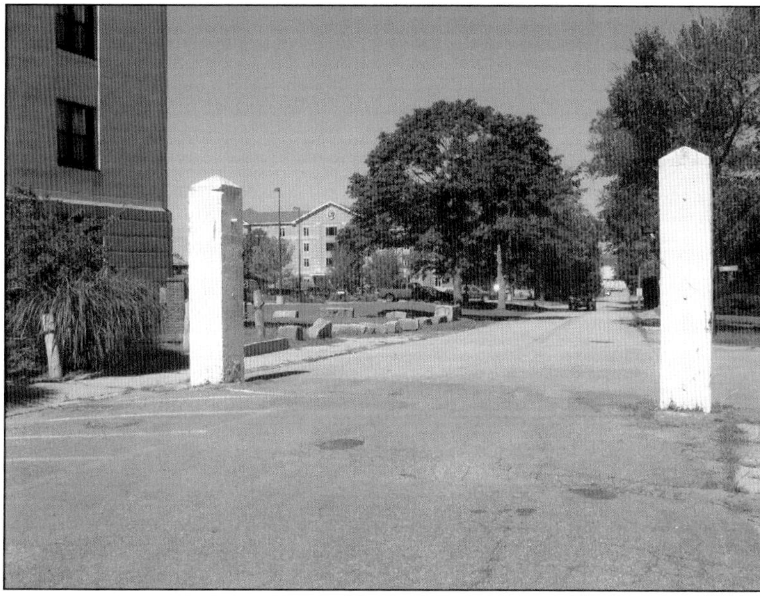

Main Gate, 2015. These pillars once held the Main Gate and were secured to the gatehouse, or Post One. (Photograph by the author.)

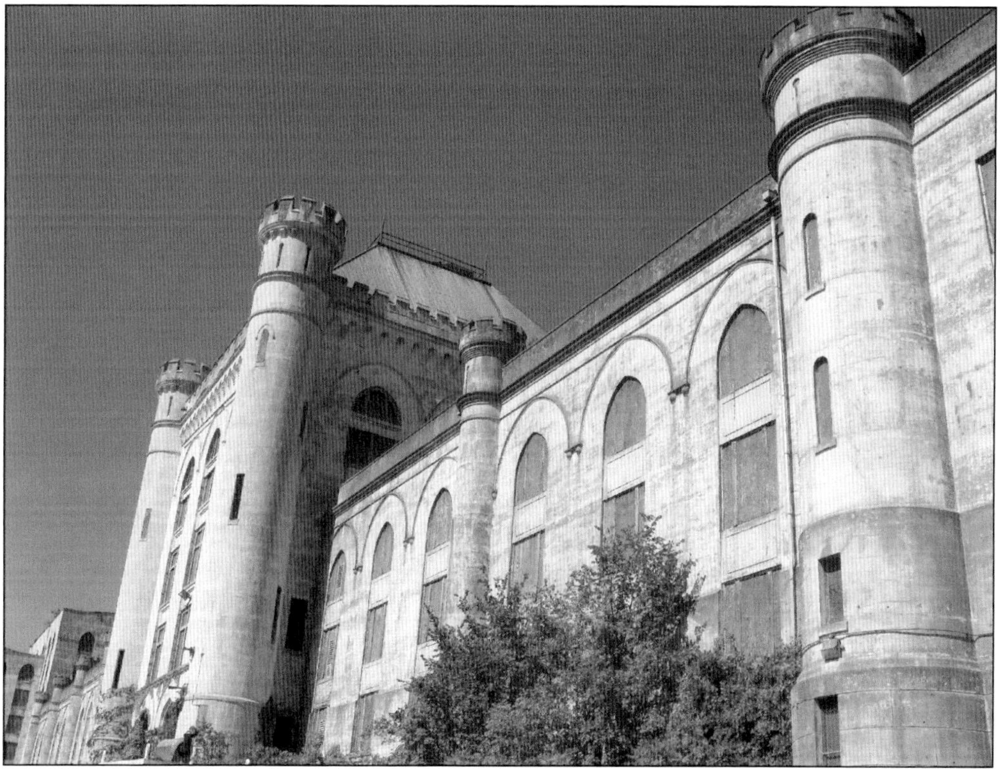

Seaside View, 2015. The decommissioning ceremony of the Naval Disciplinary Command took place on June 13, 1974, although an article in the *Navy Times* in 1966 indicates that the 27-acre prison would be phased out by 1969, not the first of several such recommendations that did not materialize. Following the Pentagon's decision to close the prison, several plans were formulated for its future use; among them was another prison, a school, and an oceanographic institute. (Photograph by the author.)

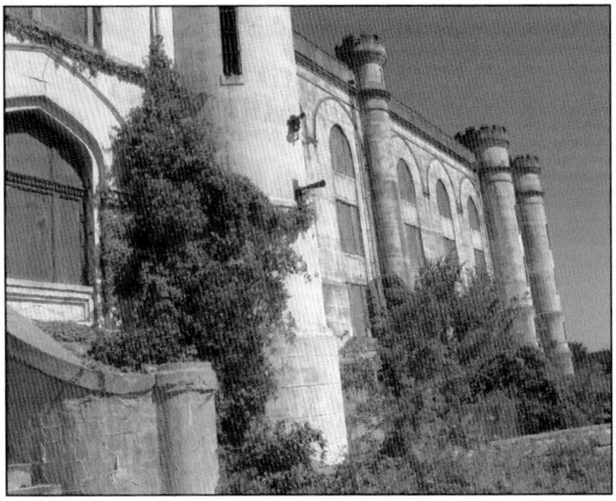

Addition and Main Entrance, Seaside View, 2015. There are significant obstacles that impede refurbishing the prison. One is that the prison contains asbestos and the cost to restore it would be formidable. Today, with the building closed and vacant for over 40 years, it is more so. Secondly, access for the general public through the secure shipyard is a significant problem: unless visitors arrive by boat, they would have to traipse through the shipyard without disrupting operations to get to the prison. (Photograph by the author.)

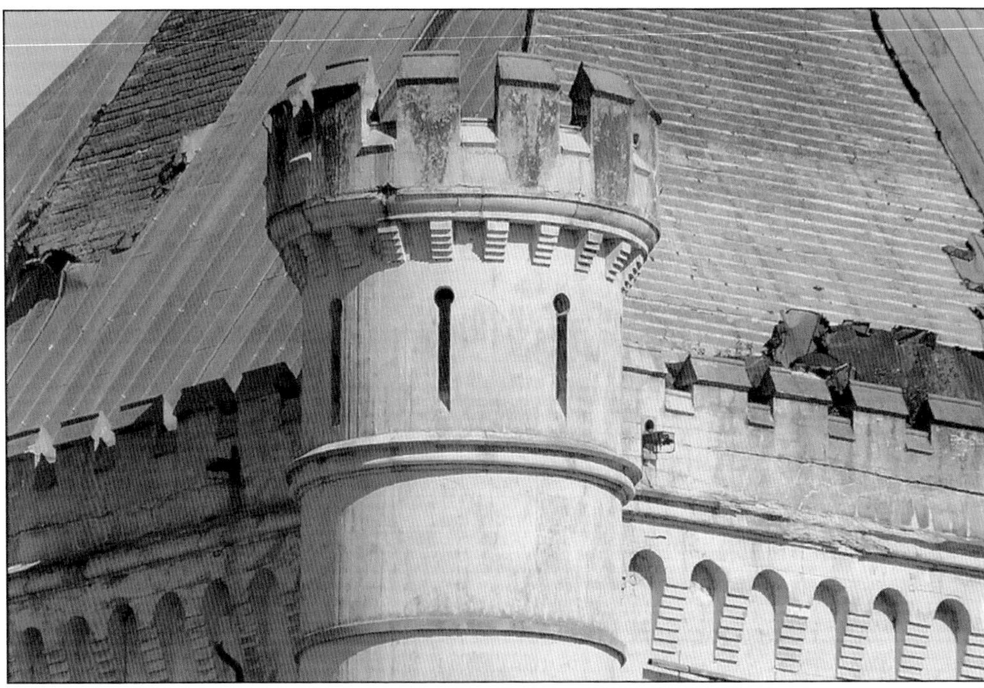

An Administration Building Tower, 2015. For 10 years, the building was vacant, unused, and closed until the 1980s when it was mothballed and sealed to prevent further damage from vandals and the elements. In June 1999, however, 70-year-old philanthropist Joe Sawtelle, a general partner of Seavey Island LLC and the Portsmouth Chamber of Commerce's 1999 Citizen of the Year, made a proposal. (JC.)

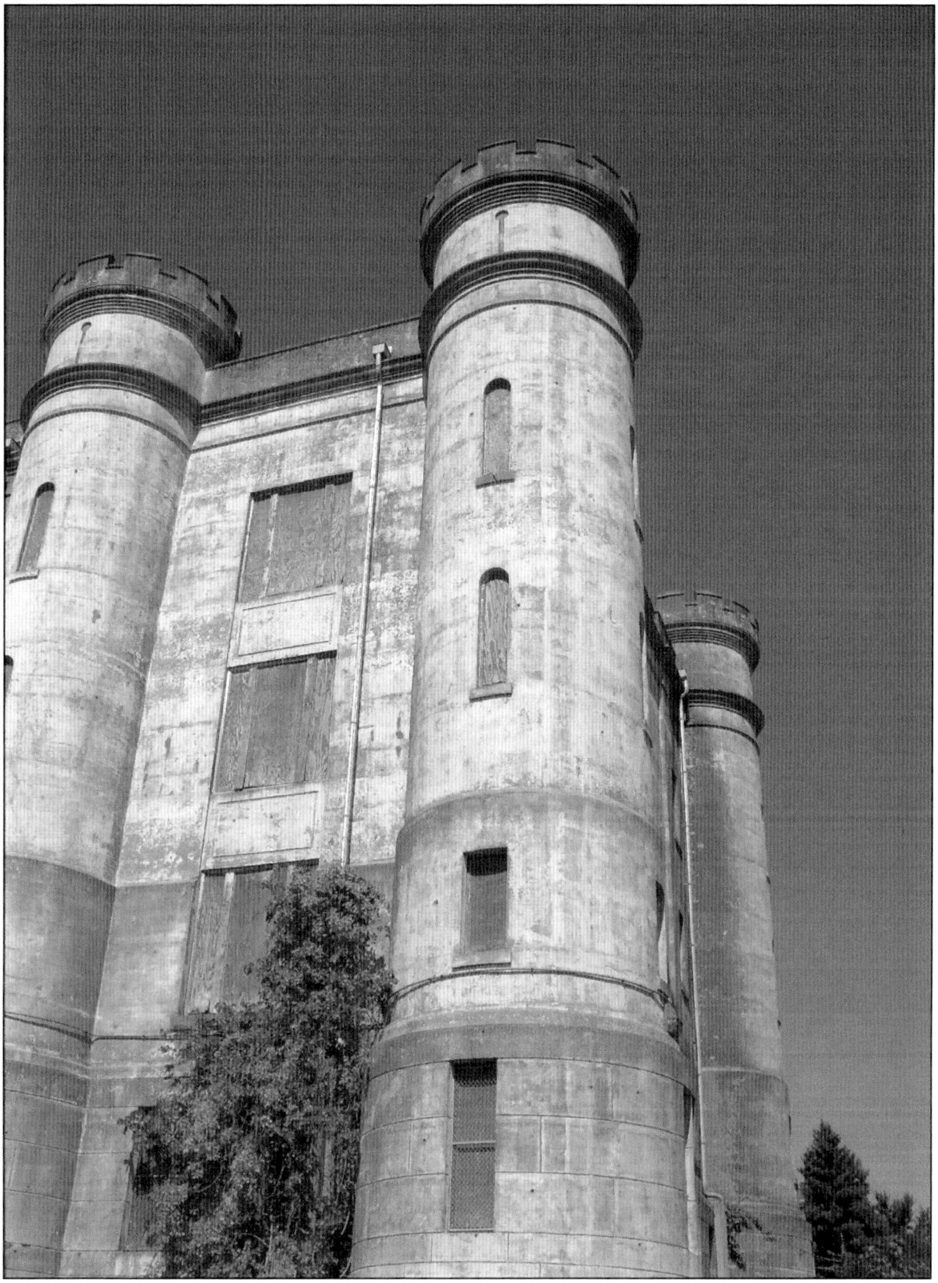

The Castle Towers, Summer 2015. Sawtelle, a New Castle resident, was not new to salvaging old buildings. He had transformed the Cocheco Falls Millworks in Dover into office space, helped rescue the historic Wentworth-by-the-Sea, and turned the experimental sub *Albacore* into a Portsmouth museum. So, signing a 15-year lease with the Naval Sea Systems Command to renovate the prison for $12 million and pay rent and utilities seemed feasible. Sawtelle planned to turn the prison into a high-tech facility, the Seavey Island Technology Center, with several companies housed there and the first tenants arriving by summer's end 2000. Demolition on the interior began. On May 2, 2000, tragically, Sawtelle died, and the project was subsequently abandoned. (Photograph by the author.)

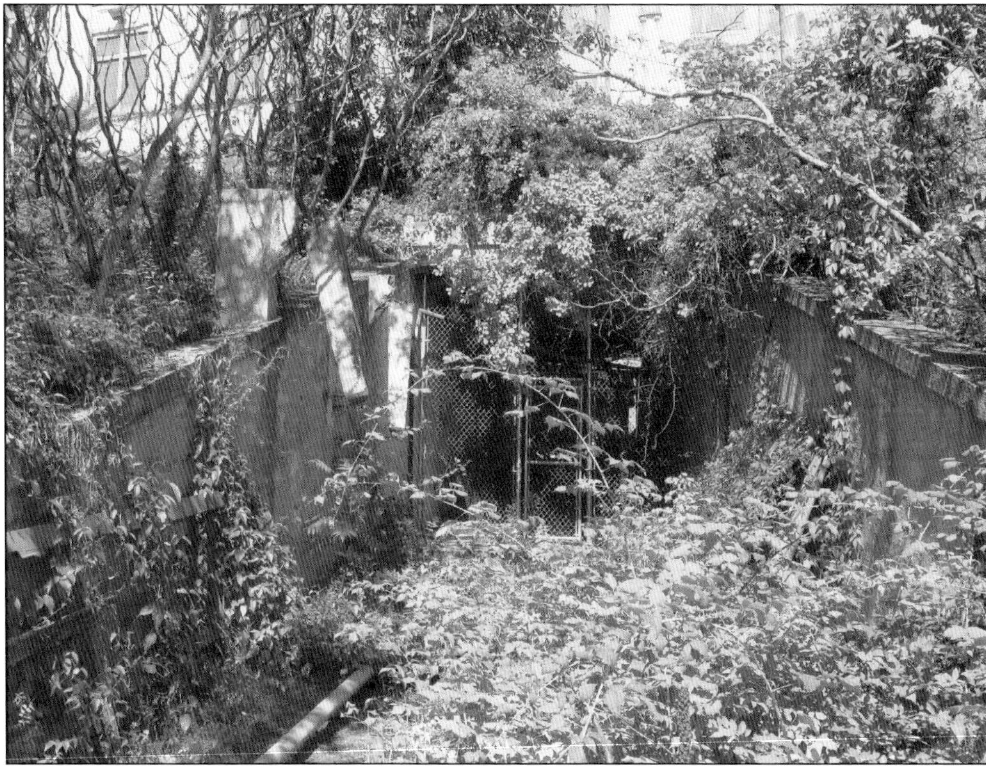

The Tunnel, Summer 2015. Although the stairs on one end and Building 121 on the other are both no longer there, the tunnel remains. (Photograph by the author.)

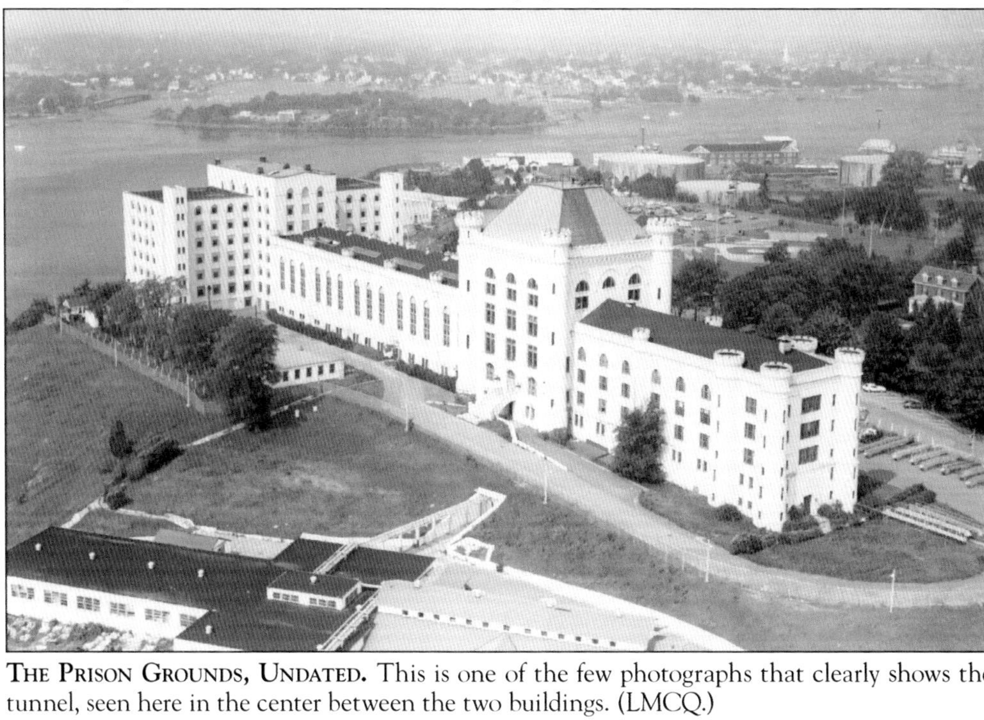

The Prison Grounds, Undated. This is one of the few photographs that clearly shows the tunnel, seen here in the center between the two buildings. (LMCQ.)

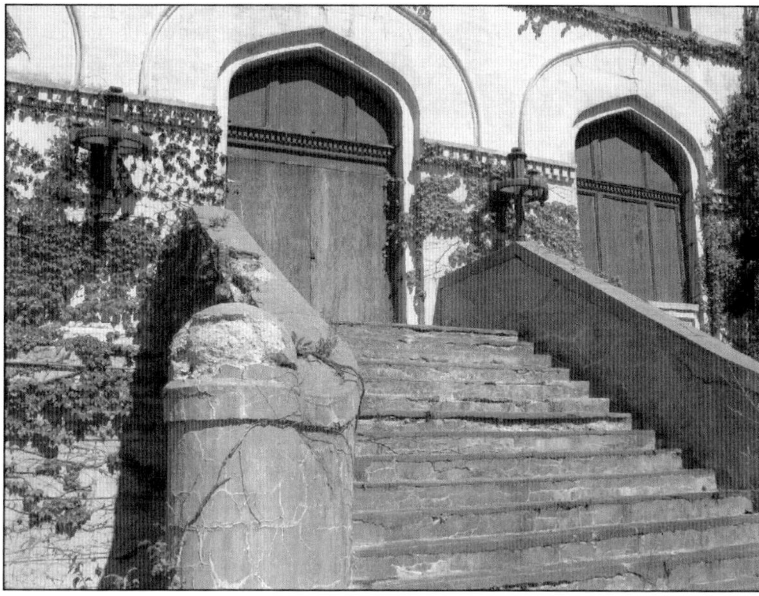

The Seaside Main Entrance, Summer 2015. Although parts of the prison now are covered in weeds and vines, at several times in its history, they were purposely planted to offset the stark appearance. (Photograph by the author.)

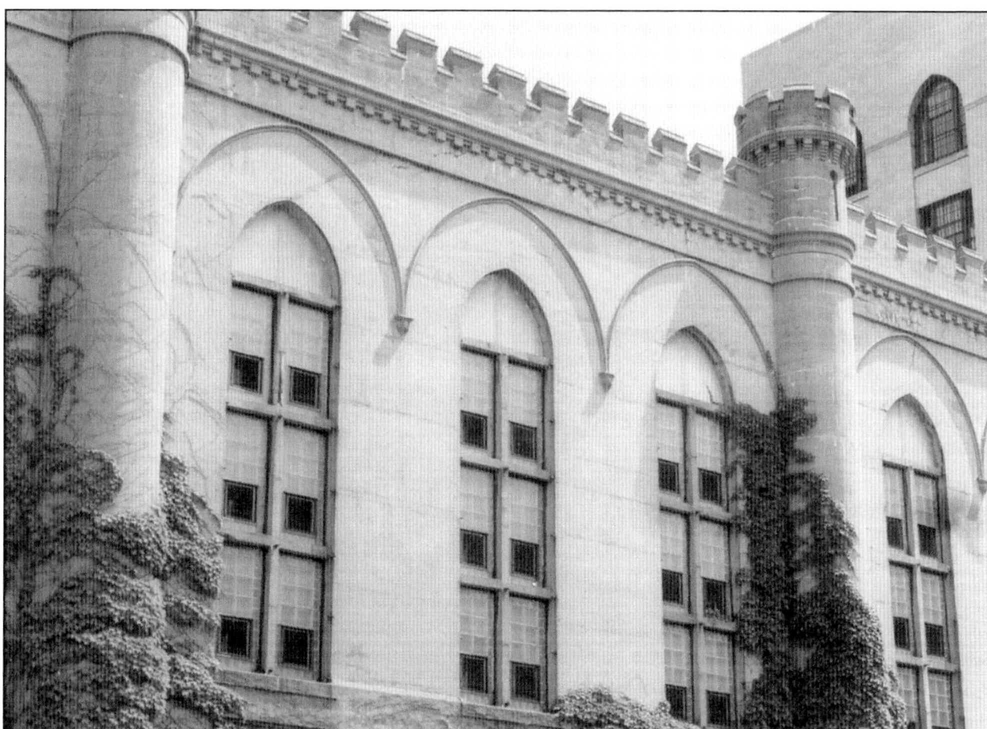

Ivy-Covered Walls. In this undated post–World War II photograph, ivy seems to be welcome. In 1908, when one of the outside jobs was to beautify the grounds, ivy was planted then as well. (NHHC.)

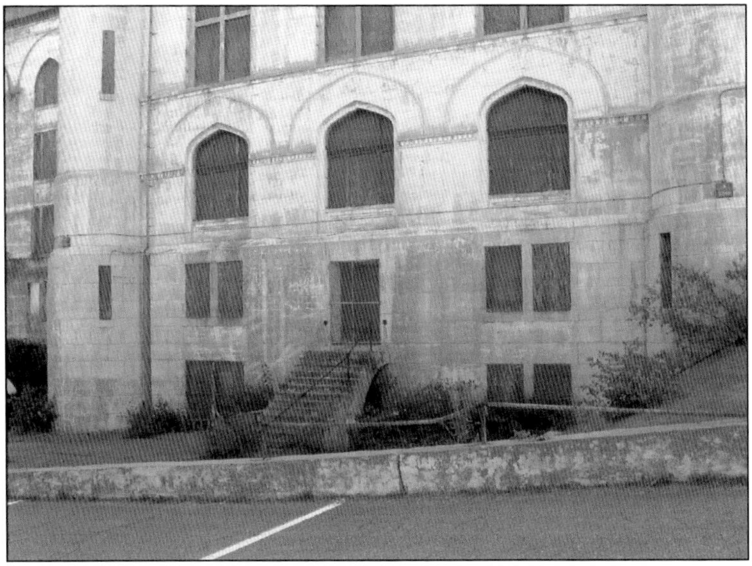

A Rear Entrance, Summer 2015. In 1943, the prisoner entrance was modified from parallel to the wall to a 45-degree angle, but still led to both the administration building and the cell block. (Photograph by the author.)

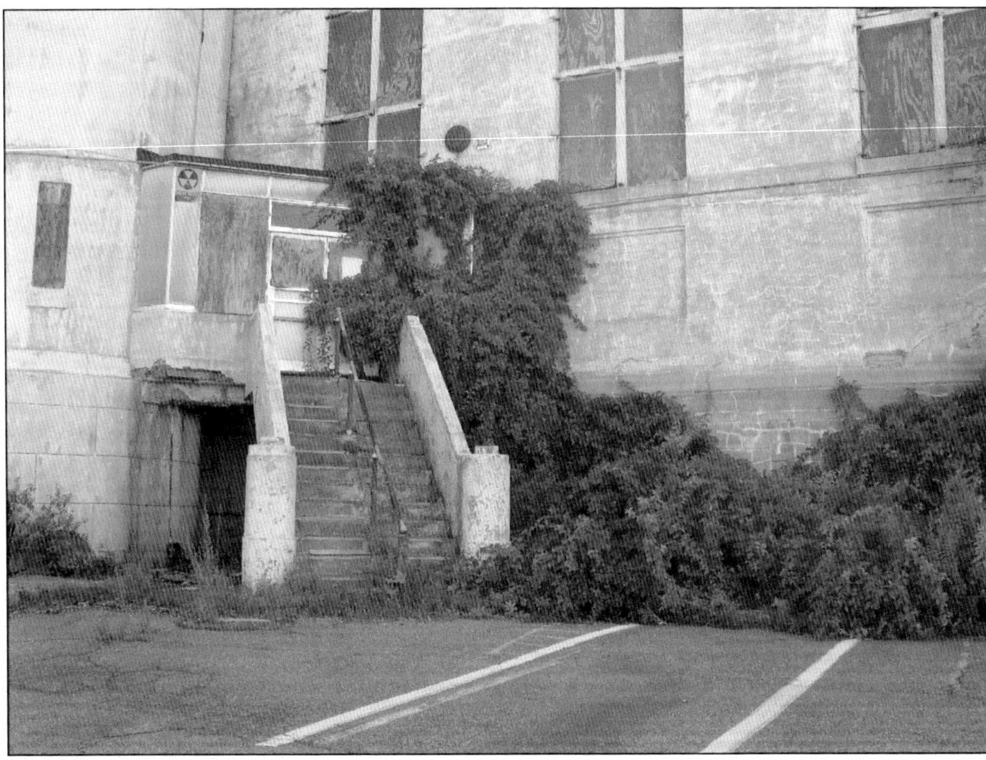

Rear Stairs, 2015. There is a myth—fact, some say—that the prison is haunted. According to an article in the final May 1974 issue of the *Castle Courier*, the inmate-authored newspaper, the ghost is a murdered former prisoner. Herman Throgwell, killed in a fight over a piece of candy, also lost an eye in the melee. The prison, then still incomplete, provided an opportunity for his assailant, a fellow prisoner, to seal Throgwell's one-eyed body in the floor of the castle. (Photograph by the author.)

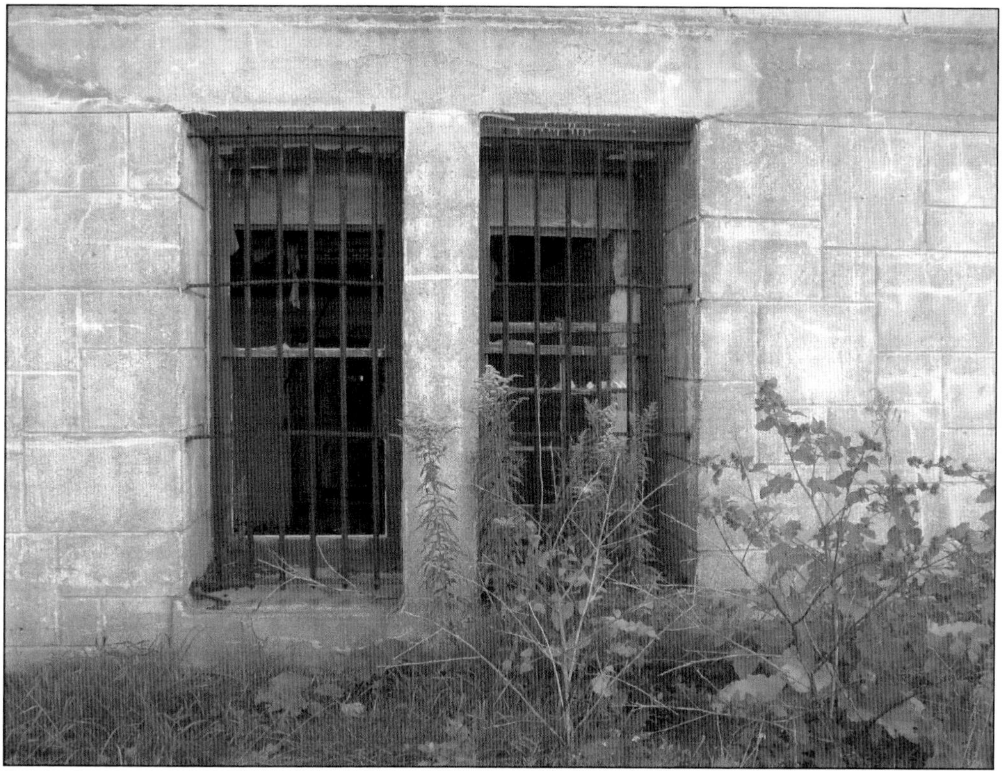

Prison Windows, Parking Lot Side, 2015. Herman, reads the *Courier* article, was "a top notch ghost. . . . His favorite pastime was to scare the new prisoners in the Screening Center. He would rattle chairs, open windows, jump up and down on the racks, and even bang the pipes." However, when the prison was slated for closure, the commanding officer arranged a work release program in a castle in Coventry, England. After the prison closed, Herman would be transferred with an escort to the ancient castle, where, supposedly, he would attract tourists. (Photograph by the author.)

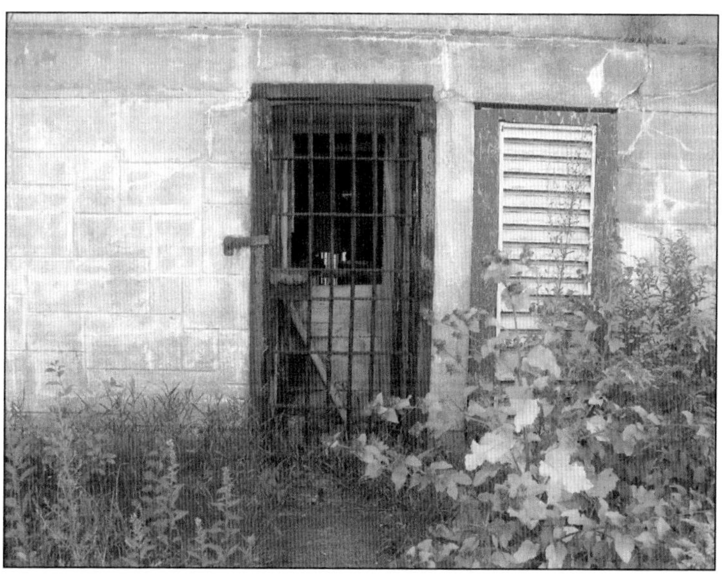

Prison Door, Parking Lot Side, August 2015. Some claim, and some Portsmouth tour guides attest, that Herman and his cronies still roam the prison. A glance through a window or a door of the empty building does nothing to diminish that assertion. In these photographs, the doorway and windows look into that screening center. (Photograph by the author.)

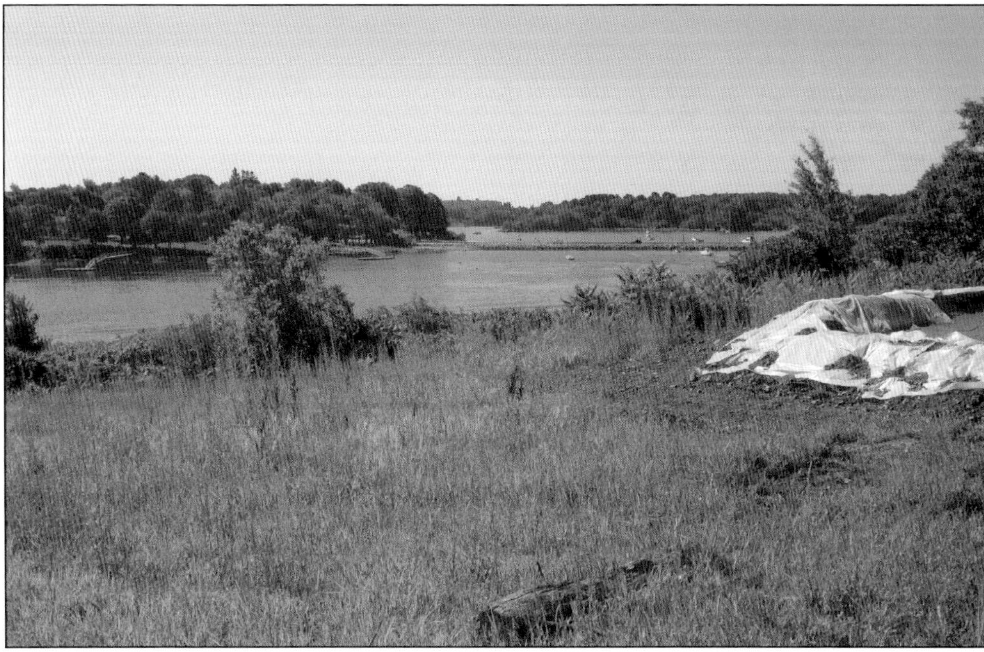

The Lower Reservation, 2015. Today, the lower reservation is just a grassy slope leading to the water's edge. The clamor of the war years, with the frequent press for facility expansion, has yielded to the quiet rhythm of an uninhabited shoreline. There is little evidence, save for several shrink-wrapped boats, escorted visitors, and occasional workmen of the continuous activity of prior decades. (Photograph by the author.)

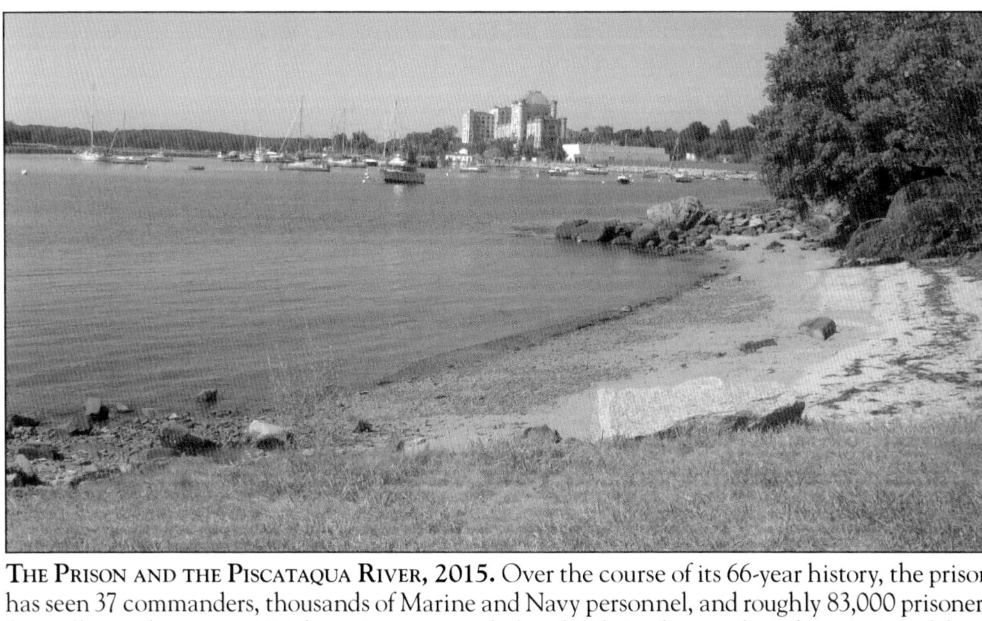

The Prison and the Piscataqua River, 2015. Over the course of its 66-year history, the prison has seen 37 commanders, thousands of Marine and Navy personnel, and roughly 83,000 prisoners from all over the country. Today, it is vacant, inhabited only in the minds and memories of those men who, for a portion of their lives, have passed through. (Photograph by the author.)

Bibliography

Bolster, W. Jeffrey, ed. *Cross Grained and Wily Waters: A Guide to the Piscataqua Maritime Region.* Portsmouth, NH: Peter E. Randall Publisher, 2002.

Filbert, Brent G. and Alan G. Kaufman. *Naval Law: Justice and Procedures in the Sea Services.* Annapolis, MD: Naval Institute Press, 1998.

Naval Facilities Engineering Command (NAVFAC), *Maine Historical Building Record Documentation: Building 93, Portsmouth Naval Prison, Portsmouth Naval Shipyard, Kittery, Maine*, December 2011.

Painter, Nell Irvin. *Standing at Armageddon: The United States, 1877–1919.* New York: W.W. Norton Company, 1987.

Ponicsan, Darryl. *The Last Detail.* New York: Dial Press, 1970.

Valle, James E. *Rocks and Shoals: Naval Discipline in the Age of Fighting Sail.* Annapolis, MD: Naval Institute Press, 1980.

Verge, Robert J.A. *A History of the U.S. Naval Prison at Portsmouth, New Hampshire.* Portsmouth, NH: U.S. Naval Print Shop, 1946.

Watterson, Rodney K. *Whips to Walls: Naval Discipline from Flogging to Progressive-Era Reform at Portsmouth Prison.* Annapolis, MD: Naval Institute Press, 2014.

Winslow, Richard Elliott. *"Do Your Job!" An Illustrated Bicentennial History of the Portsmouth Naval Shipyard, 1800–2000.* Portsmouth, NH: Marine Society, 2000.